D0778156

BESTSELLERS BY DEEPAK CHOPRA

ALSO BY DEEPAK CHOPRA

DEEPAK CHOPRA IMPRINT

Infinite Potential, by Lothar
 Schäfer
Science Set Free, by Rupert
 Sheldrake
*Supernormal: Science, Yoga,
 and the Evidence for*

*Extraordinary Psychic
 Abilities,* by Dean Radin
The Generosity Network, by
 Jennifer McCrea, Jeffrey
 Walker, and Karl Weber

QUANTUM HEALING

QUANTUM HEALING

EXPLORING THE FRONTIERS OF
MIND/BODY MEDICINE

Deepak Chopra, M.D.

BANTAM BOOKS

NEW YORK

In order to ensure the privacy of the patients mentioned in this book,
their names, circumstances, and other identifying
details have been changed.

A Bantam Books Trade Paperback Original

Copyright © 1989, 2015 by Deepak Chopra, M.D.

All rights reserved.

Published in the United States by Bantam Books,
an imprint of Random House, a division of
Penguin Random House LLC, New York.

BANTAM BOOKS and the HOUSE colophon are registered
trademarks of Penguin Random House LLC.

Originally published in hardcover in the United States by
Bantam Books, an imprint of Random House, a division
of Penguin Random House LLC, in 1989.

ISBN 978-1-101-88497-3
eBook ISBN 978-0-804-17998-0

Printed in the United States of America on acid-free paper

randomhousebooks.com

2 4 6 8 9 7 5 3

Book design by Jo Anne Metsch

CONTENTS

FOREWORD

BY DR. RUDOLF TANZI

Whenever the word *quantum* comes up, the word *physics* follows automatically. This habit of mind made *Quantum Healing* a novel and provocative title in 1989, but its author, a curious-minded endocrinologist outside Boston, was implying a legitimate question. If every atom and molecule in the universe emerges from the quantum field, doesn't this mean that our bodies do, too? The answer is undoubtedly yes. In that case, we possess a quantum mechanical body. Dr. Deepak Chopra then reasoned that the mysteries of the human body, particularly the mystery of healing, are inevitably immersed in the quantum field.

Very few scientists were thinking that way almost thirty years ago. Medical schools approached the human body essentially as a machine subdivided into the working parts of a machine—organs, tissues, and cells. When the body broke down through illness, something material was at fault. Bacteria had entered to disrupt the mechanical operation of an organ, or a worn-out part had failed. An arthritic joint was considered similar to a tire with the tread wearing thin.

Modern scientific medicine goes into sophisticated detail, but in essence it embraces the two basic principles that bind all the sciences together: materialism and reductionism. Materialism holds that there must be a physical explanation for every phenomenon. Reductionism holds that complex problems can be broken down into smaller component parts, wherein lie all solutions and answers. *Quantum Healing* blew the whistle on both principles, not because they are inherently wrong, but because they left out some extremely important things, especially when it came to the human body.

Materialism left out the mind-body connection. Mind isn't material. Yet our thoughts cause our bodies to move, something we take for granted the minute we get out of bed in the morning but which stands as a great mystery. When you break the body down into organs, tissues, and cells, you can't find the slightest trace of a thought, and yet the mind must be related to the body. How?

Reductionism left out the holistic nature of the body. Trillions of cells cooperate to sustain one another, acting to preserve overall balance and health. Up to a quadrillion neural connections in the brain generate a microscopic electrical storm, and yet the result is organized thought, not a jumble of static. As skilled as medical science is at dissecting body and brain, it has little to say about the experience of life as a whole, yet that experience impinges directly on who gets sick and who stays well.

Deepak was not the first to see these flaws and omissions, but *Quantum Healing* was very bold in becoming the first book to offer a path to new answers. He proposed that quantum physics describes an invisible domain from which mind and body both emerge and unite. *Quantum Healing* struck a nerve by focusing on the most baffling phenomenon in medicine, spontaneous remission from cancer. How could the most intractable of diseases, the object of billion-dollar campaigns to find a cure, suddenly disappear from a patient's body? Since oncology is a numbers game, it was easier simply to ignore these extraordinary cases as anomalies. But if science prides itself on going wherever reality leads us, such cases are well documented in medical journals. They force us to rethink the entire materialist, reductionist model—Deepak was willing to go there.

Even today, not everyone is willing. As a neurogeneticist, I have been fortunate to study the wondrous interplay of genes and the brain. All organic processes are coded in our DNA. Since that includes all brain processes, the mind-body connection is directly engendered in our genes. The same is true for healing, another process that cannot take place absent genetic activity. However, most geneticists don't think in such broad terms; our research studies are extremely detailed and focused (my specialty is the neurodegenerative disorder Alzheimer's disease). The mind is all too often left out of the equation, and as for *quantum*, the word has traditionally had no bearing on our training, being the province of physics.

Quantum Healing looked past this long-accepted compartmentalization, opening up genetics, along with every other corner of physiology, to quantum thinking. I didn't delve into the mind-body connection when I first began my quest to end Alzheimer's disease, but since it's a brain disorder, I discovered common ground with a broad thinker like Deepak. After getting excited about how our interests and passions overlapped, we wrote a book, *Super Brain*, together. The gist of the book, based on solid neuroscience, is that the brain is plastic, influenced by thoughts, feelings, choices, and most important, self-awareness. We also explored a radical possibility that *Quantum Healing* first proposed: What if the mind is creating the brain at the same time that the brain is creating the mind? This was a mind-blowing (or brain-blowing) idea, because it flew straight past the insistence that only physical processes matter in the brain (materialism) and that every answer lies at the level of the neuron (reductionism).

The basic research that was showing how messenger molecules carry information from the brain to every cell in the body was new when *Quantum Healing* was published. Now our knowledge in this area is extremely sophisticated. The next frontier is the mind-gene connection. Here Deepak and I have found the most exciting possibilities. We are actively pursuing the beneficial genetic changes that occur in meditation and other contemplative practices. Long portrayed as spiritual, these are actually mind-body techniques that speak to every cell and even deeper, to every gene. The implications are explosive when it comes to cutting-edge science in preventing or reversing chronic disorders, attacking the causes of aging, and fighting against the subtle imbalances that lead to inflammation, now the prime suspect in many disorders, including cancer.

We are proposing that lifestyle choices, insofar as they affect a person's genes, can lead to transformation at the level where personal evolution occurs. Genes are not the fixed, stable, immovable entities I was taught about; they are fluid and dynamic, and their activities are altered by every experience, thought, word, and action in a person's life. So, why not direct your experience to influence your genes in the most positive ways? Ground is being broken in "self-directed biological transformation" (SDBT), our phrase for personalized conscious evolution. (And a new book is emerging from this concept, titled *Super Genes,* to bring SDBT into the practicalities of daily life.)

Quantum Healing didn't set out to cure cancer or Alzheimer's or any other intractable disease. It set out to see the human body, and human existence in general, through wiser eyes. As a scientist I'm passionate about genes and the brain; as a person I'm totally fascinated by the origins of consciousness. *Quantum Healing* galvanized my intuition that these areas do not have to be separated. They belong together naturally, and once we feel secure that self-awareness is integral to the healthy workings of the body, it will be integral to existence itself. Beyond that, the possibilities are infinite.

Rudolph Tanzi, Ph.D., is director of the Genetics and Aging Research Unit and vice chair of neurology at Massachusetts General Hospital. He also serves as the Joseph P. and Rose F. Kennedy Professor of Neurology at Harvard Medical School.

INTRODUCTION

When first published, *Quantum Healing* was a provocative title based on a controversial idea. The idea was that the mind influences the body either to be sick or well. Twenty-five years ago the mind-body connection struck most doctors as weak science, bad science, or not science at all. Their medical school training taught them about systems, organs, tissues, and cells—end of story. Somewhere on the fringes lurked the placebo effect, a suspicious oddity few doctors paid attention to. Patients got better when given sugar pills they thought were drugs. Sometimes the placebo effect was just as effective as the drugs. Why?

Hardly anyone cared. Placebos were dismissed as psychosomatic. In other words, they weren't "real medicine." I vividly remember the reaction of hospital colleagues in Boston when they discovered my newfound interest in the mind-body connection. With a frown or a pitying smile they asked, "Do you really believe in such a thing?" Almost three decades later I can reply, "You don't?"

Controversial ideas have a way of becoming mainstream, and

that's what happened to the mind-body connection. No longer does anyone have to defend their belief in meditation, yoga, stress reduction, anger management, and a host of positive lifestyle changes. These measures have one thing in common: Better messages are being sent from the mind to the body. With better messages a higher state of wellbeing is possible. No one disputes this anymore.

The floodgates have opened, and today *Quantum Healing* could be doubled in size by introducing just a fraction of the new evidence supporting the mind-body connection. Medical school training is still about systems, organs, tissues, and cells, but that's no longer the end of the story. A new field known as integrative medicine has sprung up since 1989. It incorporates what used to be called alternative medicine, along with traditional healing modalities like Ayurveda, which played a large part in my own journey, as this book recounts.

Yet the mystery of healing is far from solved. I was baffled by Chitra, the first patient mentioned in the book, who somehow recovered from breast cancer without benefit of conventional treatment (only to die just as mysteriously). Such cases of spontaneous remission continue to occur. Just this month I encountered a young man who had struggled with stomach cancer for six years, finally giving up on chemotherapy because of its debilitating side effects.

His cancer had metastasized throughout his body, to the bones and liver. Given six months to live, he traveled to India, where his family originated, and renounced the hectic life of New York City for the peace and quiet of the rural countryside. He took up meditation and yoga. He became a strict vegetarian. He immersed himself in the most traditional practices of Ayurveda, practices that have roots going back thousands of years. As of three months ago his scans show that he is entirely free of cancer.

There are thousands of spontaneous remissions of cancer found in Western medical journals, and yet it's fair to say that they make hardly any difference in the routine practice of oncology, not directly at least. Cancer treatment has advanced over the past quarter century, but the path it has followed—toward genetics, sharply fo-cused drugs, and more precise statistics—has little to do with the mind-body connection.

Instead, the influence of spontaneous remissions has been indi-rect, by motivating research into healing itself. Genetics is a crucial key in cancer, and the mind can influence genes. Literally thousands of genetic markers are improved through meditation, for example. Inflammation could be just as crucial in the onset and spread of cancer, and inflammation is stress related. Stress is a reaction that begins in the mind, and a person's mindset can be changed. Life-style choices that lead to obesity, lack of sleep, and distorted bio-rhythms are being connected to cancer, and these bad choices can be reversed.°

In short, there's nothing about cancer that is separate from the mind in one way or another. This realization led the M. D. Anderson Cancer Center in Houston to announce the following in 2008: "Only 5–10% of all cancer cases can be attributed to genetic defects, whereas the remaining 90–95% have their roots in the environment and lifestyle."† This represents an enormous shift in attitude. When I was in medical school, 95 percent of cancers were considered non-preventable.

If *Quantum Healing* is to remain relevant, a new controversial idea is needed. What if *all* healing is quantum? Then every barrier separating mind and body would come down. Every cell would be conscious, not just brain cells. Beyond the boundary of the skin, all of life would be conscious, arising on a conscious planet in a con-scious universe. To the five senses, body, planet, and universe are not one and the same. But at the quantum level they have a com-mon source. To quote the great quantum pioneer Erwin Schrödinger,

---

° In 2013 the U.S. Centers for Disease Control and Prevention estimated that a third of cancer cases were related to smoking and another third to obesity.

† The cited lifestyle factors include cigarette smoking, diet (fried foods, red meat), alcohol, sun exposure, environmental pollutants, infections, stress, obe-sity, and physical inactivity.

"To divide or multiply consciousness is something meaningless. . . . In truth there is only one mind."

You and I go through life assuming that we have individual minds and bodies. When one person burns his hand on a radiator, he says "Ouch," not the person standing next to him. But at the quantum level this changes—you and I are imbedded in one mind, a cosmic intelligence that creates, governs, and controls reality. Where is this cosmic intelligence located? Schrödinger comes to our aid again by dissolving all the everyday barriers that keep us from seeing our cosmic status.

First, the barrier of separate minds: "Consciousness is a singular that has no plural." Next, the barrier of past, present, and future: "Mind is always now. There is really no before and after for the mind." Finally, the barrier between life and death: "Consciousness is pure, eternal and infinite: it does not arise nor cease to be. It is ever present in moving and unmoving creatures, in the sky, on the mountain, in fire and in air."

This last quote doesn't come from Schrödinger, however, but from one of the most ancient texts in the Indian spiritual tradition, the *Yoga Vasistha*. The fact that a sage living thousands of years ago could take an inner journey and make discoveries consistent with quantum physics wasn't news when *Quantum Healing* came out. But the world of sages, seers, and saints felt closed off from ordinary life back then. All the ensuing research in mind-body medicine has helped to build a bridge between two worlds, and the sage Vasistha, like Buddha, could be our contemporary.

What would it take to turn all healing into quantum healing? I will address this, the most burning question facing modern medicine, in the expanded edition you're now reading. After each chapter you'll find a section titled "Expanding the Topic," which approaches the mystery of healing as viewed by cutting-edge medical research and the world's wisdom traditions.

Beyond the mind-body connection there is a deeper connection between now and eternity. The human brain knows only the now.

Every electrical impulse or chemical reaction in your brain occurs right this second. The feedback between mind and body is being replenished thousands of times a minute. We can take great hope in this fact, because it means that the entire universe has conspired to bring about this very minute. Infinite creativity, intelligence, and power are supporting us once we open ourselves up to them.

When I wrote this book, I knew it was pointing in the right direction. If I felt the barbs of skeptics then (and there were many), I was confident that confirming studies were still to come. Now the idea of quantum healing has had nearly thirty years of supporting research. Let's hope this expanded edition prompts open-minded readers to revisit this concept. Hope is born from impossible ideas. To the skeptical mind, the most impossible idea is this: We are children of the universe. Our source is beyond all boundaries. Seeing ourselves as isolated, limited physical creatures is merely an assumed identity. I suppose those are three ideas, but once they are fused into a new mindset, the era of true healing will have arrived.

PART I

THE HIDDEN PHYSIOLOGY

*In the deeper reality beyond space and time,
we may be all members of one body.*

—SIR JAMES JEANS

AFTER THE MIRACLE

Several times in my medical career I have been privileged to witness miraculous cures. The most recent began last year when a 32-year-old Indian woman came to see me in my office outside Boston. She sat quietly facing me in a blue silk sari. To keep her composure, she clasped her hands tightly in her lap. Her name was Chitra, she said, and together with her husband, Raman, she ran a neighborhood import store in New York City.

A few months earlier, Chitra had noticed a small lump in her left breast that was sensitive to the touch. She underwent surgery to remove it, but unfortunately the surgeon found that the lump was malignant. When he explored further, he detected that the cancer had spread to her lungs.

After removing the diseased breast and a large portion of tissue around it, Chitra's doctor gave her initial doses of radiation and then placed her on intensive chemotherapy. This is standard procedure for treating breast cancer and saves many lives. But the lung cancer was going to be much harder to treat; it was obvious to everyone that Chitra was in a very precarious position.

Examining her, I noticed that she was very anxious. When I tried to reassure her, she surprised me with a touching statement: "I don't mind for myself if I have to die, but my husband will be so lonely without me. Sometimes I pretend to be asleep and then sit up all night, just thinking about him. I know Raman loves me, but after I'm gone, he will start seeing American girls. I can't bear to lose him to an American girl." She stopped and looked at me with suffering in her eyes. "I know I shouldn't say that, but I think you understand."

You do not get used to the sorrow that cancer creates, but I felt a deeper sorrow from knowing that time was Chitra's enemy. For the moment, she still looked healthy. She had even managed to hide her disease from her relatives, dreading having to be watched as she wasted away. We both knew it was going to be very bad for her.

No one can say that he knows a cure for advanced breast cancer. Conventional therapy had provided all that it could for Chitra. Given that her cancer had already spread to another organ, the statistics said that her chance of surviving for five years was less than 10 percent, even with the most intensive routine of chemotherapy that could be safely administered.

I asked her to start a new course of treatments, as prescribed by Ayurveda.

Like me, Chitra had grown up in India, but she had little idea of Ayurveda. Her grandparents' generation was the last to "believe" in it, I would imagine; today, every progressive Indian living in a big city would prefer Western medicine if he could afford it. To explain to Chitra why I wanted her seemingly to turn her back on progress, I told her that her cancer was not just a physical disease but a holistic one. Her whole body knew she had cancer and was suffering from it; a tissue sample taken from her lungs would show that malignant cells had migrated there, while a sample from her liver would be negative. Yet, her liver had the same blood coursing through it, and therefore it picked up the signals of disease that were coming from the lungs. This in turn affected its own functions.

Similarly, when she felt pain in her chest or had to sit down owing to shortness of breath, signals were racing throughout her body, going to and from her brain. Sensing the pain, her brain had to respond to it. The fatigue she was feeling, along with her depression and anxiety, was a brain response that had physical consequences. So it was wrong to think of her cancer as just an isolated tumor that needed to be destroyed. She had a holistic disease and for that she needed holistic medicine.

The word *holistic*, which tends to offend orthodox doctors, simply means an approach that includes the mind and body together. I believe Ayurveda does this better than any alternative, although it may not be very apparent on the surface. In fact, many well-publicized mind-body techniques such as hypnosis and biofeedback are far more flashy than Ayurveda. If Chitra had gotten sick at home in Bombay, her grandmother might have fixed her some special meals, brought home medicinal herbs in a brown paper sack from the Ayurvedic pharmacy, and insisted that she stay in bed. Various purgatives and oil massages might be prescribed to clean the body of toxins generated by the cancer. If there was a spiritual tradition in the family, she would have begun to meditate. In essence, I was going to have her do these same things, with a few additions. There is as yet no scientific reason why any of this should work, except that it does. Ayurveda has hit on something deep in nature. Its knowledge is rooted not in technology but in wisdom, which I would define as a reliable understanding of the human organism gathered over many centuries.

"I want you to go to a special clinic outside Boston for a week or two," I told Chitra. "Some things that will happen to you there will seem highly unusual. You are used to the idea of a hospital as a place with respirators, IV tubes, transfusions, and chemotherapy. By that standard, what we will do for you at this clinic will seem like nothing. Basically, I want to get your body into a deep, deep state of rest."

Chitra was a trusting person; she agreed to go. In part, of course, she had no alternative. Modern medicine had done all it could, using the strategy of physical assault on her cancer. The initial advantage of assaulting a disease is that you hope to wipe it out physically as soon as possible. The tremendous disadvantage is that the whole body is damaged in the assault on one of its parts. In the case of chemotherapy, there is the very real danger that the immune system will become so weakened that the door is opened for other cancers to develop in the future. However, untreated breast cancer is considered deadly, and today's medicine is good at wiping it out over the short run. In a climate of opinion ruled by fear, people prefer to run the risks of the cure rather than the disease.

I referred Chitra to the clinic where I work, in Lancaster, Massachusetts. She stayed for a week and received treatments; she also learned an outpatient program to use at home that included a change of diet, some Ayurvedic herbs, a specific daily routine including simple yoga exercises, and instruction in meditation. These measures look different on the surface, but underneath they all aimed at bringing her day-to-day existence to a settled, restful state, building a foundation for healing. In Ayurveda, a level of total, deep relaxation is the most important precondition for curing any disorder. The underlying concept is that the body knows how to maintain balance unless thrown off by disease; therefore, if one wants to restore the body's own healing ability, everything should be done to bring it back into balance. It is a very simple notion that has profound consequences. Chitra was also given two special mental techniques that went directly to the root of her cancer. (I will say more about these later.)

Chitra followed her program faithfully and came back to see me every six weeks. She also continued the course of chemotherapy set up by her doctor at home in New York. When we talked about that I said, "If I could confidently put you on nothing but Ayurveda, I would—the deterioration in your physical state would then be much less. But you came to me a very sick woman, and we know that the chemotherapy works as an outside approach. Let's combine the outer and the inner and hope that they add up to a real cure."

For almost a year I followed Chitra's progress. She always listened with a trusting attitude, yet as she returned for each visit, it was clear that she was not improving. Her lung X rays were still bad, her shortness of breath grew worse, and she began to look weaker and more dejected as the disease advanced. Her voice took on a note of panic. Finally the day came when Chitra did not show up for her appointment. I waited out the week and then called her home.

The news was not good. Chitra's husband, Raman, told me that she had suddenly developed a high fever and had to be hospitalized over the weekend. For some time her lungs had been seeping fluid into the pleural cavity that surrounds them, and her doctor suspected that an infection had set in. Given her grim prognosis, there was no guarantee that Chitra would ever leave the hospital.

Then a very curious thing happened. After a day or two on antibiotics, Chitra's fever went from 104 degrees F. back down to normal, which puzzled her attending physician. It is very unusual for a high-grade fever to reverse itself so rapidly if the underlying cause is an infection in a terminally ill patient. Could there be another cause besides infection? He decided to take chest X rays, and the next day Raman called me sounding both exhilarated and confused.

"She doesn't have cancer anymore!" Raman told me jubilantly over the telephone.

"What do you mean?" I asked, taken aback.

"They can't find any cancer cells at all—nothing." He was almost unable to contain himself. "Chitra's oncologist at first was sure that they had X-rayed the wrong patient and wanted to take some more pictures, but now he's convinced."

Overjoyed, relieved, and unable to explain this sudden stroke of salvation, Raman regarded his wife's recovery as a miracle. When I called Chitra in her hospital room, she kept crying into the phone,

"You did it, Deepak," while I kept insisting, "No, no, Chitra, *you* did it." I had never anticipated that such a rapid cure would result from her treatments, either conventional or Ayurvedic. In retrospect, I see that her high fever was a kind of burn-off from the dying cancer, a process known as tumor necrosis. But the exact mechanism involved has no explanation. If there is such a thing as a miraculous cure, this was one, I was certain.

Within a few weeks, however, our mutual jubilation began to change. Chitra's "miracle" wasn't holding. It eroded first within herself: instead of being able to trust in her inexplicable recovery, she became conflicted, morbidly afraid that the cancer would return. She called to ask me if she should resume chemotherapy.

"It's been two months since the cancer disappeared," I said. "Does your doctor find any new cancer cells?"

"No," Chitra admitted, "but he thinks that the chemotherapy cured me and that I should continue with it."

I began to feel frustrated. I knew, as did her attending physician, that the particular chemotherapy Chitra had received was not known to produce sudden, total recoveries of this kind, certainly not in advanced cases where the cancer had begun to spread to other sites in the body. Also, it was becoming obvious that she was being worn down past endurance. The chemotherapy had caused almost constant nausea, and her hair had fallen out in frightening amounts, adding to the shame she felt following her breast surgery. All of this compromised the Ayurvedic treatments we were trying. If even higher doses of chemotherapy were given, she would become more depressed, more prone to infections, and weaker in every way.

Yet, at the same time, I did not have a strong enough reason to tell her not to proceed. What if she suffered a relapse in six months and died?

"Go ahead with your chemotherapy," I advised, "but stick with our program, too, okay?" She agreed.

For several months more, Chitra remained free of disease, but she also remained disturbed and mystified. It seemed that Chitra's cancer was easier to defeat than the sinister doubt that was creeping back into her life, defying her to be well.

Chitra's agonizing dilemma is the real starting point of this book. For her to be well again, she needed an explanation. What had happened to her? Was her cure a miracle, as she thought at first, or only a temporary stay of execution, as she came to dread? By going deeper into the mind-body connection, I believe an answer can be found.

Research on spontaneous cures of cancer, conducted in both the United States and Japan, has shown that just before the cure appears, almost every patient experiences a dramatic shift in awareness. He knows that he will be healed, and he feels that the force responsible is inside himself but not limited to him—it extends beyond his personal boundaries, throughout all of nature. Suddenly he feels, "I am not limited to my body. All that exists around me is part of myself." At that moment, such patients apparently jump to a new level of consciousness that prohibits the existence of cancer. Then the cancer cells either disappear, literally overnight in some cases, or at the very least stabilize without damaging the body any further.

This leap in consciousness seems to be the key. It does not have to come in a flash, however. Chitra was cultivating it deliberately, through her Ayurvedic techniques. Therefore, her ability to stay at a higher level of awareness was strikingly correlated with her condition. Somehow she could motivate the absence of cancer, but just as easily she could return to it. (I think of this as being like a violin string whose pitch varies as you slide your finger up and down it.) The word that comes to mind when a scientist thinks of such sudden changes is *quantum*. The word denotes a discrete jump from one level of functioning to a higher level—the quantum leap.

Quantum is also a technical term, once known only to physicists but now growing in popular usage. Formally, a quantum is "the indivisible unit in which waves may be emitted or absorbed," the definition given by the eminent British physicist Stephen Hawking. In layman's terms, the quantum is a building block. Light is built up from photons, electricity from the charge of one electron, gravity from the graviton (a hypothetical quantum, not yet found in nature), and so on for all forms of energy—each of them is based on a quantum and cannot be broken down into anything smaller.

Both definitions—the discrete jump to a higher level and the irreducible level of a force—appear to apply to certain cases like Chitra's. Therefore, I would like to introduce the term *quantum healing* to describe what happened to her. Although the term is new, the process itself is not. There have always been patients who do not follow the normal course of healing. A tiny minority, for example, do not waste away from cancer; others have tumors that grow much more slowly than what the statistics for their diseases predict. Many cures that share mysterious origins—faith healing, spontaneous remissions, and the effective use of placebos, or "dummy drugs"— also point toward a quantum leap. Why? Because in all of these instances, the faculty of inner awareness seems to have promoted a drastic jump—a quantum leap—in the healing mechanism.

Consciousness is a force that most of us undervalue. Generally we do not focus our inner awareness or use its real power, even in the most difficult moments of crisis. That may account for why "miracle" cures are greeted with a mixture of awe, disbelief, and reverence. Yet, everyone possesses consciousness. Perhaps these miracles are extensions of normal abilities. When your body mends a broken bone, why is that not a miracle? As a healing process, it is certainly complex, far too complex for medicine to duplicate; it involves an incredible number of perfectly synchronized processes, of which medicine knows only the major ones and those imperfectly.

The reason why curing cancer by yourself is a miracle but mending a broken arm is not comes down to the mind-body connection: The broken bone seems to mend itself physically, without the intervention of your mind; yet, a spontaneous cure of cancer—so it is widely believed—depends on a special quality of mind, some deep will to live, a heroically positive outlook, or some other rare capacity.

This implies that there are two kinds of healing, one that is normal, the other abnormal, or at least exceptional.

I believe that this distinction is false. The broken arm mends because consciousness makes it mend, and the same holds true for the miraculous cancer cure, the long-term survival of AIDS, the healing by faith, and even the ability to live to a great old age without falling prey to disease. The reason why not everyone manages to take the healing process as far as it can go is that we differ drastically in our ability to mobilize it.

We can see this in the way that different people react to disease. A minute fraction, far less than 1 percent, of all the patients who contract an incurable disease manage to cure themselves. A larger fraction, but still under 5 percent, live much longer than average—this is confirmed in the 2 percent of AIDS patients who have survived longer than eight years, while the vast majority do not survive beyond two. These findings are not restricted to incurable diseases. Studies have generally shown that only 20 percent of patients with serious but treatable disorders recover with excellent results. That leaves nearly 80 percent who either do not recover or only partially recover. Why is unsuccessful healing so far out of proportion? What marks a survivor as opposed to a non-survivor?

Apparently the successful patients have learned to motivate their own healing, and the most successful have gone much further than that. They have found the secret of quantum healing. They are the geniuses of the mind-body connection. Modern medicine cannot even begin to duplicate their cures, because no cure that relies on drugs or surgery is so precisely timed, so beautifully coordinated, so benign and free of side effects, so effortless as theirs. Their ability springs from a level so deep that you cannot go any deeper. If we knew what their brains were doing to motivate their bodies, we would have the basic unit of the healing process in our hands.

As yet, medicine has not taken the quantum leap, and the word *quantum* has no clinical application. Because quantum physics works with ultra-high-speed accelerators, you may think that quantum healing uses radioisotopes or X rays. But that is the opposite of what it means. Quantum healing moves away from external, high-technology methods toward the deepest core of the mind-body system. This core is where healing begins. To go there and learn to promote the healing response, you must get past all the grosser levels of the body—cells, tissues, organs, and systems—and arrive at the junction point between mind and matter, the point where consciousness actually starts to have an effect.

The quantum itself—what it is, how it behaves—takes up the first half of this book. The second half then blends the quantum into Ayurveda, making a marriage of two cultures while trying to arrive at one answer. The scientific worldview of the West surprisingly supports the vision of the ancient sages of India. This is a journey that breaks down barriers and ignores cultural fences. To me, the whole story has to be found out. Chitra asked me for it, and so I am writing for her and all patients like her. Until they find an answer, their lives still hang in the balance.

EXPANDING THE TOPIC

Much can be said in favor of consciousness affecting the body, to the extent that the gap between "normal" healing and "miraculous" healing has closed even more over the past few decades. The main obstacle, as far as mainstream medicine is concerned, is a fixed belief that the body operates entirely like a physical machine. If that were so, the following experiment would have failed.

The experiment was the brainchild of the pioneering work of Harvard psychologist Ellen Langer, who as far back as 1981 was testing the possibility that aging has a major mental component. (The notion is actually ancient in origin. The medieval Indian philosopher and sage Adi Shankara declared that people grow old and die because they see other people grow old and die.)

In 1981, Langer took eight men in their seventies, all in good health but exhibiting signs of age, and immersed them for five days in an environment that was like time travel going back to 1959, including the music and television of the period, along with the movies and events in the news. The men were told to act as if they were their younger selves, because Langer had already done experiments in which memory loss in the elderly could sometimes be reversed by giving subjects an incentive to remember. In other words, the mind was being motivated to affect the body.

Before entering the time-capsule environment, the men were tested on various markers of aging such as grip strength, dexterity, and how well they could hear and see. At the end of the five days, the group had improved on seven out of eight measures, including better vision, a startling finding. They looked younger as assessed by outside judges. Thirty-three years ago Langer was proceeding more or less intuitively, without the knowledge into gene expression and neuroplasticity that we can turn to today (more on those breakthroughs in later "Expanding the Topic" sections).

In another startling experiment, Langer went into a retirement home and divided her subjects into two groups. Both were given some houseplants for their room. One group was told that they were responsible for keeping the plants alive, and that they could make choices in their own daily schedule. The other group was told that the staff would tend the plants, and in addition they were given no choice in their fixed daily schedule. At the end of eighteen months, twice as many subjects in the first group were still alive compared with the second group. (The same rationale lies behind the accepted practice of giving the elderly a pet to take care of. At the very least it improves their mood and quality of life. It may prolong their lives as well.)

Aging and healing have in common that they have long been viewed as fixed processes based on strict physical limitations. An invisible factor like making your own choices about how to spend your day never figured into the calculation. This bias has been shifting for quite a while, but only the beginning signs were evident when *Quantum Healing* appeared. Today what's important isn't the acceptance of consciousness as a factor in healing—that battle has been won, more or less. Instead we need a set of new assumptions about how far consciousness can go to alter healing and aging, not to mention intractable chronic pain, addictions, dependency on prescription drugs, recovery from surgery, and so on.

Here are the basic assumptions I'd suggest:

1. Mind comes before matter.
2. Mental choices originate the messages that change organs, tissues, and cells.
3. The body is fluid and dynamic, not fixed and determined.
4. Genes express whatever a person desires. They operate through switches that the mind can access.
5. The mind-body system is a feedback loop where input and output have many determinants, including lifestyle, environment, behavior, beliefs, and past conditioning.
6. Through self-care, a higher state of wellbeing is attainable. Self-care makes daily use of the mind-body feedback loop.
7. Ultimately, the evolution of future humanity depends on internal balance (homeostasis) that is balanced with the whole ecology of the planet.

There's much more to say about each of these points, as we'll discover in coming chapters. But the general conclusion is that "normal" isn't as far from "miraculous" as both camps, believers and skeptics, used to think. The choices you make today are the key to your wellbeing for life. Every cell in your body is eavesdropping on your thoughts. Consciousness research is constantly gaining new ground, so it's best to assume that your potential for mind-body mastery is much greater than anyone now supposes.

2

THE BODY HAS A MIND
OF ITS OWN

When I said that no one can honestly claim to know the cure for breast cancer, I was telling a half-truth. If a patient could promote the healing process from within, that would be *the* cure for cancer. Healing episodes like Chitra's come about when a radical shift takes place inside, removing fear and doubt at the same time as it removes the disease. Yet, the exact location of this shift opens up profound mysteries. It defies medical wisdom to answer even the most basic question: Was the shift in Chitra's mind, in her body, or both? To find out, Western medicine has recently begun to move away from drugs and surgery, the mainstay of every doctor's practice, toward the amorphous, often perplexing field loosely known as "mind-body medicine." The move was almost a forced one, because the old reliance on the physical body alone had begun to crumble.

Mind-body medicine makes many doctors extremely uneasy. They feel it is more a concept than a true field. Given a choice between a new idea and a familiar chemical, a doctor will trust the chemical—penicillin, digitalis, aspirin, and Valium do not need any new thinking on the patient's part (or the doctor's) to be effective. The problem comes in when the chemical isn't effective. Recent surveys taken in England and America have shown that as many as 80 percent of patients feel that their underlying complaint, their reason for going to the doctor, was not satisfactorily resolved when they left his office. Classic studies going back to the end of World War II showed that patients left the Yale Medical School hospital sicker than the day they arrived. (These are paralleled by similar studies that showed that patients with psychiatric complaints improved more while they were on the waiting list to see a psychiatrist than after they actually saw him—so the situation isn't simply one of exchanging a body doctor for a head doctor.)

A miracle cure, then, simply throws into high relief the need to reexamine some of medicine's basic concepts. Our current logic of healing can be impressive, or at least good enough, as when we apply penicillin to cure an infection, but nature's logic can be awe-inspiring. Many physicians have stood in wonder witnessing such cures as Chitra's without having a clue how to explain them; the standard term for them is *spontaneous remission*, a convenient tag that says little more than that the patient recovered by himself. Spontaneous remissions are quite rare—one study in 1985 estimated that they occur once in every twenty thousand diagnosed cancer cases; some specialists believe they are much rarer (fewer than ten per million), but no one knows for sure.

Recently I spent an evening with a leading oncologist, or cancer specialist, from the Midwest, a doctor who treats thousands of patients every year. I asked him if he knew of any spontaneous remissions. He shrugged and said, "I feel uncomfortable with that term. I have seen tumors completely regress. It's very rare, but it happens."

Did these regressions sometimes happen totally by themselves? He admitted that they occasionally did. He thought for a moment and mentioned that certain kinds of melanoma—an extremely lethal skin cancer that kills very quickly—are known to disappear by themselves. He couldn't explain why this happened. "I don't stop to think about these rare incidents," he said. "Treating cancer is a matter of statistics—we go with the numbers. A huge majority of patients respond to certain lines of treatment, and there just isn't time to find out about the infinitesimal minority who recover for some unknown reason. Besides, it is our experience that many of these regressions are only temporary."

Did he think complete regressions were rarer than one in a million? No, he answered, not that rare.

Then, as a scientist, didn't he want to find out the mechanism that lies behind them, even if the odds are one in a million, or one in ten million? Again he shrugged. "Of course there must be a mechanism behind it," he conceded, "but my practice is not set up to look into that. Let me give you an example: eight years ago, a man came to see me complaining of a painful chest cough. We X-rayed him, and it turned out that he had a large tumor between his lungs. He was admitted to the hospital, we took a biopsy, and the pathologist's report diagnosed the tumor as oat-cell carcinoma. This is an extremely deadly, very fast-growing malignancy.

"I told my patient that he must have immediate surgery to relieve the pressure that his tumor was creating, followed by radiation and chemotherapy. He was quite disturbed by the prospect of treatment and refused. I completely lost track of him after that. Eight years later, a man came to see me with an enlarged lymph node in his neck. I took a biopsy, and it turned out to be oat-cell carcinoma. Then I realized that it was the same man.

"We took chest X rays, and there was no trace of lung cancer. Normally, 99.99 percent of untreated patients would have died in six months; as many as 90 percent would not live five years even with maximum therapy. I asked him what he had done for the earlier cancer, and he told me he hadn't done anything—he had just decided he was not going to let himself die of cancer. And he may refuse treatment again with this second cancer."

By definition, scientific medicine deals in predictable results.

Yet, whenever spontaneous remissions appear, their behavior is completely unpredictable. They can occur without the presence of any therapy, or they can accompany conventional cancer treatment. The myriad alternative approaches to cancer available in the United States today may each have distinct merits, but no one has proven that they promote spontaneous remissions any better than standard radiation and chemotherapy, nor are they apparently any worse. How advanced the cancer is seems not to matter, either. Both tiny tumors and extremely large masses of malignancy can disappear, virtually overnight. Because of their rarity and because they happen as if by chance, spontaneous remissions have so far taught us very little either about the cause of cancer or about how an "impossible" cure is achieved.

It seems reasonable to suppose that the body is fighting cancer all the time and winning a huge majority of the battles. Many kinds of cancer can be induced, either in test tubes or in laboratory animals, using toxic substances (carcinogens), fatty diets, radiation, high doses of stress, and viruses, among other things. Since we are subjected to all of these at a furious rate, they must be causing damage inside us. DNA is known to break down under these extreme conditions; usually, however, it knows how to repair itself or to detect the damaged material and discard it.

This means that early cancers are probably being detected and combatted in the body on a regular basis. If you take this process and step it up in intensity, you have the "miracle" of a spontaneous remission. It is no miracle at all, in fact, but a natural process that has yet to be explained, just as curing pneumonia with penicillin would be a miracle if you could not explain it through the germ theory of disease. The point is that the mechanism behind miracle cures is not mystical or random—and it deserves to be investigated.

In ordinary practice, once the miracle is over, the doctor goes back to his routine, including his routine concepts. Even these, however, the stock-in-trade of medical school, have buckled. To give just one example: Since its inception as a field of rational scientific study, medicine has accepted the degeneration of brain function in elderly people as a natural occurrence. This deterioration was thoroughly documented with "hard" findings—as we age, our brains shrink, grow lighter, and lose millions of neurons every year. We have our full complement of neurons by age 2, and by age 30, the number starts to decline. The loss of any single brain cell is permanent, since neurons do not regenerate. On the basis of this well-known fact, brain decline seemed to be scientifically valid; sadly but inevitably, to grow old must lead to memory loss, decreased reasoning ability, impaired intelligence, and related symptoms.

These time-honored assumptions, however, have now been shown to be wrong. Careful study of healthy elderly people—as opposed to the sick, hospitalized ones whom medicine habitually studied—has revealed that 80 percent of healthy Americans, barring psychological distress (such as loneliness, depression, or lack of outside stimulation), suffer no significant memory loss as they age. The ability to retain new information can decline, which is why old people forget phone numbers, names, and the reason for walking into a room; but the ability to remember past events, called long-term memory, actually improves. (One authority on aging quotes Cicero, who declared, "I've never heard of an old man who forgot where his money was hidden.")

In tests where 70-year-olds were matched with 20-year-olds, the older people performed better than the younger in this area of memory. After they practiced the other kind of memory—called short-term memory—for a few minutes every day, the older group could almost match the younger subjects, who were at their prime of mental functioning.

Perhaps the "prime of life" should be extended. The secret, as with almost every other "natural" decline in old age, depends on habits of mind, not the circuitry in the nervous system. As long as a person stays mentally active, he will remain as intelligent as in youth and middle age. People will still lose over one billion neurons throughout their lifetime, at an average rate of 18 million per year, but this loss is compensated for by another structure, the branchlike filaments called dendrites, which connect the nerve cells to one another.

A nerve cell tends to be highly individual in shape, but typically it has a bulbous central section from which thin arms radiate, like an octopus. These arms, or axons, end in a swirl of tiny filaments that looked treelike to the early anatomists, so they named them dendrites after the Greek word for "tree." Dendrites, which can vary in number from less than a dozen to more than a thousand per cell, serve as contact points, allowing the neuron to send signals to its neighbors. By growing new dendrites, a neuron can open new channels of communication in every direction, like a switchboard sprouting extra lines.

It is not known how a thought is actually formed among brain cells or how the bewilderingly vast number of connections interrelate—millions of dendrites come together at major junction points in the body, such as the solar plexus, not to mention the billions upon billions in the brain itself. But experiments have shown that new dendrites can be grown throughout life, up to advanced old age. The current view is that this new growth easily provides us with the physical structure for unimpaired brain function. In a healthy brain, senility is not physically normal. A rich multiplication of dendrites might even lie behind growing wise in old age, a time when more and more of life is seen in its totality—in other words, more interconnected, just as the nerve cells are more interconnected through their new dendrites.

This example illustrates how radically wrong medicine can be if it insists that matter is superior to mind. To say that a nerve cell creates thoughts may be true, but it is just as true to say that thinking creates nerve cells. In the case of the new dendrites, it is the habit of thinking, remembering, and being mentally active that creates the new tissue. Nor is this an isolated finding. Curiously enough, as soon as the concept of the "new old age" was permissible in the eyes of doctors, our views of many forms of degeneration began to alter.

As long as you exercise, for example, your body's musculature will not wither, and your strength will be unimpaired for life, although there will be a slow decline in stamina. You can train for a marathon at 65, provided you are in good physical shape and train sensibly. Similarly, your heart changes with age, growing less resilient and pumping less blood per beat, but heart disease and hardening of the arteries, thought absolutely normal with old age a few decades ago, are now seen as avoidable, too, depending on diet and lifestyle. Strokes, another given of old age, have declined by 40 percent just in the last decade, thanks to better control of hypertension and less fat in our diets. A large percentage of "unavoidable" senility has been traced to vitamin deficiency, poor diet, and dehydration. The overall result of these findings is that old age is being drastically reconsidered; a less obvious result is that the whole body, at any stage of life, has to be rethought.

What is happening on every front in medicine is that the healthy body is showing itself to be more resilient and versatile than was hiterto suspected. Whereas medical school teaches that germ A causes disease B and is treated by drug C, nature seems to feel that this is only one option among many. The mental approach to treating cancer, for instance, would have been ridiculed a decade ago. But people do seem able to participate in their cancer treatment, and even to control the course of the disease, by using thoughts. In 1971, Dr. O. Carl Simonton, a radiologist at the University of Texas, met a 61-year-old man with throat cancer. The disease was very far progressed; the patient could hardly swallow, and his weight had dropped to 98 pounds.

Not only was the prognosis extremely poor—the doctors gave him a 5 percent chance of surviving five years after treatment—but the patient was already so weak that it seemed unlikely he would respond well to radiation, which is the standard therapy for this condition. In desperation, but also curious to try a psychological approach, Dr. Simonton suggested that the man enhance his radiation therapy through the use of visualization. He was taught to visualize his cancer as vividly as possible. Then, using any mental picture that appealed to him, he was asked to visualize his immune system as the white blood cells successfully attacked the cancer cells and swept them out of the body, leaving only healthy cells behind.

The man said he envisioned his immune cells as a blizzard of white particles, covering the tumor like snow burying a black rock. Dr. Simonton had him go home and repeat this visualization at intervals throughout the day. The man agreed, and soon his tumor seemed to be shrinking. In a few weeks it was definitely smaller, and his response to radiation was almost free of side effects; after two months, the tumor was gone.

Naturally, Dr. Simonton was surprised and baffled, though elated that the psychological approach had been so powerful. How does a thought defeat a cancer cell? The mechanism was totally unknown—in fact, given the fiendish complexity of the immune system and the nervous system, both of which were obviously involved here, the mechanism might be unknowable. For his part, the patient accepted his cure without undue surprise. He told Dr. Simonton that arthritis in his legs kept him from going stream-fishing as much as he liked. Now that the cancer was gone, why not try visualizing the arthritis away too? Within a few more weeks, that is exactly what happened. The man remained free of both cancer and arthritis for a follow-up period of six years.

This now-famous case is a landmark in mind-body medicine, but unfortunately it is not the whole story. Dr. Simonton's visualization therapy (it has branched out into a broad mind-body program) does not reliably cure cancer. One of my patients used it with success to cure herself of breast cancer, I believe, although she practiced the technique on her own and not under a doctor's scrutiny. Long-term statistical studies, however, dispute whether such sporadic results are any better than those of conventional treatment. At present, conventional therapy has a big edge. If a woman with breast cancer, for example, detects the tumor while it is still very small and localized, the chances of curing her (a "cure" means surviving at least three years without a recurrence of the disease) are currently better than 90 percent. In comparison, the number of spontaneous remissions, at the most generous estimate, would be well below $\frac{1}{10}$ of 1 percent. Until a mental or other alternative therapy outperforms radiation and chemotherapy, it will not become the treatment of choice. Although patients may long for such approaches, most doctors still fear and distrust them.

But even if Dr. Simonton's patient were one of a kind, he is enough to rock our conception of how the body cures itself, for here is nature finding a way to combat death that no doctor had ever tried—and here also is the dark possibility that what the doctor usually tries is not helping nature but stifling it.

Curious and adventurous doctors have flocked to experiment with mind-body innovations over the last decade, from biofeedback and hypnotism to visualizations and behavior modification. The results across the board have been amorphous and hard to interpret. Psychologist Michael Lerner spent three years conducting an in-depth study of forty clinics offering alternative approaches to cancer, whose methods ranged from herbs and macrobiotics to visualization of positive mental images. He found that these "complementary cancer centers" were sought out by patients who were generally well educated and prosperous, that the doctors running the clinics were also serious and well intentioned, but that nothing close to a cure for cancer had been discovered anywhere he visited.

When he interviewed the patients, a fairly large proportion (40 percent) thought that they had experienced at least a temporary improvement in the quality of their lives. Another 40 percent reported that they experienced actual medical improvements in their condition, lasting from a few days to a number of years. About 10 percent fell at the extreme ends of the spectrum, one group saying that they got nothing from the treatment and the other that they were now partially or wholly recovered from their disease. Generally, the record of alternative approaches is that they give a measure of comfort and relief to patients, but disappointingly, the remission rates are not radically different from those of standard therapy.

There are other problems that run deeper than inconsistent results: the mind-body field continues to be plagued by an inability to rigorously prove its basic tenet, that the mind influences the body toward either health or disease. It seems utterly self-evident that sick people and healthy people enjoy different states of mind, but the causal connection is still elusive. In 1985 a major study of breast cancer conducted at the University of Pennsylvania failed to find any correlation between the mental attitude of patients and their chances of surviving their disease beyond two years. In an editorial accompanying the study, which appeared in the prestigious *New England Journal of Medicine*, the whole concept of emotions affecting cancer was denounced. "Our belief in disease as a direct reflection of mental states," the editorial declared, "is largely folklore."

In response, letters deluged the journal, most of them from physicians who heatedly disagreed with the editorial's conclusion. It certainly seems unreasonable to discount mental attitudes as a factor in illness, much less as folklore. Every practicing physician knows that the patient's will to recover plays a vital part in his treatment. Wedded as they are to "hard" medicine, most doctors nonetheless cannot condone the idea that attitude, belief, and emotions do not play their part. Hippocrates stated at the dawn of Western medicine that "a patient who is mortally sick might yet recover from belief in the goodness of his physician." Numerous modern studies have corroborated this, by showing that people who trust their doctor and surrender themselves to his care are likelier to recover than those who approach medicine with distrust, fear, and antagonism.

In the wake of the editorial, tempers flared and lines of allegiance were drawn, while the issues became even more confused. Three separate studies of breast-cancer survival rates from the mid-1980s came up with three entirely different results. In one, the women who displayed strong positive attitudes tended to outlive those who were negative, and it did not matter if their diseases were more advanced—positive emotions, it seemed, helped them re-cover from a late-stage, metastasized cancer, while patients with negative emotions died from small tumors that had been diagnosed relatively early.

A second study, however, found that any strong attitude, if ex-pressed rather than held back, helped in survival of this very deadly disease. While the first finding bolsters common sense—the idea that positivity is better than negativity—the second does much the same from another angle, the idea being that it is better to fight than to give up. Publicity was given to a so-called cancer personality, who bottles up emotions and somehow converts repression into malig-nant cells. The opposite would be the "strong will to live" type, who can be either positive or negative.

All of this follows a certain logic, except for the study that ap-peared in the *New England Journal of Medicine* to begin with, sec-onded by supporting studies, which found no correlation between *any* emotional pattern and surviving breast cancer beyond two years. Even as it grew in popularity, becoming one of the most wel-come innovations since the Salk vaccine, the concept of mind-body medicine was shaken. Now, a familiar pattern has emerged, in which the public is informed of some elating breakthrough, followed by disappointing clinical results that are generally known only in re-stricted medical circles.

A classic example was the division of heart-attack patients, more than three-quarters of them middle-aged males, into high-risk Type A personalities and low-risk Type B's. The Type A personality was supposed to be a hard-driving, compulsive worker, constantly racing deadlines and churning his system with stress hormones, as opposed to the relaxed, tolerant, more balanced Type B. Type A suffered from "the disease of being in a hurry"; therefore, it seemed logical that his heart would eventually rebel, leading to a coronary.

Unfortunately, controlled studies have indicated that this widely accepted division is not so neat. It turns out that most people have some Type A in them and some Type B, and that tolerance for stress varies widely, with certain groups stating that they thrive on it. Finally, a 1988 study found that if a man actually has a heart attack, Type A's survive better than Type B's. Their drive to succeed apparently turns into a benefit once the coronary strikes.

The intricacies of the mind-body relation were not to be easily solved. If one asks why a positive mind cannot be easily correlated with good health—it appears to be one of the most obvious facts of life—the answer has to do with what you mean by "mind" in the first place. This is not a philosophical question but a practical one. If a patient comes in with cancer, is his mental state judged by how he feels on the day of the diagnosis, long before, or long afterward? Dr. Lawrence LeShan, author of the pioneering studies from the 1950s correlating emotions to cancer, went back into the childhoods of cancer patients to find the black seed that poisoned their psychology, and he theorized that it lay dormant in the subconscious for years before inducing their disease.

In my own practice, I saw a lung-cancer patient who had lived comfortably with a coin-sized lesion in his lungs for five years. He did not even suspect that it was cancerous, and since he was in his sixties, the lesion was growing quite slowly. However, as soon as I told him that the lesion was consistent with a diagnosis of lung cancer, he became terribly agitated. Within a month he started to cough up blood; within three, he was dead. If his state of mind contributed to this untoward haste, it apparently acted quickly. This patient could live with his tumor, but he couldn't live with the diagnosis.

Even more basic is this question: Is the "mind" that a doctor is interested in the patient's overall personality, his subconscious, his attitudes, his deepest beliefs, or something not yet understood and defined by psychology? It may be that the relevant aspect of the mind involved in getting sick or getting well is not even specifically human.

An Ohio University study of heart disease in the 1970s was conducted by feeding quite toxic, high-cholesterol diets to rabbits in order to block their arteries, duplicating the effect that such a diet has on human arteries. Consistent results began to appear in all the rabbit groups except for one, which strangely displayed 60 percent fewer symptoms. Nothing in the rabbits' physiology could account for their high tolerance to the diet, until it was discovered by accident that the student who was in charge of feeding these particular rabbits liked to fondle and pet them. He would hold each rabbit lovingly for a few minutes before feeding it; astonishingly, this alone seemed to enable the animals to overcome the toxic diet. Repeat experiments, in which one group of rabbits was treated neutrally while the others were loved, came up with similar results. Once again, the mechanism that causes such immunity is quite unknown—it is baffling to think that evolution has built into the rabbit mind an immune response that needs to be triggered by human cuddling.

There is even a possibility, many doctors would contend, that the mind is a fiction, medically speaking. When we think that it is sick, what is really sick is the brain. By this logic, the classical mental disorders—depression, schizophrenia, and psychosis—are actually brain disorders. This logic has obvious inadequacies: it is like saying that car wrecks should be blamed on automobiles. But the brain, being a physical organ that can be weighed and dissected, makes medicine feel more secure than does the mind, which has proved impossible to define after many centuries of introspection and analysis. Doctors are quite happy not to be called upon as philosophers.

The ability of today's psychotropic, or mind-influencing, drugs to relieve the major symptoms of mental illness, such as depression, mania, anxiety, and hallucinations, is much greater than any treatment available in the past. Chemical psychiatry is likely to vie with its exact opposite, mind-body medicine, as the medical revolution of our time. It has hard clinical results to back it up, including numerous indications that chemical imbalances in the brain are directly linked to mental illness.

Nothing could appear to be more all-encompassing than the fullblown madness of a chronic schizophrenic, who suffers from hallucinatory visions and inner voices, distorted thinking, and often complete physical and mental disorientation. To ask a schizophrenic what day it is can throw him into bewilderment and shivering terror. However, the structural difference between this state of mind and sanity may be traceable to one minute biochemical called dopamine, which is secreted by the brain. The dopamine connection, known for two decades, held that schizophrenics overproduce this chemical, which plays an important role in processing both emotions and perceptions—a hallucination would thus be a perception of the outside world that has gotten scrambled in the brain's chemical coding.

This hypothesis was further simplified in 1984 when a psychiatrist at the University of Iowa, Dr. Rafiq Waziri, reviewed what was known about the brain chemistry of schizophrenics and narrowed the defect down to an even smaller molecule called serine, a common amino acid found in most protein foods. Serine is thought to be an early link in the manufacture of dopamine. Unable to metabolize serine correctly, the brains of schizophrenics apparently overproduce dopamine to offset the lack—the exact process is still unknown. Could it be that full-blown schizophrenia, considered the most bizarre and complex of mental disorders, depends on how well you digest your food? Earlier findings at M.I.T. have already shown that the brain's basic chemistry is so variable that it can be modified by a single meal.

Dr. Waziri bolstered support for his theory by taking a group of long-term schizophrenics and feeding them a dietary supplement of glycine, a chemical that serine is supposed to build as part of the dopamine mechanism. Perhaps the extra glycine would bypass the serine defect, Waziri reasoned, and bring dopamine back into balance. In the trial group, a few schizophrenics responded quite dramatically—they were able to stop their medications without having any psychotic episodes. For the first time in years, their thinking was free from both their disease and the mind-numbing drugs used to treat it.

A dietary approach to mental illness would be far more benign than current therapies. The possibility of finding more dietary links is also tantalizing. At least one best-selling diet book has jumped the gun by listing "happy foods" and "sad foods," on the theory that the amino acids in these foods go directly to the brain and are made into chemicals that produce either positive or negative moods. Milk, chicken, bananas, and leafy greens are among the happy foods, because they stimulate dopamine and two other "positive" brain chemicals. Sugary and fatty foods, on the other hand, are typically sad foods, because they stimulate acetylcholine, a "negative" chemical. Critics say, quite justifiably, that brain chemicals are not so simple—can a schizophrenic's high dopamine levels be considered positive? Nor does it seem that changing the intake of amino acids leads directly to more of a desired brain chemical, just as the amount of cholesterol in your diet does not directly correlate with the amount in your blood.

If you can eat your way to sanity, or even a better mood, then the basic issues in mind-body medicine become even more confused. Can you trust the mind to cure arthritis and at the same time hold that eating chocolate will make you depressed? This would imply a self-contradiction, that mind is dominant over matter except when matter is dominant over mind. In the current atmosphere of ambiguous findings, the two opposite positions—treat the body through the mind, treat the mind through the body—are equally up in the air.

None of the confusion has been adequately clarified, and as a result, the subjective world of the mind remains a treacherous force, capricious in its ability to heal, equally capricious in its ability to bring illness. Many doctors, because of their materialistic bias, would be thrilled to conclude that chemicals must be the answer to all our mental and physical mysteries.

I don't think they can be. In my specialty of endocrinology, some of the first chemicals that affect the mind, the endocrine hormones, were discovered. Every day I see patients who display mental symptoms that are traceable to defects in their hormonal balance—the distorted thinking of a diabetic going into a low-blood-sugar reaction, the mood shifts of the menstrual cycle, and even a characteristic depression that is the earliest warning sign of certain cancers (a tumor in the pancreas, for example, may be too small to detect, yet it will release cortisol and other "stress hormones" into the bloodstream, causing the patient to feel depressed).

Despite this, I see too many flaws in the argument that a deeper knowledge of body chemistry is all we need—the body has too many chemicals (literally thousands of them), they are produced in bewilderingly complex patterns, and they come and go too fast, often in fractions of a second. What controls this constant flux? We cannot leave the mind out of the mind-body connection altogether. To say that the body heals itself using only chemicals is like saying that a car shifts gears using only the transmission. Clearly it takes a driver who knows what he is doing. Although medicine has spent several centuries trying to hold on to the idea that the body runs itself alone, like a self-motivated machine, there must be a driver here, too. Otherwise, our body's chemistry would be a jumble of floating molecules instead of the incredibly ordered and precise machinery that it so obviously is.

In a more naïve age, the driver was thought to be a tiny man, called the homunculus, who sat in the heart and performed all the gear shifts needed to run the body. The homunculus went out in the Renaissance, when anatomists began for the first time to dissect cadavers and verify what was inside them. The homunculus wasn't found inside the heart (neither was the soul), but that left a huge, glaring gap between the mind and the body. Many scientists since have tried to fill the gap with the brain, saying that the brain's function is to order and control all other functions in the physiology; but this answer begs the question, because the brain is just another machine. The driver still needs to be there. I will argue that he is, but he has become something much more abstract than the homunculus or even the brain—he is built into the intelligent power that motivates us to live, move, and think.

Can that be proved? The next step for us is to work our way deeper into the body's inner intelligence, to try to find out what motivates it. The territory of mind-body medicine has no givens and no inflexible rules, which is all to the good. For decades, medicine has known that much disease has a psychosomatic component, yet dealing with that component has been like trying to harness the wind. Inside us there must be a "thinking body" that responds to the mind's commands, but where could it be and what is it made of?

EXPANDING THE TOPIC

One of the most baffling mysteries touched upon in this chapter— where does a thought come from?—remains just as baffling today. It may surprise you, but there is no evidence that the brain is thinking. In fact, if you assume that the mind arises from the brain, which is the standard working assumption in neuroscience, consciousness is just an inference. Imagine an old-time player piano, the kind that performed music by inserting a paper roll into the mechanism. Punched holes in the paper roll activate the keys, giving the appearance that an invisible pianist is playing the "Maple Leaf Rag" or a Mozart sonata.

No one would propose that the piano roll manufactured itself. There must be a musician whose actual intentions lie behind the "invisible" pianist. We infer his existence without seeing him. The same is true about the mind when you observe the brain. As its quadrillion connections activate, using chemical signals and faint electrical charges, the vast activity of mind—thoughts, feelings, sensations, and images—appears. To claim that this happens automatically seems strange, but it's the materialist position, while in *Quantum Healing* I said the opposite: An invisible intelligence, complete with intentions, desires, hopes, dreams, and so on, is at work. The fact that you can't see this entity, known as the self, doesn't prove that he doesn't exist. It only proves that he doesn't exist if you are a strict materialist, who will accept nothing except physical phenomena.

The bulk of this chapter was devoted to the reality of the mind-body connection, which is unassailable now. Over the past thirty years the network that transmits messages throughout the body has been studied in much greater detail, leaving no doubt that every thought, feeling, mood, and belief crosses the bridge from mental to physical. But these detailed researches into hormones, neurotransmitters, immunomodulators, peptides, and thousands of products expressed by genes has obscured the simplicity of the mind-body connection.

In simple terms, the entire system is a feedback loop, with only two factors to consider, input and output. Input enters the brain, output exits. This is the nexus where every process, mental or physical, meets every other, like trillions of train tracks converging on a train station and then exiting the station to go their separate ways. The reason for simplifying the almost infinite complexity of a living mind and body comes down to practicalities. Each of us wants to know the right and wrong kind of input that will affect us.

Positive Input

Pure food, air, and water
Positive emotions
Strong self-esteem
Low stress, good coping skills in the face of stress
Moderate exercise
Good sleep (eight to nine hours every night)
Loving, supportive relationships
Inner contentment, lack of conflicts and tensions
Satisfying work
Meditation and other contemplative practices
Abstaining from alcohol, tobacco, and recreational drugs

    Minimizing the use of prescription drugs

    Healing old wounds and self-destructive conditioning from the
       past

The reason that little or none of these things seem new is that they don't need to be. After decades of public information about prevention and the rise of the wellness movement, we know a great deal about positive lifestyle changes (this isn't the same as knowing all we need to know about why these changes work). Input, positive or negative, registers in every cell of the body, down to the expression of your genes (that is, their complex chemical output).

The fly in the ointment is that information isn't the same as motivation. People may know what's good for them, but they continue to live otherwise. The most common kinds of negative input remain a mainstay in the lives of people who sincerely want to change, including overuse of alcohol, tobacco, and drugs; eating processed and junk foods; tolerating a high level of stress; going short on sleep; taking little or no exercise. The Gallup organization, which surveys the wellbeing of populations around the world, has a top category known as "thriving." These are the people who describe themselves as happy, safe, financially secure, and healthy—in short, they are enjoying a level of wellbeing that most Americans would consider a basic minimum. Yet the percentage of people who are thriving around the world is dismally low, often under 10–15 percent, and even in the prosperous developed West, it rarely rises above 33 percent. The fact that the United States continues to consume antidepressants and tranquilizers in record numbers attests to our inner unease, and by some estimates the abuse of prescription painkillers is now a cause of death surpassing the total deaths from illegal substances.

No amount of preaching about these things will work over the long run. Prevention implies a level of fear, and fear is a bad motivator except in short bursts. The body resists being in a state of chronic stress, and worrying about your health is a form of stress. The only successful long-term motivation is inspiration. It, too, can flicker out quickly. But there's a secure kind of inspiration that comes from valuing yourself with such conviction that you like and enjoy the experience of giving your mind and body positive inputs all the time.

When I wrote *Quantum Healing* I wanted to give the human side of the mind-body connection, realizing that a term like *feedback loop*, adopted from computers and information theory, sounds cold and abstract. But the whole game comes down to input-output in the end.

Without dwelling on the negative, let's say that you've had a stressful day. You feel wiped out by five o'clock, so you grab a burger and fries instead of cooking at home. You settle in with a drink or two to unwind. Your workload is heavy, so you catch up by taking some of it home with you, and by bedtime you find your mind is still so active that getting to sleep takes a while. Your alarm clock goes off at the usual time the next morning, but you've managed only six hours of sleep. No matter, it's time to start the whole routine over again. In the back of your mind you promise yourself to do better, a promise you may or may not keep.

Yet as normal as this daily routine has become for millions of people, adapting to it is a challenge for the human body, because as we now realize, each deviation from a positive lifestyle registers at the cellular level. Here's a summary of what is happening. The consequences of negative input are daunting.

What Negative Input Does

Disturbs overall balance, leading to inflammation.

Moves erratically though the body, obstructed by chronic stress and the toxic debris of negative input from the past.

Reinforces old neural pathways, making it much harder to break bad habits.

Contributes to abnormal cell function, including precancerous
   anomalies.
Weakens the immune system, impairing resistance to disease.
Contributes to premature aging.
Creates a general sense of dullness, discomfort, and dis-ease,
   the opposite of wellbeing.

Because *Quantum Healing* focused on the drama of spontaneous remissions from cancer—so-called miracle cures—the bigger
message might not have struck with enough force. So let me state
it in unmistakable terms: Input is under your control. Without
anticipating cancer or any other disorder, your chief aim every
day should be to maximize positive input and minimize negative
input.

We are badly in need of a new model for wellbeing. Most people
segment their lives into work, leisure, and family. Little time is left
for self-care. Yet caring for yourself today is exactly what determines
your life for decades to come.

True self-care embraces a person's entire life. Taking charge of
your own wellbeing reaches into every corner because it has to.
Your brain processes every experience, physical, mental, and spiritual, as input. Look at the contrast that self-care makes when compared to self-neglect.

10 Keys to Self-Care

1. Making happiness a high priority.
   Versus: Coasting along with our present state of happiness and
   unhappiness.
2. Making sure your life has purpose and meaning.
   Versus: Focusing on daily practicalities, even those that seem
   routine and meaningless.
3. Living according to a higher vision.

Versus: Living for externals like a better job, more money, a bigger house, etc.

4. Expanding your awareness in every decade of life.
Versus: Viewing youth as the peak of life and old age as a dwindling decline.

5. Devoting time and attention to personal growth.
Versus: Staying the same as you always were and feeling proud about it.

6. Following a sensible regimen of good diet and physical activity.
Versus: Eating a diet high in sugar, fat, and calories. Promising yourself to exercise tomorrow, or next week.

7. Allowing your brain to reset by introducing downtime several times a day.
Versus: Working your brain to the point of exhaustion before allowing yourself to take a break.

8. Getting to know your inner world through meditation, contemplation, and self-reflection.
Versus: Avoiding what you really feel. Fearing what you might find if you dared to look inside yourself.

9. Practicing gratitude and appreciation.
Versus: Grabbing as much as you can for yourself. Never forgetting to look out for number one.

10. Learning how to love and be loved.
Versus: Leaving romance behind in the past. Not looking into the deep source of love in yourself.

As you can see, self-care goes far beyond eating our vegetables and signing up for the gym. It amounts to a new model for success and happiness, a model that abundant medical evidence supports. I'll say more about that as we proceed. There's a reason for giving these general principles first. In a world where massive attention is given to the next fad diet, the gym-honed body, and the beauty of youth, the truth is that a shift in consciousness produces far greater benefits.

Getting people to turn inward is an important aspect, but they have to know why. What *Quantum Healing* aimed at was far more radical: seeing yourself in a new way, as a child of the universe. On the basis of that realization, self-care cannot help but begin at the source, where your consciousness merges with cosmic consciousness. You can't truly value yourself until this happens, and then self-care is like caring for Nature itself.

3

THE SCULPTURE OR
THE RIVER?

Counting the number of cells in the human body is no easier than counting the number of people in the world, but the accepted estimate is 50 trillion, or about 10,000 times the Earth's present population. Isolated and placed under a microscope, the various kinds of cells—heart, liver, brain, kidney, et cetera—look rather alike to the untrained eye. A cell is basically a bag, enclosed by an outer membrane, the cell wall, and filled with a mixture of water and swirling chemicals. At the center of all but the red blood cells is a core, the nucleus, which safeguards the tightly twisted coils of DNA. If you hold a speck of liver tissue on your fingertip, it looks like calf's liver; you would be hard-pressed to discern that it is specifically human. Even a skilled geneticist would detect only a 2 percent difference between our DNA and a gorilla's. Of the liver cell's many functions, over five hundred at latest count, you would not have a clue simply by looking at it.

As clouded as the mind-body issue has become, one thing is in-

disputable: somehow human cells have evolved to a state of formidable intelligence. At any one time, the number of activities being
coordinated in our bodies is quite literally infinite. Like the Earth's
ecosystems, our physiology appears to operate in separate compartments that in fact are invisibly connected: we eat, breathe, talk,
think, digest our food, fight off infections, purify our blood of toxins,
renew our cells, discard wastes, vote for Republicans, and much
more besides. Each of these activities weaves its way into the fabric
of the whole. (Our ecology is more planetlike than most people realize. Creatures roam our surface, as unmindful of our hugeness as we
are of their minuteness. Colonies of mites, for example, spend their
entire life cycle in our eyelashes.)

Within the body's vast array, the functions of any single cell—
such as one of the 15 billion neurons in the brain—fill a good-sized
medical text. The volumes devoted to any one system of the body,
such as the immune system or the nervous system, take up several
shelves in a medical library.

The healing mechanism resides somewhere in this overall complexity, but it is elusive. There is no one organ of healing. How does
the body know what to do when it is damaged, then? Medicine has
no simple answer. Any one of the processes involved in healing a
superficial cut—the clotting of the blood, for example—is incredibly complex, so much so that if the mechanism fails, as it does with
hemophiliacs, advanced scientific medicine is at a loss to duplicate
the impaired function. A doctor can prescribe drugs that replace the
missing clotting factor in the blood, but these are temporary, artifi-
cial, and have numerous undesirable side effects. The body's perfect
timing will be absent, as well as the superb coordination of a dozen
related processes. By comparison, a man-made drug is a stranger in
a land where everyone else is blood kin. It can never share the
knowledge that everyone else was born with.

The body, we must admit, has a mind of its own. Once we understand this mysterious aspect of our basic nature, then the mi-

raculous nature of curing cancer should disappear. Everyone's body knows how to heal a cut, yet apparently only a few people have bodies that know how to cure cancer.

Every doctor realizes that it is nature who cures disease, a statement first written by Hippocrates two thousand years ago. What is the difference, then, between nature's ordinary form of healing and unusual or "miraculous" healing? Perhaps the difference is small and exists only in our heads. If you are peeling potatoes and cut your finger with a slip of the knife, the cut heals by itself, and obviously you are not wonder-struck, because the process of healing—the clotting of the blood to close the wound, the formation of a scab, and the regeneration of new skin and blood vessels—seems altogether normal.

Yet, we should be aware that this feeling of normalcy is not the same as knowing what healing is or how to control it. It is sobering to consider how much of the knowledge in medical books pertains not to life but to death. By performing autopsies on cadavers, examining tissue slides under a microscope, and analyzing blood, urine, and other isolated by-products of the body, the majority of medical knowledge has been obtained. True, patients are examined when they are alive, and tests can be run on many isolated functions in their bodies. But the knowledge so acquired is rudimentary compared to the volumes of super-sophisticated data devoted to death. The poet Wordsworth wrote this memorably terse line: "We murder to dissect." No truer statement has ever been made about the limitations of medical research.

The first thing that is killed in the laboratory is the delicate web of intelligence that binds the body together. When a blood cell rushes to a wound site and begins to form a clot, it has not traveled there at random. It actually knows where to go and what to do when it gets there, as surely as a paramedic—in fact, more surely, since it acts completely spontaneously and without guesswork. Even if we break down its knowledge into finer and finer bits, looking for the secret in some minute hormone or messenger enzyme, we will not find a protein strand labeled "intelligence," and yet there is no doubt that intelligence is at work.

Part of this intelligence devotes itself to healing, and it seems to be a very powerful force. Every fatal disease has its mysterious survivors, not just cancer. Although I know of no spontaneous cures of AIDS, there are long-term survivors—those who remain alive after five years—whose immune systems have somehow defended themselves against a disease that under normal conditions is totally devastating. Researchers tend to approach such extraordinary physiologies as biochemical freaks of nature. By taking samples of their blood and isolating any unusual components that can be detected in the immune cells, molecular biologists hope to discover the unknown ingredient that is protecting these people. If that can be accomplished—it is an extremely tedious, difficult task, given the complexity of the immune system—then after years of testing and millions of dollars, a new drug may emerge that can benefit the population as a whole.

Yet, what everyone really needs is the ability to make this wonder drug himself, just as the person who first produced it did, and that ability cannot be synthesized. Isn't buying the drug as good as making it? Not by a long shot. The so-called active ingredient in a man-made drug contains very little know-how compared to the original chemical produced by the body. It would almost be fairer to call the drug an inert ingredient.

The reason for this lies at the level of our cells. The outer membrane of each cell, or the cell wall, is outfitted with numerous sites called receptors. The cell wall itself is smooth, but these receptors are "sticky"—they are made of complex molecular chains whose last links are open-ended, each one waiting for another molecule to come along and bind with it. In other words, receptors are like keyholes into which only very specific keys will fit. For a drug to work—whether morphine, Valium, digitalis, or almost anything else—it must be the key that fits some precisely chosen receptor on the cell wall and no other.

The hormones, enzymes, and other biochemicals produced by our bodies have superb knowledge about which receptors they should fit into. The molecules themselves actually seem able to pick and choose among various sites—it is uncanny to follow their tracks under an electron microscope as they make a beeline to where they are needed. Also, the body can release hundreds of different chemicals at a time and orchestrate each one with regard to the whole.

If you hear a hot rod backfire on the street outside your window and jump in your chair, your instantaneous reaction is the outcome of a complex internal event. The trigger for the event is a burst of adrenaline from your adrenal glands. Carried into the bloodstream, this adrenaline signals reactions from your heart, which starts to pump blood faster; from your blood vessels, which contract and force up your blood pressure; from your liver, which puts out extra fuel in the form of glucose; from your pancreas, which secretes insulin so that more glucose can be metabolized; and from your stomach and intestines, which immediately stop digesting food so that more energy can be shunted elsewhere.

All this activity, happening at a furious pace and with powerful effects everywhere in your body, is coordinated by the brain, which uses the pituitary gland to guide many of the hormonal signals just described, not to mention various other chemical signals that go racing down your neurons to focus your eyes, prick up your ears, jerk your back muscles upright, and swivel your head in alarm.

To make this whole reaction happen and then to make it go away again (for the body, unlike a man-made drug, knows how to reverse every one of these processes just as neatly as it began), the same key-in-the-lock mechanism is employed everywhere. It is all so deceptively simple, yet if you attempt to duplicate this event with a drug, the results are nowhere near as precise, orderly, and beautifully orchestrated. In fact, they are chaotic. Injecting adrenaline, insulin, or glucose separately into the body gives it a crude jolt. The chemicals immediately flood all the receptor sites without coordination from the brain. Instead of talking to the body, they assault it with single-minded insistence. Even though the chemical make-up of adrenaline is identical no matter where it is derived, the critical ingredient of intelligence must be present; otherwise, the drug's action is a mockery of the real thing.

Here is a related example to show the complicated results of giving a drug that seems simple. Hypertension patients are generally told to bring down their elevated blood pressure with diuretics—drugs that take water from the cells and pass it out of the system through urination. This is exactly what the kidneys do all the time as they delicately monitor your blood chemistry to make sure that the balance of water, waste products, and the necessary salts, or electrolytes, is precisely maintained. A diuretic, however, has only one idea in mind, and obsessed with that one idea, it careens through the body, demanding, "Water! Water!" from every cell it meets.

The result is that the fluid tension in the blood vessels is reduced, which is what the doctor wants to happen, but the water level everywhere else is affected at the same time. The brain may be forced to give up some of its water, which under normal conditions it does only in the direst emergency, causing the patient to feel dizzy and drowsy. In many cases nothing more serious happens, but sometimes other brain functions may also then be thrown off, especially in older patients: if they happen to drink alcohol, even in moderation, these people can become so confused that they forget to drink enough water or to eat properly. This can lead to malnutrition combined with severe dehydration. In the view of some endocrinologists, the dehydration induced by diuretics in the presence of alcohol or tranquilizers is the leading cause of death among older Americans.

All of these consequences, whether mild or severe, are usually called the undesirable "side effects" of diuretics, but that is not an accurate name. They are just its effects—the good and bad ones necessarily come together in the same package. A diuretic basically works by latching onto sodium atoms, causing the body to discard excess salt, and this in turn indirectly brings down the water level in the tissues, since water is bound up with salt in our bodies, just as in sea water. The diuretic cannot help it if too much salt is taken where water is still needed. Since potassium is close to sodium in its atomic structure, the diuretic also causes it to be depleted, leading to weakness, fatigue, and leg cramps. (Less-adverse effects are generally noticed by the leaching of other trace elements, such as zinc and magnesium.) Besides these common signs of potassium deficiency, there can be other complications—digitalis, the drug commonly given to heart patients to strengthen their weak heartbeat, becomes more toxic if the body is low on potassium. Ironically, a potassium deficiency is now suspected to be a causal link in high blood pressure, which means that the diuretic may be promoting the very condition it was meant to cure.

The frustrating reality, as far as medical researchers are concerned, is that we already know that the living body is the best pharmacy ever devised. It produces diuretics, painkillers, tranquilizers, sleeping pills, antibiotics, and indeed everything manufactured by the drug companies, but it makes them much, much better. The dosage is always right and given on time; side effects are minimal or nonexistent; and the directions for using the drug are included in the drug itself, as part of its built-in intelligence.

Thinking about these well-known facts has led me to three conclusions. First, that intelligence is present everywhere in our bodies. Second, that our own inner intelligence is far superior to any we can try to substitute from the outside. Third, that intelligence is more important than the actual matter of the body, since without it, that matter would be undirected, formless, and chaotic. Intelligence makes the difference between a house designed by an architect and a pile of bricks.

For the moment, let's keep our definition of the word *intelligence* as simple and practical as possible. Rather than referring to the intelligence of a genius, which may seem both exalted and abstract, I define it simply as "know-how." There is no doubt, whatever you think about intelligence in the abstract, that the body must be credited with an immense fund of know-how.

The body's inner intelligence is so powerful that when it goes awry, the physician is faced with a truly formidable antagonist. Every cell in the body is programmed by its DNA, for example, to divide at a certain rate, producing two new cells after the mother cell splits in half. Like everything else regulated by our inner intelligence, this process is not purely mechanical. A cell divides in response to its own internal need combined with signals generated from the cells around it, the brain, the faraway organs that are "talking" to it via chemical messages. Cell division is a carefully considered and well-thought-out decision—except in the case of cancer.

Cancer is wild, anti-social behavior, whereby a single cell reproduces itself without check, heeding no signals from anywhere except, apparently, its own demented DNA. Why this occurs, no one knows. It is a good bet that the body itself knows how to reverse the process, but for some reason, equally unknown to science, it doesn't always succeed. It is only a matter of time, once the process begins, before the cancer cells overwhelm a vital organ, crowd out its normal cells, and cause death. When the final crisis comes, the cancer cells perish with the rest of the body, doomed by their ungoverned appetite for self-expansion.

Medicine has so far not figured out a way to send a message to the cancer cells in time to ward off the tragic fate they have created. The chemicals a physician might use against cancer are not at all effective on the level of intelligence. Cancer is endowed with mad genius, while drugs are simple-minded. So the oncologist resorts to a much cruder assault, a form of poisoning. The anti-cancer drug that is administered is generally toxic to the entire body, but because cancer cells are growing at a much faster rate than normal cells, they ingest more of the poison and die off first. The whole strategy is a calculated risk. The patient must be fortunate; his physician must be extremely knowledgeable about the dosage and timing of the chemotherapy, both of which are absolutely vital. Then the cancer may be defeated, adding years of useful life to the patient's existence.

Ironically, the therapy may fail because it strips the body of the very intelligence that usually guards it from disease. Many anti-cancer drugs are extremely damaging to the body's immune system; they directly suppress the bone marrow, which manufactures our white cells, with devastating effect on the white-cell count in the blood. As the course of chemotherapy continues, the patient becomes more and more susceptible to new forms of cancer, and in a certain number of cases—as high as 30 percent for breast cancer—new cancer appears and the patient dies. Moreover, it is sometimes not statistically possible to kill every malignant cell. It has been estimated that a typical cancer patient may have 10 billion cancer cells. If his chemotherapy is 99.99 percent effective, there would still be 1 million survivors, more than enough to start over again.

Cancer cells are not created equal; some are hardier than others and therefore more difficult to kill. It may be that destroying the weaker cells acts as a kind of Darwinian selection, leaving the fittest to survive. In that case, chemotherapy would actually promote a more virulent disease than it cured. (Likewise, the persistent staphylococcus infections that patients come down with in hospitals are often highly resistant to antibiotics, because only the most vicious bacteria can live in the sterile environment of operating rooms and withstand the continual bombardment of penicillin injections.) One can easily conceive of a strain of "super cancer" that might arise from one or two malignant cells that had the strongest resistance to treatment.

In any case, the early promise that chemotherapy would wipe out cancer in our generation, widely believed in the 1950s, has sobered. Now a few cancers at a time are defeated, such as lymphocytic leukemia in children and some kinds of Hodgkin's lymphoma, while other major killers, such as lung and brain cancers, are virtually untouchable through chemotherapy.

Nothing I have said so far about the body's know-how is hypothetical. We have all been informed, doctors and public alike, about the body's wondrous intricacy. Yet we persist in thinking of the body in an obsolete mold, as basically matter, but with a smart technician inside who moves the matter around. This technician was once called a soul; now it tends to be demoted to a ghost inside the machine, but the same emphasis remains. Because we see and touch our bodies, carry their solid weight around with us, and bump into doors if we don't watch out, the reality of the body appears to be primarily material—such is the bias of our world.

But the bias has a huge blind spot in it. Despite the overwhelming superiority of the body's know-how, which scientists freely acknowledge, a minute amount of time and money is spent trying to grasp the living body as a whole, and for very good reason. The Greek philosopher Heraclitus made the famous remark, "You cannot step into the same river twice," because the river is constantly being changed by new water rushing in. The same holds true for the body. All of us are much more like a river than anything frozen in time and space.

If you could see your body as it really is, you would never see it the same way twice. Ninety-eight percent of the atoms in your body were not there a year ago. The skeleton that seems so solid was not there three months ago. The configuration of the bone cells remains somewhat constant, but atoms of all kinds pass freely back and forth through the cell walls, and by that means you acquire a new skeleton every three months.

The skin is new every month. You have a new stomach lining every four days, with the actual surface cells that contact food being renewed every five minutes. The cells in the liver turn over very slowly, but new atoms still flow through them, like water in a river course, making a new liver every six weeks. Even within the brain, whose cells are not replaced once they die, the content of carbon, nitrogen, oxygen, and so on is totally different today from a year ago.

It is as if you lived in a building whose bricks were systemically taken out and replaced every year. If you keep the same blueprint, then it will still look like the same building. But it won't be the same in actuality. The human body also stands there looking much the same from day to day, but through the processes of respiration, digestion, elimination, and so forth, it is constantly and ever in exchange with the rest of the world.

Certain atoms—carbon, oxygen, hydrogen, and nitrogen—pass through the body very quickly, being an essential part of the things we use up the fastest—food, air, and water. If it were up to only these four elements, we would be creating new bodies for ourselves literally every month. However, the pace of renewal is slowed by other elements that do not flow through us very rapidly. The calcium bound into our bones can take a whole year to replace itself—some authorities extend the time to several years. Iron, the component that makes red blood cells red, is held onto quite tenaciously, being lost mainly through the sloughing of dead skin cells or the actual loss of blood.

Even though the rates of change may differ, change is always there. What I am calling "intelligence" takes on the role of guiding this change so that we do not collapse into a heap of bricks. That is one of the most obvious facts about the physiology, but intelligence is so changeable, so quick on the move—in other words, so *alive*— that medical textbooks devote almost no space to it at all.

To get an idea of how limited our current knowledge is, consider the structure of a neuron. The neurons that compose the brain and central nervous system "talk" to one another across gaps called synapses. These gaps separate the tiny branchlike filaments, the dendrites, that grow at the ends of each nerve cell. Everyone possesses billions of these cells, divided between the brain and the central nervous system, and as we saw, each one is capable of growing dozens or even hundreds of dendrites (the total estimated at 100 million million), meaning that at any one time, the possible combinations of signals jumping across the synapses of the brain exceed the number of atoms in the known universe. The signals also communicate with one another at lightning speed. To read this sentence, your brain takes a few milliseconds to arrange a precise pattern of millions of signals, only to dissolve them instantly, never to be repeated again in exactly the same way.

In medical school, we were taught a simple model of how neurons communicate: an electrical charge forms on one side of the synapse, and when the charge is large enough, it jumps like a spark across the gap to deliver a signal to another nerve cell. Assuming that this is the correct mechanism (in reality it isn't), the description we learned in our neurology textbook in 1966 told us next to nothing about how neurons act in real life; the book model makes sense only for a single nerve cell, isolated, stopped in time, and stripped of context. In truth, the action taking place at the gaps in the nervous system is like that of a cosmic computer reduced to a microcosmic scale. This awesome computer operates continuously, handles hundreds of programs at a time, deals in multiple billions of "bytes" of information every second, and, most miraculously of all, knows how to run itself.

It is not really our medical training that was at fault here. How can any textbook possibly describe this whole process? To think is to form patterns inside ourselves that are just as complex, fleeting, and rich in their diversity as is reality itself. Thinking is the mirror of the world, and nothing less. Science simply does not have the tools to look at such a phenomenon, which is at once infinite and alive. The living body will not stop to be studied, certainly not as a whole. So when it delivers a shock to science, as in a spontaneous cure of cancer, medicine all but halts in its tracks, bewildered to find that life does not behave as neatly as the laboratory model.

In 1986, a shock was delivered that could turn the whole field of brain research on its head: a Mexican neuro-surgeon, Dr. Ignacio Madrazo, successfully implanted healthy new cells into the brain of a patient with Parkinson's disease.

Not only did the transplant take, which previously was considered impossible, but the patient showed an amazing 85 percent return to normal functioning. Before the surgery, the patient, a Mexican farmer in his late thirties, had been rendered virtually helpless by his disease. Parkinson's strikes about 1 percent of people over age 50. It begins with muscle tremors, rigidity of the limbs, or a tendency to move very slowly. The immediate cause of these symptoms is a deficiency of dopamine, the same brain chemical that leads to schizophrenia when it is in oversupply. For reasons not yet known, the nerve cells that produce dopamine, located in a part of the brain stem called the substantia nigra, begin to die, creating the deficiency. Without enough dopamine, the brain's ability to regulate muscle movement is impaired and finally lost.

Any or all three of Parkinson's symptoms grows worse over time, until the patient is totally incapacitated. The playwright Eugene O'Neill contracted Parkinson's in his fifties. It became increasingly difficult for him to write as his shaking became more severe. He had planned a cycle of four plays that were to be his masterpiece, but his disease destroyed everything: one glance at the surviving manuscripts reveals that O'Neill could barely form the cramped, spidery, pathetically illegible letters. Through heroic endurance, he managed to commit his words to paper, but no one has ever been able to decipher what they say.

In Mexico, Madrazo's patient, though considerably younger than most Parkinson's victims, had been confined to his bed, suffering from constant, rhythmic tremors that made him unable to walk without assistance. After the surgery, he could walk, run, feed himself, work in his garden, and, as a moving film of him shows, once again take his young children in his arms.

Dr. Madrazo's operation opened the door for other Parkinson's patients, of which there are over a million in the United States alone. By the end of 1987, two hundred similar operations had been performed throughout the world. Madrazo performed twenty of these, all with considerable success. (Previous attempts at the same surgery had failed, as have many since. Madrazo believes that his success is due to the exact location he chooses for his implants.) But the long-term consequences are just now being considered— suddenly, and with little warning, neuro-researchers are confronted with the science-fiction possibility of a "brain transplant."

What makes any brain-tissue graft such a shock is that medicine has always believed that the brain could not heal itself—which is why almost all brain damage, either by accident or disease, has been considered irreversible. Only in 1969 did a researcher in Cambridge, Godfrey Raisman, prove with an electron microscope that damaged nerve cells can sprout new growth. Now Madrazo has shown that the brain not only can heal itself but will accept tissue from other organs. His transplant for Parkinson's was done with cells from the adrenal gland, which also produces dopamine; the surgery can also be performed using brain tissue from another person or even from a pig fetus.

Neuroscientists currently hypothesize that the brain is endowed with a complex chemical repair system that was almost totally unknown a few years ago. A Swedish research team has shown that memory loss in rats can be reversed by injecting them with one of the brain's major repair chemicals, a key protein called NGF, or nerve growth factor. By analogy, the brain damage associated with Alzheimer's disease, which also involves memory loss, may be treatable in the same way. The Swedish experiment also implies an advance over the brain-tissue graft, because it did not use live tissues or require surgery.

One after another, the basic tenets of brain physiology are having to be reconsidered and drastically modified. The breakthroughs continue to be revolutionary: another Swedish team has shown that nerve cells can be implanted onto the retina of the eye, whose surface is just an extension and spreading out of the optic nerve. After they are implanted, the cells begin to grow new branches, confirming that regeneration in the brain is possible and normal. Once again, this research involved laboratory animals and not human subjects, but the applications for treating blind people are obvious; likewise, other grafts may benefit victims of traumatic brain injury, strokes, and various brain disorders.

I want to emphasize that none of these advances would have been possible without a change of concept on the part of science. It is disturbing to think that the same doctors who confidently speak today of healing the brain just as confidently pronounced it impossible in 1985. The roots of the brain graft actually go back many years, to 1912, when Elizabeth Dunn, a researcher at Rockefeller Institute, successfully implanted nerve cells into a mouse's brain. Her research was greeted with total indifference. (One is reminded that penicillium mold was observed to kill bacteria more than 140 times, and accordingly written up in the literature, before Alexander Fleming "discovered" this fact. Previous to him, all the other researchers had been annoyed that their carefully grown laboratory cultures were being spoiled by the intrusion of the green mold. Fleming himself threw out his infested bacteria cultures, only later realizing that he had a wonder drug in the making.)

Another pioneer in brain-graft research, Don M. Gash, now at the University of Rochester, was pulled aside by a senior faculty member at the beginning of his career and told, "Dr. Gash, you're a young man with a promising career ahead of you. Don't waste your time on a silly idea that can't be true."

The very notion that there is a transplant at work arouses intense skepticism. Critics of Madrazo's procedure have noted that the recovery time of his patients, which begins within a few weeks after the brain cells are implanted, is far too fast for the new tissue to "take." It may be that the brain is repairing itself totally on its own, releasing chemicals in response to the surgical wound rather than from the new cells (rather like an oyster releasing mother-of-pearl in response to a bit of grit under its shell).

Perhaps these findings are telling us not so much to perform more transplant surgery but rather to look for new abilities in the brain as a living, dynamic organ. For all that it has been glorified by modern medicine, the brain has been the most frozen part of the frozen sculpture model of the body, since it alone could not repair itself. On the face of it, this is a suspicious claim. All the cells in your body, whether a hair follicle, a neuron, or a heart cell, grew out of one double strand of DNA at the moment of conception. Everything you can do—think, speak, run, play the violin, or rule a country— builds on a capacity programmed into that one original molecule. Therefore, to say that a neuron cannot heal itself is the same as saying that its DNA has been crippled. Is this a reasonable assumption? Certainly the DNA has decided to become a brain cell instead of a heart cell, and that involves expressing certain parts of its potential while suppressing others.

But this is totally different from saying that any ability in the DNA has been lost. Nothing is lost in DNA. Each cell in the body contains all of DNA's infinite possibilities all of the time, from the moment of conception until the moment of death. Proof of this exists in the procedure called cloning: theoretically, one can take a cell from the inside of your cheek and, given the right conditions, produce an identical copy of you, or a million identical copies. The genius of nature is that she did not settle for a million identical clones; indeed, only the lowest organisms consist of identical cells, and most of them are single-celled, like the amoeba. Yet, the distinction between an amoeba and a human being breaks down at the level of DNA, in this sense: all of the amoeba is contained in its little packet of DNA, and all of you is contained in yours. So it should not be so surprising that a neuron actually can (under circumstances we do not quite understand) decide to drop its rule about not repairing itself and suddenly begin to do just that. Its DNA is not crippled.

The truth of the matter is that the brain is too complex to be turned into a model, and science by definition works with models. Models are useful, but without exception they have blind spots built into them. To see brain function, or any function in the body, without a model, you would have to see it as a very abstract and seemingly contradictory thing, as non-change being preserved in the midst of dynamic change.

As non-change, the body is solid and stable, like a frozen sculpture. As change, it is mobile and flowing, like a river. In the scientific worldview inherited from Newton, it has been almost impossible to hold both these aspects together in one's mind at the same time. I remember a physicist remarking that for Newton, nature was like a billiard game. What he meant was that classical physics studies a collection of solid objects—the billiard balls—moving along straight lines propelled by fixed laws of motion. The game is to predict their paths, speed, momentum, and so on, like an English gentleman at his evening game of snooker. To make these calculations, however, you have to stop the game and draw a model of it, complete with formulas for the proper angles, trajectories, and so on.

Science has accepted essentially a frozen, geometric way of mapping out everything that happens in the material world, so quite naturally the idea of the sculpture took precedence over the idea of the river. But the river has not stopped just to please science—the beauty of the human body is that it is new every moment. Yet, how do you make a map of the body for every moment? That is the next dilemma we have to confront. If we can solve it, we will come much closer to what we want, not more knowledge to put into libraries, but new abilities to program into our cosmic computer.

EXPANDING THE TOPIC

The theme of this chapter is that the body should be freed from any fixed model of how it works. In a word, you should think of your own body as a verb, not a noun. If change were the only constant, obviously we'd all desire positive change. I've already simplified this into positive inputs versus negative inputs. But I was trained in medical school to treat fixed processes, with the primary focus on those processes that have become so impaired that disease has begun to appear. Not just a model of the human body is involved in such training but an entire worldview, which is why *Quantum Healing* had to be so ambitious in its aims.

Fortunately, steady progress has been made in the area of wellness, and now a totally disease-oriented approach isn't as dominant. Self-directed change, conducted outside the doctor's office, has caught on. Pioneering studies by Dr. Dean Ornish, first published in the British medical journal *The Lancet* in 1990, tested the proposition that lifestyle changes could create radical improvements in the body. Starting with a one-year study, Ornish took patients already suffering from coronary artery disease, the primary cause of heart attacks.

One group of subjects was followed with normal medical care while the others were enlisted in a lifestyle program that consisted of whole foods, stress management, moderate exercise, and social support. The specific form of stress management was yoga and meditation. The program's diet included a drastic reduction in the amount of fat consumed per day. These measures sound rather routine today, but Ornish produced a result that astounded the medical community at the time. The patients in the control group showed no improvement in their heart disease, and quite often the stenosis in their coronary arteries (narrowing due to the buildup of fatty plaques) had worsened after a year. In the group following the lifestyle protocols, however, the coronary vessels had slightly opened, which was the first time that coronary artery disease had ever been reversed by any means, including drugs.

The door had opened to a new world of self-care, as other studies replicated Ornish's results. Recent progress has been even more dramatic. In 2008, Ornish, working in collaboration with Nobel laureate Elizabeth Blackburn, showed that lifestyle changes improve gene expression. That is, the genes responsible for disease prevention were turned on while the genes responsible for cancer and heart disease were turned off. This simple statement hardly conveys the magnitude of the finding. It would have seemed utterly impossible when *Quantum Healing* was written that the way a person thinks and acts has a direct influence on their genes.

Nor are we talking about minor changes. Within three months of undertaking Ornish's program, hundreds of genetic changes were observed. One of the most exciting has to do with the production of an enzyme known as telomerase, which seems to be crucial in the aging process. Each strand of DNA is capped at the end, like a period ending a sentence, by a structure known as a telomere. With age, it appears that telomeres weaken, causing the genetic sequence to fray at the ends.

It is thought, with considerable supporting research, that increased telomerase, the enzyme that builds telomeres, might significantly retard aging. The Ornish-Blackburn study discovered that telomerase did in fact increase in subjects following the positive lifestyle program. I was excited by these findings and wondered how far they might extend. In collaboration with a number of universities, the Chopra Center for Wellbeing is conducting an ongoing study, the largest of its kind to date, that focuses primarily on consciousness.

Subjects are divided into two groups, with one group spending a week at the center learning to meditate and engaging in a multidimensional program that deals with mind, body, and spirit. The control group spends the week engaging in an unstructured spa program that is a pleasant change from their ordinary routine. Dozens of biomarkers are carefully analyzed, and the results are a magnification of the original Ornish-Blackburn findings. Even more genetic markers were found to improve, and the changes occurred within mere days of beginning to meditate.

The beneficial effects of meditating were well enough known

that I had confidence in them when writing *Quantum Healing*. These new findings, however, go far beyond the accepted understanding that meditation can lower blood pressure, decrease heart rate, increase immunity to disease, and reduce the effects of stress. Those key findings haven't changed, but now we know that meditation leads to far more holistic benefits, and that they occur very quickly—it's not a matter of dedicating years at a time to master an esoteric Eastern discipline.

The chart below summarizes what happens when any kind of positive input enters the mind-body feedback loop.

What Positive Input Does

Promotes overall balance, or homeostasis.

Moves easily through the system, without obstruction or blockages.

Generates new neural pathways.

Promotes the production of new brain cells.

Improves gene expression.

Allows every cell to function normally, without anomalies or aberrant behavior.

Supports the immune system, increasing resistance to disease.

Counteracts the effects over time of entropy and aging.

Increases a sense of wellbeing: The person feels healthy, vibrant, and alive.

The shape of the future is becoming clear. Two new concepts are emerging. The first is radical wellbeing, the notion that through lifestyle modification a person can attain a state of wellness that reaches far beyond disease prevention. The second is self-directed biological transformation (SDBT), the notion that the genetic switches that create and govern every cell can be consciously directed. In a word, you can consciously guide your own personal evolution. Unlike conventional wellbeing, in radical wellbeing making the right choices isn't optional. Every thought you have is already encoding a biological choice right this minute, pointing to a positive outcome (wellbeing) or a negative one (imbalance, physical decline, disease, or death).

That our cells change by the instant holds the key to a higher state of health and the possibility of conscious evolution. If you want to see what your thoughts were like yesterday, look at your body today. If you want to see what your body will be like tomorrow, look at your thoughts and feelings today. Benign neglect isn't good enough—once you see that mind and body form a continuous, all-embracing feedback loop, there is nothing that *doesn't* have an effect. The cell membrane of all 50 trillion cells in the body is a vast communication center that is responsive to every aspect of your life. Although the brain has traditionally been considered the seat of mind, there is intelligence in every cell, with an equal complexity and ability to respond to the environment.

These are the themes I broached in *Quantum Healing*, and they have become only more potent over time.

4

MESSENGERS FROM INNER SPACE

To climb to Machu Picchu, the fortress city of the Incas, is a formidable task. One crosses a sixteen-thousand-foot pass in the high Andes, where the oxygen is already low enough to cause giddiness, and once the city is in sight above the clouds, its walls are reached by three thousand stone steps. This was the last stronghold captured by Pizarro when he conquered Peru in 1532. One is astonished to think that foot-runners connected Machu Picchu with every village along the two thousand miles of the Incan empire. They were swift messengers of almost inhuman endurance. They ran barefoot, covering immense distances every day—at times the equivalent of two or three Olympic marathons. Some of their trails began at the height of a mountain peak in the Colorado Rockies and ascended more than a mile higher.

It must have been these runners, the eyes and ears of the emperor Atahualpa, who warned him of the approaching Spanish. By treachery, Pizarro collected a fortune in ransom when he kidnapped (and later murdered) Atahualpa. One hopes the legends are true which say that the most priceless Incan gold was secreted away in time. (Pizarro, who was unusually greedy, even for a conquistador, was himself murdered by jealous rivals in 1541.)

If you think of the human brain as the fortress at Machu Picchu, then it too must have runners to carry its commands to the farthest outposts of its empire—in this case, the big toe. The physical routes are certainly visible—the central nervous system runs down the spinal column, branching out on either side at each vertebra in the backbone; these major nerves then branch into millions of tinier pathways that communicate to every region of the body. The early anatomists saw the major nerves in the sixteenth century, but the nervous system kept a secret. Who were the runners that took the messages to and from the brain?

Many people still think that the nerves work electrically, like a telegraph system, because until fifteen years ago, that is what medical texts contended. However, in the 1970s, a series of important discoveries began, centering on a new class of minute chemicals called neurotransmitters. As their name implies, these chemicals transmit nerve impulses; they act in our bodies as "communicator molecules," whereby the neurons of the brain can talk to the rest of the body.

Neurotransmitters are the runners that race to and from the brain, telling every organ inside us of our emotions, desires, memories, intuitions, and dreams. None of these events are confined to the brain alone. Likewise, none of them are strictly mental, since they can be coded into chemical messages. Neurotransmitters touch the life of every cell. Wherever a thought wants to go, these chemicals must go too, and without them, no thoughts can exist. To think is to practice brain chemistry, promoting a cascade of responses throughout the body. We have already seen that intelligence, as know-how, pervades the physiology—now it has acquired a material basis.

That gives away the plot of this chapter, but with none of the drama. In truth, no other recent event in biomedicine has been as revolutionary as these discoveries. The arrival of neurotransmitters on the scene makes the interaction of mind and matter far more mobile and flowing than ever before—far closer to the model of the river. They also help fill the gap that apparently separates mind and body, one of the deepest mysteries that man has faced since he began to consider what he is.

At first, around 1973, it seemed that only two neurotransmitters were needed, one to activate a distant cell, such as a muscle, and the other to slow down the activity. Two brain chemicals, acetylcholine and norepinephrine, do just that; they are the "go" and "slow down" signals of the nervous system. They were considered revolutionary at the time, because they proved that the impulse sent from one nerve cell to the next was not electrical but chemical in nature. All at once, the accepted notion of tiny sparks jumping from neuron to neuron was rendered obsolete. But the new chemical model at first continued to preserve the basic theory that only two signals were necessary. Man-made computers operate using just this kind of binary switch, and apparently so did the brain.

Then, as molecular biologists around the world began to investigate more deeply, numerous new neurotransmitters cropped up, each with a different molecular structure and apparently a different message to deliver. Structurally, many of them were related, being built up as peptides, complex chains of amino acids of the same kind as those which appear in the proteins that make up every cell, including brain cells.

A great many riddles began to be solved, directly or indirectly, as these discoveries emerged. If you take a sleeping cat, remove a tiny portion of its spinal fluid, and inject it into a cat that is awake, the second cat will immediately fall asleep. This is because a cat's brain puts its body to sleep chemically, with its own internal sleeping potion. In order for the animal to wake up again, the opposite chemical, a wake-up signal, must be injected into the spinal column.

In humans, where the same chemical mechanisms operate, the

body is awakened in the morning not by a rude internal alarm but by a series of timed signals, at first mild, then progressively stronger, that lift us from deep sleep by stages. The whole process involves a gradual transition, in four or five waves, from the biochemistry of sleep to the biochemistry of wakefulness. If this process is interrupted, you do not come as fully awake as you should—the biochemistry of two distinct phases has been mixed. That is why parents of newborns, having to get up several times during the night, feel that they are never quite normal during the day. Alarm clocks also jolt us out of our natural wake-up patterns, giving rise to grogginess that may persist all day, until the next round of sleeping-and-waking readjusts the mind-body chemistry.

Here is a related example. All camels exhibit an unusual tolerance for high levels of pain—they can calmly chew on thorns while at the same time being beaten with a stick by an irate camel driver. Curious researchers examined camels' brain cells and found that they produce large quantities of a specific biochemical that, if injected into other animals, causes them to ignore pain, too. Sleep and pain tolerance, it is now known, thus depend on precise chemical messengers produced in the brain.

One by one, various other functions that were once "all in your head" have been connected to specific neurotransmitters. Schizophrenics suffering acutely from hallucinations and psychotic thoughts often improve dramatically if put on a kidney dialysis machine, which filters impurities from the blood. As we saw, brain researchers have established that a neurotransmitter called dopamine exists in abnormally high levels in the brains of schizophrenics. Current chemical treatment of the disorder entails using psycho-active drugs that suppress dopamine; perhaps the dialysis machine is actually removing it, or a related by-product, from the bloodstream.

By the mid-1980s, barely ten years after the original breakthrough, more than fifty such neurotransmitters and neuropeptides were known. All fifty can be manufactured on one side of the synapses between our neurons, and once they cross the synapses, all fifty can be received by the receptor sites on the other side. This implies an incredible flexibility to communicate from cell to cell. The individual neuron was now seen to be a producer of messages that did not just say "yes" or "no," as a computer does. The brain's vocabulary is far larger, encompassing thousands of combinations of separate signals, with no end in sight, since new neurotransmitters continue to be discovered at a fast rate.

What kind of messages do nerve cells exchange with one another? The answer is tantalizing, for certain segments of our chemical vocabulary seem to be just as specific as ordinary speech, while others are highly ambiguous. Our tolerance for pain, like the camel's, depends on the class of biochemicals discovered in the 1970s called endorphins and enkephalins, which act as the body's natural painkillers. The word *endorphin* means "internal morphine," and *enkephalin* means "inside the brain." And that is their story: they are like a version of morphine produced by the brain itself.

This hitherto unknown ability to make internal opiates proved very exciting. It was already suspected that the body must be able to regulate the sensation of pain. Although insistent, pain does not always register on our awareness. Strong emotions, for example, can override pain signals from the body, as when a mother rushes to save her child from a burning house or a wounded soldier fights on, ignoring the pain of his injuries. Under more ordinary circumstances, all of us to some extent can take our attention away from a minor pain—we don't notice a sore throat, for instance, if we are talking to someone with intense interest.

Despite this common experience of having the pain threshold rise and fall, no mechanism had ever accounted for it. Now medicine could explain it by using these internal painkillers, the endorphins and enkephalins, which every neuron in the body is able to produce at will. Very quickly the general public was told that the brain produces narcotics up to two hundred times stronger than anything you can buy on the street, with the added boon that our own painkillers seemed to be nonaddictive. Perhaps in the future a physician would anesthetize his patients by stimulating some region in their brains, giving Western medicine a scientific form of Chinese acupuncture.

Morphine and endorphins both block pain by filling a certain receptor on the neuron and preventing other chemicals that carry the message of pain from coming in. Without these chemicals, there can be no sensation of pain, no matter how much physical provocation is present. Using this model, a molecule of endorphin is like a specific word, the word *painkiller*. One can imagine that whenever the word *pain* comes to the brain's attention, it has the option of sending *painkiller* back as its answer. Unfortunately, this simple picture was clouded over by later research.

It was found that levels of endorphins in the body do not correspond on a one-to-one basis with how much pain is being felt. This can be proved with placebos, or dummy drugs. Patients who are in pain can often be relieved by receiving a placebo, usually a coated sugar pill, which they are told is a powerful painkiller. Not everyone will respond to this, but generally between 30 percent and 60 percent will report that their pain went away. This result, called the placebo effect, has been noted for centuries, but it is highly unpredictable. The doctor cannot tell in advance which patients will benefit or to what extent.

Why should a totally inert sugar pill relieve pain in the first place, even the stabbing pain of peptic ulcers or traumatic surgery? Endorphins, it was now discovered, must hold the answer. A drug called naloxone acts as a chemical antagonist to morphine, meaning that it has the ability to knock morphine molecules out of a receptor site. When naloxone is administered on top of a painkiller, the sensation of pain instantly floods back. As it turns out, the same thing will happen with the placebo. The patients whose pain went away from the sugar pill reported that it returned again after they took naloxone. This implied that endorphins and morphine must basically be the same drug, the difference being that one is manufactured by the body and the other by the opium poppy.

But once again, it was only a certain percentage of patients who showed this result. Naloxone made the pain return in full force for certain patients; for others, the placebo effect still worked totally; and for still others, only a little of the pain came back. Researchers found themselves in a state of renewed confusion, where they remain today. Endorphins are certainly internal painkillers, but uncovering these new molecules was not the whole answer.

Pain studies have now shown that morphine is not chemically identical to endorphins, that endorphins interact in a more complex way than narcotic drugs, and that any form of treatment for pain relief—morphine, endorphins, acupuncture, or hypnosis—is highly variable in its effectiveness. It was also discovered that endorphins cannot be made into satisfactory pharmaceuticals: our internal painkillers are just as addictive as heroin if given by injection.

Soon, the same frustrating complications that scientists ran up against with the endorphins and enkephalins spread to all the other neuro-transmitters. It turns out that a neuron does not simply catch a signal from a neighboring nerve cell and pass it along untouched to the next synapse. That is only one of its choices. Although no one can describe exactly how neurons receive their chemical messages or how they transport them down their own axons, or trunks, it is known that the process must be very flexible. The nerve cell can change the message en route, turning the chemical it received at point A into a different one at point B. The receptor sites on the ends of nerve cells can also modify themselves to receive different types of messages; the sending station on the other side of the synapse is equally versatile.

For our purposes, this confusion is actually a highly encouraging state of affairs, because it proves that the body cannot be understood without the missing ingredient of intelligence. The physical makeup of endorphins, or any other neurochemical, is not nearly as important as their know-how—how they choose their sites, what triggers them to act, how they "talk" to the rest of the body in precise coordination, and so on. Even in the midst of a genuine chemical revolution, mind is superior to matter. In fact, it now appears that the molecular structure of any neuro-transmitter is completely secondary to the brain's ability to employ it.

It came as a tremendous surprise to cell biologists that, as far as molecules go, neurotransmitters are nothing special. All of the protein in our bodies is built up from chains of twenty basic amino acids, and these chains can be further arranged into longer strands called peptides. Neuropeptides have their own signature, making them distinct from the other peptide chains in the body, but the same factory, our DNA, makes all of them. DNA is the source for all the proteins that repair cells, build new ones, replace missing or defective pieces of the genetic code, heal cuts and bruises, and so forth.

Without bothering to invent a new class of chemicals, the DNA has figured out another use for its familiar raw materials, the amines, amino acids, and peptides. Once again, it is just the *ability* to make these different products that is crucial. There is nothing special about the molecules themselves, even though their discovery by a molecular biologist may be special to science.

Where does the ability to make the neurotransmitters come from, then? Perhaps we should look to the contribution made by the mind. After all, it is not really the adrenaline molecule that makes a mother rush into a burning building to save her child or an endorphin molecule that protects her from feeling the flames. Love makes her rush in, and single-minded determination protects her from pain. It just happens that these attributes of her mind have found a chemical pathway that the brain can follow to talk to the body.

Now we have arrived at the heart of the matter. Mind by any definition is nonmaterial, yet it has devised a way to work in partnership with these complicated communicator molecules. Their association is so close, as we have seen, that mind cannot be projected into the body without such chemicals. Yet these chemicals are not mind. Or are they?

The whole paradoxical situation was wittily summarized several years ago when the eminent English neurologist and Nobel Prize winner Sir John Eccles was asked to address a conference of parapsychologists, who were discussing the usual topics of ESP, telepathy, and psychokinesis—the ability to move physical objects with the mind. If you want to see real psychokinesis, he told his audience, then consider the feats of mind-over-matter performed in the brain. It is quite astonishing that with every thought, the mind manages to move the atoms of hydrogen, carbon, oxygen, and the other particles in the brain's cells. It would appear that nothing is further apart than an insubstantial thought and the solid gray matter of the brain. The whole trick is somehow done without any apparent link.

The mystery of mind-over-matter has not been explained by biology, which prefers to push on to more and more complicated chemical structures operating at finer and finer levels of the physiology. It is still obvious that no one is ever going to find a particle, however minute, that nature has labeled "intelligence." This is all the more apparent when we realize that *all* the matter in our bodies, large or small, has been designed with intelligence as a built-in feature. DNA itself, although acknowledged as the chemical mastermind of the body, is made up of essentially the same basic building blocks as the neurotransmitters it manufactures and regulates. DNA is like a brick factory that is also made out of bricks. (The great Hungarian mathematician John von Neumann, besides being a founder of the modern computer, was interested in robots of all types. He once invented, on paper, a truly ingenious machine, a robot that could build robots identical to itself—in other words, a self-reproducing machine. Our DNA has accomplished the same thing on a grand scale, since the human body is nothing more than variants of DNA built by DNA.)

You may find it easy to think of DNA, with its billions of genetic bits, as an intelligent molecule; certainly it must be smarter than a simple molecule like sugar. How smart can sugar be? But DNA is really just strings of sugar, amines, and other simple components. If these are not "smart" to begin with, then DNA couldn't become smart just by putting more of them together. Following this line of reasoning, why isn't the carbon or hydrogen atom in the sugar also smart? Perhaps it is. As we shall see, if intelligence is present in the body, it has to come from somewhere, and that somewhere may be everywhere.

If we follow the next step of the neurotransmitter story, we find ourselves faced with another quantum leap in complications, but surprisingly, the relation between mind and matter actually begins to clear up. The areas of the brain that mediate our emotions—the amygdala and the hypothalamus, which is also known as "the brain's brain"—were both found to be particularly rich in all the substances in the neurotransmitter group. This implied that where thinking processes are abundant (meaning that many neurons are tightly clustered), so will be the chemicals associated with thinking. At this point there was still a rather well-defined division between chemicals that jumped the gap between brain cells and those that traveled from the brain down the bloodstream. (In my field, endocrinology, one of the defining qualities of a hormone is that it floats through the blood, a process that is generally much slower than the transmission speed of a nerve cell, which has been clocked at 225 miles per hour; a signal sent from head to toe takes less than 1/50th of a second.)

Just when science thought it could isolate brain chemicals and categorize their sites, the body cropped up with its own complication. Researchers at the National Institute of Mental Health found receptors in equal abundance at other sites outside the brain. Starting in the early 1980s, receptors for neurotransmitters and neuropeptides were discovered on cells in the immune system called monocytes. "Brain" receptors on white cells in the blood?—it would be hard to exaggerate the significance of this discovery. In the past, it was thought that the central nervous system alone relayed messages to the body, rather like a complicated telephone system connecting the brain to all the organs it wanted to "talk" to. In this scheme, the neurons function like telephone lines conveying the brain's signals—that is their unique function, shared by no other system in the physiology.

Now it was seen that the brain does not just send impulses traveling in straight lines down the axons, or trunks, of the neurons; it freely circulates intelligence throughout the body's entire inner space. Unlike the neurons, which are fixed in place along the nervous system, the monocytes of the immune system travel through the bloodstream, giving them free access to every other cell in the body. Outfitted with a vocabulary to mirror the nervous system's in its complexity, the immune system apparently sends and receives messages that are just as diverse. In fact, if being happy, sad, thoughtful, excited, and so on all require the production of neuropeptides and neurotransmitters in our brain cells, then the immune cells must also be happy, sad, thoughtful, excited—indeed, they must be able to express the full range of "words" that neurons do. Monocytes can be thought of in effect as circulating neurons.

With this one discovery, the concept of the intelligent cell took on full-fledged reality. One kind of localized intelligence was already well known, that possessed by the DNA in every cell. Since Watson and Crick mapped the structure of DNA in the early 1950s, investigation had proved that this remarkable, almost infinitely complex molecule encoded all the information necessary to create and sustain human life. But the intelligence of genes was seen primarily as fixed, because DNA itself is the stablest chemical in the body, and thanks to that stability, each of us is able to inherit genetic traits from our parents—blue eyes, curly hair, facial patterns, et cetera—and preserve them intact to pass on to our children.

The know-how carried by the neurotransmitters and neuropeptides represented something else altogether: the winged, fleeting, sentient intelligence of the mind. The wonder is that these "intelligent" chemicals are not only made by the brain, whose function is to think, but by the immune system, whose primary role is to protect us from disease. From the standpoint of a brain chemist, this sudden expansion of messenger molecules adds a new order of complexity to his work. But for us, the discovery of "floating" intelligence confirms the model of the body as a river. We needed a material basis for claiming that intelligence flows all through us, and now we have it.

Anyone can see that his mind is filled with a bewildering flood of impressions that are far too amorphous to pin down. To describe it, psychology is reduced to equally amorphous terms like the famous phrase *stream of consciousness*. Today, as if to fill that stream with water you can actually see and touch, brain researchers have found cascades of brain chemicals. But unlike a stream, these cascades have no banks; they flow anywhere and everywhere. They never cease this flow, either, for the smallest fraction of a second. A brain scientist in effect stops time to examine a cascade's components. The chemicals he wants to find are extremely minute—it took three hundred thousand sheep brains to yield a single milligram of the molecule the brain uses to stimulate the thyroid. Nor are the cell receptors easy to grasp. They constantly dance on the surface of the cell walls and change their shape to receive new messages; any one cell may contain hundreds or even thousands of sites, only one or two of which can be analyzed at a time. Science learned more about brain chemistry in the last fifteen years than it knew in all of previous history, but we are all still like foreigners trying to learn English from scraps of paper found in the street.

No one has yet been able to grasp how the cascade of chemicals exactly patterns itself to do all the things a mind can do. Memory, recollection, dreaming, and all the other everyday activities of the mind remain a profound mystery as far as their physical mechanics is concerned. But now we know that the mind and body are like parallel universes. Anything that happens in the mental universe must leave tracks in the physical one.

Recently brain researchers have found a way to photograph a thought's tracks in 3-D, like a hologram. The procedure, known as

PET (positron-emission tomography), is done by injecting the bloodstream with glucose whose carbon molecules have been tagged with radioisotopes. Glucose is the brain's sole food, which it uses much faster than do ordinary tissues. Therefore, when the injected glucose reaches the brain, its marker molecules of carbon can be picked out as the brain uses them, and thus pictured in three dimensions on a monitor, much the same way a CAT scan is produced. Watching these marker molecules shift around while the brain thinks, scientists saw that each distinct event in the universe of mind—such as a sensation of pain or a strong memory—triggers a new chemical pattern in the brain, not just at a single site but at several. The image looks different for every thought, and if one could extend the portrait to be full-length, there is no doubt that the whole body changes at the same time, thanks to the cascades of neurotransmitters and related messenger molecules.

As you see it right now, your body is the physical picture, in 3-D, of what you are thinking. This remarkable fact escapes our notice for several reasons. One is that the physical outline of the body does not change drastically with every thought. Even so, the whole body quite obviously projects thoughts. We literally read other people's minds from the constant play of their facial expressions; without marking it, we also register the thousandfold gestures of body language as a sign of their moods and intentions toward us. Films made by sleep laboratories disclose that we change position dozens of times during the night, obeying commands from the brain that we are unconscious of.

Secondly, we don't see our bodies as projected thoughts because many physical changes that thinking causes are unnoticeable. They involve minute alterations of cell chemistry, body temperature, electrical charge, blood pressure, and so on, which do not register on our focus of attention. You can be assured, however, that the body is fluid enough to mirror any mental event. Nothing can move without moving the whole.

The latest discoveries in neurobiology build an even stronger case for the parallel universes of mind and body. When researchers looked further, beyond the nervous system and the immune system, they began to discover the same neuropeptides and receptors for them in other organs, such as the intestines, kidneys, stomach, and heart. There is every expectation of finding them elsewhere, too. This means that your kidneys can "think," in the sense that they can produce the identical neuropeptides found in the brain. Their receptor sites are not simply sticky patches. They are questions waiting for answers, framed in the language of the chemical universe. It is very likely that if we had the whole dictionary and not just our few scraps, we would find that every cell speaks as fluently as we do.

Inside us, the questions and answers go on forever. Just by itself, a single gland like the thyroid has so much to say to the brain, to its fellow endocrine glands, and through them to all the body, that its cascade of conversation influences dozens of vital functions, such as growth, metabolic rate, and much more. How fast you think, how tall you are, and the dimensions of your eyes, for example, all depend in part on advice from the thyroid. We can safely conclude, then, that mind is not confined to the brain by some neat division set up for our own convenience. Mind is projected everywhere in inner space.

One of the most forward-looking and accomplished researchers in the field of brain chemistry, Dr. Candace Pert, director of the brain biochemistry division at the National Institute of Mental Health, has pointed out that it is quite arbitrary to say that a biochemical like DNA or a neurotransmitter belongs to the body rather than the mind. DNA is almost as much sheer knowledge as it is matter. Dr. Pert refers to the entire mind-body system as a "network of information," shifting the emphasis away from the gross level of matter toward the subtler level of knowledge.

Is there really any reason to keep mind and body apart at all? In her own writings, Pert prefers to use one term for both—*bodymind*. If this word sticks, it will clearly indicate that a wall has come crashing down. Pert does not have all of medical science behind her yet, but that may change very quickly. It is becoming clearer every day that the mind and body are amazingly alike. Insulin, a hormone always identified with the pancreas, is now known to be produced by the brain also, just as brain chemicals like transferon and CCK are produced by the stomach.

This shows that our neat division of the body into nervous system, endocrine system, digestive system, and so on is only partially right and may soon be outmoded. It has now been absolutely proved that the same neurochemicals influence the whole bodymind. Everything is interconnected at the level of the neuropeptide; therefore, to separate these areas is simply bad science.

A body that can "think" is far different from the one medicine now treats. For one thing, it knows what is happening to it, not just through the brain, but everywhere there is a receptor for messenger molecules, which means on every cell. This explains a great deal about drugs and their side effects that had not been known. Some drugs have a bewildering number of side effects. If I consult my *Physician's Desk Reference*, which comprehensively lists the medications that a doctor can prescribe, I can find page after page under the listing for corticosteroids. The most familiar corticosteroid (or just steroid) is cortisone, but the whole family is widely prescribed to treat burns, allergies, arthritis, postoperative inflammation, and dozens of other conditions.

If you didn't know about receptor sites, steroids would appear highly peculiar. Let us say that I prescribe steroids to a woman who is suffering from a difficult case of arthritis. The steroids would bring down the inflammation in her joints dramatically, but then a host of strange things might happen. She could begin to complain of being fatigued and depressed. Abnormal fatty deposits might begin to show under her skin, and her blood vessels could become so brittle that she would develop large bruises that are very slow to heal. What could link these entirely divergent symptoms?

The answer lies at the level of the receptors. Corticosteroids replace some of the secretions of the adrenal cortex, a yellowish pad on the top of the adrenal glands. At the same time, they suppress the other adrenal hormones, as well as secretions from the pituitary gland, which is located in the brain. As soon as it is given, the steroid rushes in and floods all the receptors throughout the body that are "listening" for a certain message. When a receptor becomes filled, what follows is not a simple action. The cell can interpret the adrenal "message" in many ways, depending on how long the site stays filled. In this case, the receptor stays filled indefinitely. (The fact that other messages are not being received is important, as is the loss of innumerable connections with the other endocrine glands.)

The cell can exhibit extreme reactions from filling one receptor. By analogy, look at a moth hanging under the eaves on a summer night. In a male moth, the fuzzy antennae on its head are actually receptor sites that have extended outside the body. As the sun sets, the moth waits for a signal from a female moth in his vicinity, who is emitting a special molecule called a pheromone. Moths are tiny creatures, and the number of pheromones they can send through the air is infinitesimal compared to the total volume of air and its immense freight of pollen, dust, water, and other pheromones being secreted by animals of every kind, including man. One would hardly suspect that two moths can communicate over any sizable distance.

But when a single pheromone molecule lands on the male's antenna, his behavior is transformed. He swiftly homes in on the female, begins an elaborate courtship ritual in the air, and proceeds with the act of mating. Biologically speaking, the only thing that causes this complicated behavior is *one* molecule.

When I give steroids to an arthritis patient, trillions of molecules and receptor sites are involved. That is why the blood vessels, skin, brain, fat cells, and so on all exhibit their different responses. If I go to my desk reference, the long-term consequences of staying on steroids include diabetes, osteoporosis, suppression of the immune system (making a person more susceptible to infections and cancer), peptic ulcers, internal bleeding, elevated cholesterol, and much more. One might even include death among these side effects, because taking steroids for a long period causes the adrenal cortex to shrivel (an example of how an organ will atrophy if not used). If the steroid is withdrawn too quickly, the adrenal gland does not have time to regenerate. The patient is left with inadequate defenses against stress, which adrenal hormones help to buffer. He can go to the dentist to have a wisdom tooth extracted, a stress that is usually well within the normal limits, but deprived of adrenal hormones, he can go into shock. A tooth extraction could even kill him.

Take all of these details together, and what you see is that steroids can cause literally *anything* to happen. They may be the immediate cause or just the first domino—the distinction makes little difference to the patient. To her, there is no difference between the osteoporosis caused by steroids and the "real thing." The same holds for depression, diabetes, or death. A single messenger has caused them all. In truth there is no such thing as a single messenger—each one is a strand in the body's web of intelligence. Touch one strand, and the whole web trembles.

I realize that this makes drugs look much more dangerous than we had thought, even in an era that is obsessed with cataloging medical disasters. We are used to a more limited idea of what a side effect is—a touch of the bitter with the sweet, like the thorn that comes with the rose or the hangover with the bottle of wine. Instead, a side effect balloons out into anything the body can think of. Generally we are protected from serious harm because the body reacts along certain narrow lines. A patient who takes an aspirin might experience bleeding in his stomach lining but not a heart attack. However, every cell in the body has a wide latitude for action—it is a conscious being who understands the world around it. The side effects in my desk reference are just the ones that have been observed so far.

I recently read a story of an internist who was baffled when one of his patients, a man in his late seventies, suddenly began to act paranoid. The man was obsessed by the idea that robbers were going to break into his house, and he bought a gun to keep under his pillow. One night he terrified his wife by leaping out of bed at three in the morning, running downstairs with his pistol, and searching wildly for the intruders he thought were behind every chair. Knowing that he was hallucinating dangerously, the wife rushed him to the internist. The patient had no prior history of mental illness and was on no medications other than digitalis, which he took to stabilize his heart rhythm. Considering the patient's age, a diagnosis of Alzheimer's disease seemed imminent.

However, the internist consulted a neurologist to read the patient's CAT scan. Nothing abnormal appeared on it, but the neurologist said, "I bet this man is hallucinating from the digitalis." In thirty years of practice, the internist, who is also a professor of medicine in New York City, had never seen this side effect, although he had heard of it, barely. He reduced the digitalis, and within ten days the patient returned to normal. It seems quite freakish that a highly specific heart medication should lead to insanity. If this patient had hallucinated a few decades ago, when the desk reference did not list such a bizarre side effect, no doctor would have believed it; today, the internist believed it only after an extensive battery of tests ruled out everything else.

What this case teaches is that you can never tell what the body is thinking, or where. It is entirely possible that the man's heart went insane, in the sense that it toppled the first domino and triggered the onset of his paranoia. The brain and the heart share many of the same receptor sites; more important, they share the same DNA, which implies that a heart cell can behave like a brain cell, a liver cell, or any other kind of cell. After open-heart surgery, patients sometimes have psychotic breaks and begin hallucinating. Flat on their backs, groggy from deprivation of oxygen to the brain, and locked into the blank sterility of an intensive care unit, they suddenly think that little green men are marching up and down the sheets—such is the accepted explanation for their episodes. Could it be that in fact it is the heart that is hallucinating here? Simply the trauma of the surgery could make the heart think that reality has run wild, and that is what it tells the brain.

The discovery of neurotransmitters, neuropeptides, and messenger molecules of all kinds has vastly extended our concept of intelligence. But if every cell has an endless number of messages it can send and receive, it is also clear that only a small fraction are activated at one time. Who or what controls the messages? That turns out to be an explosive question. In a chemistry lab, reactions will run automatically as soon as the experiment starts; it is just a matter of mixing one chemical with another. Yet, someone has to take the chemicals off the shelf to begin with.

Medicine has traditionally preferred to ignore this fact as it applies to the human body. Now we see that with thousands of chemicals on its shelf, a cell has not only to choose some, mix them together, and analyze the results. It has to make the chemicals in the first place, finding thousands of ways to create new molecules out of basically a handful of elements—carbon, hydrogen, oxygen, and nitrogen. To do that requires a mind. So, by following the story of neuropeptides, we have ultimately arrived at a dramatic shift in worldview. For the first time in the history of science, mind has a visible scaffold to stand upon. Before this, science declared that we are physical machines that have somehow learned to think. Now it dawns that we are thoughts that have learned to create a physical machine.

EXPANDING THE TOPIC

Placing mind before brain, the main point of this chapter, remains very hard for some people, in particular the researchers who devote their entire careers to exploring the brain. By developing ever more sophisticated brain scans, such as fMRI, which can look at brain activity "lighting up" in real time, neuroscience has entered a kind of golden age. New findings emerge literally by the month, and in some circles it is confidently promised that very soon the mystery of the mind will be completely solved.

This is a promise that will never be kept if science proceeds by assuming that brain = mind. Think about music. A piano sonata is written by Mozart, using a completely mental process. He writes the notes down on paper, and the sonata can be performed on the piano. Now imagine that a scientist comes along and says, "I've been examining how pianos work. I've looked at the keys and strings down to the molecular level. I can tell you how the piano's mechanism registers the finest nuances of Mozart's sonata. Very soon we will know exactly how he composed everything he ever wrote."

The claim is nonsense, because dissecting a piano tells you nothing about how music is composed. Likewise, examining the human brain down to the subtlest chemical reactions inside neurons and across the synaptic gaps that separate them says nothing about where thoughts come from. This is the simplest refutation of materialism one can offer, and yet it has profound consequences.

Let's ask the most basic question. How does the brain produce the sights, sounds, smells, tastes, and textures of the three-dimensional world? In other words, when you see a red apple, where does its redness come from? Your brain is completely dark inside; there is no light anywhere in any part of the visual cortex, much less the color red. This mystery doesn't bother most scientists, even brain scientists. They would simply respond that apples are red, and how the brain registers this fact comes down to chemical reactions in the visual cortex. But the notion that the color red exists "out there" in Nature is simply wrong.

Light is transmitted by photons, which are colorless; in fact, they are invisible. There is no brightness "out there" as photons sweep from the stars and certainly no brightness inside the brain's total darkness. So if light's brightness is neither "in here" nor "out there," why is the sun so bright that you can't look at it with the naked eye for more than a few seconds?

Light's brightness and color, along with everything else we perceive, come from "conscious agents," a term coined by the farseeing
cognitive scientist Donald D. Hoffman of the University of California, Irvine. He proposes that the only reality we can know is the
reality created by consciousness. If there is anything that is real but
beyond the human mind, then it won't be accessible. A conscious
agent doesn't have to be human. Every animal species experiences
a reality that conforms to its nervous system, so that a dog's image of
sound reaches much higher than the human ear can perceive, while
the hearing of a humpback whale reaches much lower (whales can
hear one another's songs for hundreds of miles underwater). Some
snakes, including pythons and rattlesnakes, can detect infrared light
through specialized "pit organs" located in their jaws, and so they
"see" into a dimension entirely closed off to human perception.

Conscious agents fascinated me because the ancient Vedic rishis
were in complete agreement with the notion that consciousness is
the source of reality. They didn't push the everyday world of the five
senses completely out of the picture. Instead they gave it a lower
status known as Maya, a Sanskrit word usually translated as
"illusion"—it comes up later in this book. Maya is the apparent reality "out there" that all of us naïvely accept at face value, but which
turns out to be no more real than the movie projected on the screen
in a cinema. Consciousness serves as the projector whose light casts
these images while itself remaining pure light, with no images at all.

Let me go into this subject a little more philosophically than I
did in the original *Quantum Healing*. The ancient sages of India,
and all philosophers since then, explored the mind by going inward.
But in a scientific age, we have to ask: How can thinking about the
mind be better than gathering hard facts about the brain?

Because data only has meaning given a certain way of seeing it.
This point was made in the one book almost every college student
reads (if they read any) in the philosophy of science, Thomas S.
Kuhn's *The Structure of Scientific Revolutions*, published in 1962.
Kuhn shattered the notion of objective progress in science by argu-

ing that given their starting assumptions, every scientific scheme for explaining Nature—what he called a paradigm—is right on its own terms.

This groundbreaking insight went back to 1947, when Kuhn, then a graduate student at Harvard, was wrestling with how wrong Aristotle had been. Aristotelian physics was the first systematic explanation of Nature in mechanical terms, the cornerstone of Western science that made Copernicus, Newton, and Einstein possible. And yet a brilliant mind like Aristotle's arrived at completely wrong conclusions about such basic things as why objects fall to earth or what heat is. Suddenly Kuhn had an epiphany: What we call Aristotle's mistakes in fact weren't mistakes at all. If you accept the starting assumptions behind Aristotelian physics, its description of Nature was valid.

Kuhn seemed to be saying that Aristotle was just as right as Newton, which to most people, including probably every physicist, makes no sense. In our time, the acceptance of scientific progress is all but universal, and the triumphs of modern technology are undeniable. Yet no one has rebutted Kuhn's point that we view Nature through our own paradigm, our worldview. The history of science is a constant stream of shifting paradigms, one after another. There is no way to step outside the paradigm you totally believe in.

But what if the current paradigm happens to be absolutely right? A Theory of Everything has been on the horizon for decades, and we are told that it's only a matter of time before the theory is complete. Kuhn's point is that an absolutely correct theory, no matter how much data you feed into it, cannot be achieved. All you can achieve is the fulfillment of the paradigm you believe in. Eventually problems will arise that cannot be solved without shattering the present paradigm so that a new one can be formed.

To a doctor, spontaneous remission from cancer posed just such a problem. As long as your medical paradigm separated mind and body, no way existed for consciousness (including beliefs, expectations, fears, wishes, faith, and hope) to influence the daily life of cells. Looking beyond medicine, we have to consider consciousness as a whole. If the mind can influence the body, what do we mean by mind? If brain = mind, the answer to all ills should be a host of super-pills that alter brain function, steering it in the direction we want it to go. In effect, this is where neuroscience thinks it's heading, because the old paradigm says so. There is literally no room for consciousness being the agent of change.

In the years since *Quantum Healing* was first published, my own thinking has become more sophisticated about the so-called hard problem of connecting mind and brain. Anyone who flatly says that brain = mind is turning their backs on what the philosophy of science teaches.

1. Theories are right about what they include and wrong about what they exclude.
2. No model of reality is big enough to explain reality.
3. Data has no meaning unless it is interpreted, and interpretations are bound by the observer's starting assumptions.

In a word, everyone has a story, and everyone believes their story. Even contradictory stories can be valid and fit the same data. This startling conclusion applies to everyday life all the time. Competing stories are told in divorce court when marriages break apart, in criminal court when prosecution and defense do battle, and in the corridors of medicine when two doctors have different concepts of healing. Sticking to your story convinces you that you're telling the truth when in fact you are just defending a way of seeing.

The story told by neuroscience, that brain = mind, is particularly weak. There is absolutely no data to indicate that neurons can think; they merely light up on an fMRI as thinking occurs, which isn't the same thing. You could construct a setup so that a 100-watt bulb lights up over your head every time you have a bright idea, but that doesn't mean the light bulb *caused* the idea. Neuroscience ignores this obvious flaw when it arrives at the same false conclusion, using neurons instead of a lightbulb.

The current state of total confidence in neuroscience requires thick blinders. Brain scientists don't see the dead end they are walking toward when they promise that neurons are going to explain where thoughts come from. Not just thoughts, but no color, shape, sound, taste, and smell will ever be located in neurons, and what isn't in a neuron isn't in the brain, either.

It would be pointless to tear down the old paradigm without having something better to offer. In that regard, *Quantum Healing* pointed in the right direction. All the things the brain is credited with actually should be assigned to the mind. Once this shift is made, enormous untapped potential becomes available. Neuroscience will continue to do valuable things, in particular fixing the abnormalities and disorders of the brain connected to a wide range of diseases. You can't play Mozart on a broken piano. Yet the mystery of Mozart's genius, like all mysteries of the mind, must be solved on a different plane, beyond the physical.

5

GHOSTS OF MEMORY

R ecently a young woman in her late twenties, a part-time model, came to my office in Boston. After years of hiding the fact that she had an eating disorder, her family had finally persuaded her to seek treatment. Since adolescence she had been obsessed with her figure, and over time this concern had become more and more abnormal until it blossomed into a double sickness, anorexia nervosa and bulimia.

Looking at this attractive, bright woman, who to all appearances was normal, I was not lulled into thinking that her problem was easy. Despite extensive research and publicity in recent years, both anorexia and bulimia remain highly puzzling. Why should young women, many of them well educated and from high-income backgrounds, nurture an uncontrollable obsession with diet and weight? Anorexics develop a fear of food and a horror at the act of eating. Confined to a rigidly ritualized pattern of behavior that leads them to voluntary starvation, they will deny that they are too thin, even to the point of death.

The companion disease, bulimia, can be separate from anorexia or can coexist with it, as in this woman's case. In bulimia, the horror of food takes a weird turn in the form of bingeing. The secret food binges that a bulimic goes on are often enormous—anywhere from 2,000 to 50,000 calories at a sitting (2,000 calories is enough food to sustain a vigorous 150-pound person for a day). This huge amount of food is then vomited back up, causing tremendous stress on the digestive system and the body as a whole.

This particular woman's disorder had advanced to the point where she was vomiting every day in order to maintain the normal but still low weight needed for her work. The very sight of a dessert, she told me, caused her to break out in a cold sweat and sent her heart racing. She was extremely intelligent and listened closely when I said that at the root of her disorder was a mistake in her self-image. Because our society is obsessed with the ideal of thinness, many women try to live up to an inner image of their bodies that is simply not right for their physical makeup. In her case, however, the image was not saying, "I have to be thin." It was saying, "I can never be thin enough."

To explain this paradoxical illness, one has to drop the distinction between mind and body and think of one system, the "body-mind." This is because an eating disorder is a holistic disease, the cruel opposite of holistic health. In anorexics, the distorted idea, "I must be thinner," takes over the bodymind like a malevolent and elusive phantom. Even after long hospitalization and exhaustive psychiatric treatment, the patient rarely eats like a normal person. A normal person would have to struggle to starve himself—once the body went past a certain point of deprivation, its hunger signals would take precedence over everything else in the bodymind, until the desire for food became overpowering. For someone with anorexia, the same thing happens but in reverse—the compulsion to avoid eating is all but irresistible.

As I was talking about this, the young woman looked at me sorrowfully and whispered, "So there really are such things as ghosts, aren't there?"

I was startled, and after a moment I answered, "It's true, but this ghost can be exorcised." What we were talking about is a ghost of memory, a memory picked up and stored in the body. Memory sounds very abstract, while food is very concrete. But the memory is far more real in this case. Whether a person is compulsively too thin or too fat does not depend primarily on how much food he takes in. This is true for conditions that are less bizarre than anorexia. For centuries, obesity has been seen as a flaw in character, which religious ages called the sin of gluttony. The implication was that if fat people were just strong enough and used a little self-discipline, they could be as thin as the rest of us simply by eating less.

Now it is generally recognized that for the chronically obese, diets do not solve the problem (just as, at the opposite extreme, filling an anorexic with food does not solve that problem), because the brain of a fat person is actually sending out overpowering signals for too much food. How these messages are triggered and how to turn them around are open questions. Unless some degree of control is gained at a very deep level, obese people can spend their whole lives forcing themselves to diet, a self-defeating tactic that only makes the mental distortion worse. The loss of 10 pounds is registered in their brains as a famine, and the next time food is offered, the brain will not stop until 15 pounds is put back on, adding an extra 5 as a safety margin against the next famine. Obese people have been known to gain weight on diets where no extra calories are offered beyond the bare minimum to sustain basal metabolism. The reason for this is that the brain can actually alter the metabolism in such a way that the calories are stored as fat instead of being burned up as fuel.

No one knows why the intellect is so powerless to change these distortions in self-image. The ghost gets stronger the more you fight it. Although anorexics will persistently deny that they have a problem, once the doctor pierces this defense, it is clear that a profound split in the bodymind is involved, with one part of the system struggling to maintain rationality while another sends up wildly irrational impulses.

I once spent an hour counseling another anorexic woman in her thirties who weighed less than 80 pounds, had given birth at that weight, and was going into rapid physical decline (10 percent of anorexics die from deliberate starvation or from causes related to malnutrition). Her case was made particularly bizarre by the fact that she loved nothing better than going home to cook for her large Italian family, doling out pasta and olive oil to a dozen brothers, sisters, cousins, aunts, and uncles.

Our conversation had been rather eerily reasonable until she suddenly snapped at me, "Do you really think you can talk me out of this? I already understand the whole thing perfectly, you know, and it hasn't done me a damn bit of good. Leave me alone. This is how I have to eat."

She glared at me with unconcealed hostility. "Tell me," she demanded, "how many people do you cure of smoking by talking to them? They know what nicotine does and the danger of lung cancer and all that. It doesn't do them any good to talk, and you won't do me any good, either."

I sat back, feeling the cold blasts of despair and the hot blasts of hatred in what she had said. How horrible to have to live with both, in a weird, poisonous tangle.

"The real question isn't whether I can help you, is it?" I pointed out after she calmed down. "It's whether you can help yourself." She started to soften just a little, and I added gently, "You know, you're not hurting me by not eating. You're not hurting anyone real at all, but someone who is an image. It is all inside you, and that is the part that is so tough, both for you as a person and for me as your doctor."

This story does not have an immediate happy ending. Certainly my patient was right about the futility of talking about her disease. She remains a very hostile, confused person, and my best hope is that joining a peer group with other anorexics and bulimics will help. To get her to exorcise the ghost of memory, she will have to reach the level where the ghost lives. Until the ghost is gone, patients like her do not feel that they have a disease—they *are* their disease.

I mean this quite literally. What happens to you when you see a snake and jump out of its way? The frightened thought, *Look out, a snake!* comes to mind at exactly the same instant as adrenaline makes you jump. Usually the thought and the action are so closely tied together that the conscious thought doesn't even have time to say its words—you just see the snake and you jump. So there is no space where you can drive in a wedge between the two. In the case of an anorexic, the mere sight of food sets up a wave of revulsion. Perhaps the sight and smell of a fresh loaf of bread sends the thought, *Ugh, I can't eat this*, while at the same time the stomach turns, the salivary glands dry up, and the whole digestive tract is alerted not to function.

Naturally, this is a twisted reaction, but the thought and the reaction come packaged together, and there is no place to drive in a wedge between them. What is at work here is something we can call an "impulse of intelligence," which means a thought and a molecule tied together, like a two-sided coin. Once the impulse starts to rise, there is no turning it back. The thought is the molecule; the molecule is the thought. At the time it takes place, an impulse of intelligence constitutes the patient's whole inner reality. When an anorexic is repelled by food, her reaction is all there is (at least for that instant)—she *is* her disease at the moment. The same holds true for the obese person trying to resist food, the smoker trying to resist another cigarette, and so on.

You cannot change a thought after you have had it—the entire inner struggle of such patients is totally futile. But there is another component to an impulse of intelligence besides the thought and the molecule. The third component is silence; this is the unseen component. Like all of us, the anorexic must fetch thoughts from the region that lies deeper than thought, and it is there that a cure might be found.

The anorexic's dreaded realization, *I am my disease*, may be true, but it is not the final truth. If the anorexic could transcend her compulsions, looking on them without involvement, her disease would end. Becoming a silent witness would be enough to disentangle her from the ghost. Archimedes said that if he had a lever long enough and a place to stand on, he could move the Earth—presumably, he would have to stand in outer space. The anorexic needs just such a place; unfortunately, a human being is confined to inner space. No one has a spare nervous system hanging in the closet in case his primary one gets strange ideas. Sadly but inevitably, there is no place outside to stand on.

Without realizing it, we count very heavily on the fact that our thoughts will trigger the right chemicals in our bodies; the mind and its messenger molecules are automatically and perfectly matched. But this process can break down, and then the resulting confusion is like running two programs on the same computer—when the input is scrambled, it is no wonder that the printout, your body, becomes garbled. For example, one of the most ambiguous drugs ever devised is Valium.

Valium belongs to a class of chemicals called benzodiazepines, which are used as both tranquilizers and sleeping pills. These substances were greeted in their day as revolutionary. Their predecessors, the barbiturates, had many notorious drawbacks: they were highly addictive; they induced poor-quality sleep because they blocked REM, or dream sleep; and overdoses could prove fatal. Valium and its relatives, on the other hand, produced better sleep with less hangover, were much harder to overdose on, and at first seemed nonaddictive. At the height of its immense popularity, Valium was said to account for one-quarter of all new prescriptions written in America.

Now it is known that Valium is itself addictive, that it produces sleep irregularities of its own (interfering with the third and fourth stages of deep, dreamless sleep), and that serious withdrawal symptoms occur after prolonged use. If you look at the level of the receptors on the cell wall, none of this is surprising, because Valium acts by outcompeting the body's own neurochemicals and taking over their receptor sites. This kind of interference would perhaps be advantageous if Valium competed only with the neuropeptides responsible for causing the feelings of anxiety (called octadeca-neuropeptides). But the calming effect of the drug does not come by itself; Valium confuses the nervous system as a whole. Moreover, it was recently discovered that the monocytes of the immune system also are attracted to Valium. So when a doctor gives what he thinks is a sleeping pill or a tranquilizer, he is affecting the immune system at the same time, adding more confusion at the level of the receptors.

No one knows if this has caused any harm, largely because the finding about the immune system is too new. In all likelihood, we will discover that nature has already provided our bodies with an exact internal analogue to Valium, which means that we are clumsily reproducing something that already exists in nearly perfect form. If I ask myself whether I like the idea of plugging the same chemical into my immune cells every day, in the indiscriminate fashion that Valium was doled out to millions of patients, primarily women, for thirty years, the answer is obvious.

The immune cells have a reason for each receptor; they use them to think, act, perceive, and respond in precise ways. A person uses the same two eyes to view the whole world; a cell, however, has a different eye for each thing it needs to see. In other words, a constantly filled receptor renders the cell blind to one specific thing. At a time when the incidence of many cancers, such as breast cancer, is still rising, sending unknown messages into the immune system seems very risky.

Currently there is a "chemical revolution" under way in the treatment of mental disease, and it seems as miraculous as Valium did thirty years ago. Doctors now widely give their mental patients mind-altering, or psychotropic, drugs to clear up the overt symptoms of their sickness, mainly depression, mania, and hallucinations. The symptoms are often relieved, sometimes quite dramatically and suddenly, although many patients cannot tolerate the mental numbness and fatigue that are common side effects (not that the side effects are simple: certain antidepressants can make the patient's depression worse for the first few weeks, or swing it in the opposite direction until it turns into wild mania).

Critics of drug therapies call them "chemical lobotomies" and charge that they strip the patient of his human dignity. Doubtless there are many abuses, particularly in large, understaffed public hospitals for the insane. It takes very careful fine-tuning to stabilize the correct dosage of any psychotropic drug, and horror stories abound of depressed patients who reacted so badly to their medication that they committed suicide rather than endure the cure. Still, the success in this field implies that drugs will be used to cure schizophrenia and depression altogether, if not today, then in the future.

A "cured" schizophrenic does not yet exist through chemical means. This is because there is more to being normal than not having hallucinations. Once you suppress a schizophrenic's bizarre visions or the strange voices he hears in his head, you do not find a normal person facing you, but a shell. Altering the chemical level of dopamine, even if it could be done a hundred times better than it is done today, will not lead to a cure. The reason is contained in the lesson learned from the neurotransmitters themselves: for every chemical breakthrough, there is also a chemical barrier.

The good news about neurotransmitters is that they are material. A thought, whether sane or mad, is hard to grasp because it is so intangible; it is not something you can touch or feel. The neurotransmitters, however, are certainly tangible, although they are extremely tiny and often short-lived. It is the neurotransmitter's role to match up with a thought. To do that, its molecules must be just as flexible as thoughts, just as fleeting, elusive, changeable, and faint.

Such flexibility is a kind of miracle but also a curse, in that it throws up a barrier that is almost impossible to pass. No man-made drug can duplicate this flexibility, either now or in the foreseeable future. No drug actually pairs up with a thought. This is apparent just by looking at the structure of the receptor. Receptors are not fixed: they have been accurately described as looking like lily pads that have floated up from the depth of the cell. Like lily pads, their roots sink downward, reaching the cell's nucleus, where the DNA sits. DNA deals in many, many kinds of messages, potentially an infinite number. Therefore, it makes new receptors and floats them up to the cell wall constantly. There is no fixed number of receptors, no fixed arrangement on the cell wall, and probably no limit to what they are tuned in to. A cell wall can be as barren of lily pads as a pond in winter, or as crammed as one in full flower in June.

The only thing constant about a receptor is its unpredictability. Researchers recently discovered, for example, that a neurotransmitter called imipramine is produced abnormally in the brains of depressed people. While looking for the distribution of imipramine receptors, they were startled to find them not just on the brain cells but on skin cells. Why should the skin create receptors for a "mental molecule"? What did these skin receptors have to do with depression?

One plausible answer is that a depressed person is depressed everywhere—he has a sad brain, sad skin, sad liver, and so on. (Likewise, researchers have examined patients who complain of feeling jittery all the time and discovered abnormally high levels of two chemicals, epinephrine and norepinephrine, in their brains and adrenal glands. However, high concentrations were then found in their blood platelets, meaning that they had "jittery blood cells," too.)

It has been frustrating for doctors to realize how complex the

whole business is becoming. Hopes for a quick cure of schizophrenia, depression, alcoholism, drug addiction, and other disorders
were dashed in the mid-1970s, just a few years after the original
endorphins had been isolated in 1973. Now the chemical barrier is
stronger than ever, as the true flexibility of the messenger molecules
is being divined.

Thinking about this problem, I have to ask myself a deeper question: Can a drug really exorcise the ghost of memory? My medical
experience says no—I have seen too many depressed patients who
were "cured" by drugs and yet who still radiate a feeling of hollow
sickness. Instead of trusting drugs, one needs to find out how the
patient's sick memory got into his chemical system to begin with.
For it is absolutely clear that the nonmaterial memory is there. It
may be taking a ride on a molecule, but its life does not depend on
that. The following case serves as an example.

Walter grew up on the streets of south Boston in the late 1960s;
he felt the edge of hatred that greeted black people who moved into
that neighborhood. To escape this and the poverty that had dogged
him all his life, Walter joined the Army at 18. Within six months he
found himself in Vietnam. He fought in combat and survived, but
when he bounced back onto the street again two years later, he was
hooked on heroin, which many soldiers used to make the war less
traumatic. Unlike most soldiers, Walter had no reason to quit when
he got home. Eventually the police caught him, and by order of the
court he came under my care at the V.A. hospital for his addiction.

Our main focus was simply to detoxify Walter. In the normal
course of things, he would have passed through the revolving door
and back out onto the street. But while he was staying in the hospital
I began visiting with him. It was clear that he was an exceptional
person. Despite his desperation, he did not seem eaten up by inner
violence, and he was courageously willing to fight his habit. Walter
made friends with me. He also made quick progress medically, and

a year after detox he was still holding a steady job and talking eagerly about the normal life he longed for and loved.

Then a strange incident occurred. One day Walter's car broke down, forcing him to take the subway to work, which he hadn't done in several months. He got on the train to Dorchester, an old, clattery line with screeching rails. He hated the noise and couldn't manage to ignore it. The fan was broken, and it was July. Within a few minutes of being shut up in the hot, stifling compartment, he found the train intolerable. He went from feeling uneasy to agitated to extremely agitated, and by the time he got off he was in a completely wild, irrational state. Nothing he could do would make his agitation go away. By the time I saw him, two days later, Walter was completely hooked on heroin again, and this time he had hardly any will to recover.

What happened to this man? A chemical explanation for the train incident is not sufficient. I keep thinking of him wearing his pinstriped business suit, confidently outfitted for a new life, but then having to step onto the same train that he had ridden when he was troubled and addicted. In some treacherous turn of memory lane, the past came back, and with it came his craving. Where did the craving hide out for a year before it returned? In some way that medicine is just beginning to unravel, a cell's memory is able to outlive the cell itself.

At any point in the bodymind, two things come together—a bit of information and a bit of matter. Of the two, the information has a longer life span than the solid matter it is matched with. As the atoms of carbon, oxygen, hydrogen, and nitrogen swirl through our DNA, like birds of passage that alight only to migrate on, the bit of matter changes, yet there is always a structure waiting for the next atoms. In fact, DNA never budges so much as a thousandth of a millimeter in its precise structure, because the genomes—the bits of information in DNA—remember where everything goes, all 3 billion of them. This fact makes us realize that memory must be more permanent than matter. What is a cell, then? It is a memory that has built some matter around itself, forming a specific pattern. Your body is just the place your memory calls home.

This conclusion is difficult to argue with, in light of all that we now know about forms of chemical intelligence, but medicine stubbornly resists these implications. For instance, it is generally believed that people who are addicted to alcohol, cigarettes, or drugs have a "chemical addiction," meaning that their cells are hooked on nicotine, alcohol, heroin, et cetera. But if you look at the level of the body's chemistry, you find that heroin or nicotine fits into the same receptors on the cell walls that everyone has. An addict does not have receptors that exhibit abnormal cravings.

By analogy, a fat man's stomach lining isn't addicted to food—it just accepts what is given to it. The truth seems to be that the cell's memory for the addictive substance is what is hooked, and it keeps creating distorted cells that reflect its weakness. In other words, an addiction is a distorted memory. It is just our material bias that keeps looking to the cell. (These pernicious memories may be inherited, since addiction runs in families, but even if there is a specific "addiction gene," one is forced to consider the nonmaterial conditions that caused the DNA to express the gene. Your ears are formed because a gene encodes them, but the reason the ear was developed in the first place, millions of years ago, was certainly nonmaterial—some organism started to respond to sound.)

If you take an addict, detoxify his body, and keep him away from alcohol or drugs for several years, all the old cells that used to be "chemically addicted" are totally gone. Yet the memory persists, and if you give it a chance, the memory will latch onto the addictive substance once again. A good friend of mine, a cardiologist from Colombia, gave up smoking fifteen years ago. This spring he went back home and happened to go to a movie, a rare event in his life. He is an extraordinarily busy man, even for a heart doctor, and had not seen a movie since he could remember. There was an intermission in this particular show, and when he walked into the lobby he was seized by an almost uncontrollalble urge to smoke.

"You see, when I was a teenager in Bogotá," he told me, "we used to smoke in the lobby between movies. All I did was step back into that scene, and the urge to smoke came back in a flash. I found myself in front of the cigarette machine fumbling for change, and only by clutching myself inside and repeating, 'This is *crazy*, you're a cardiologist,' was I able to resist." Even so, he had to rush out of the theater and now wonders ruefully how the movie ended.

What makes any addiction so frightening is that the brain's receptors are always willing to cooperate with the mind's instructions. Think back to the stress reaction where a car backfires and adrenaline is released into your bloodstream. We noted that as part of the overall reaction, the stomach and intestines stop digesting food. As long as the stress reaction is temporary, this is a completely normal and correct thing for the body to do, and it happens automatically.

However, if you choose to stay in an environment where there is ·constant stress, the time must come when your body wants to return to digesting food. Then a deep conflict will arise, because the stress reaction will still be saying "no" to the stomach while another part of the brain (probably the hypothalamus) is saying "yes." The resulting turmoil ties the stomach in knots and churns up the intestines. These organs begin to lose their natural rhythm, and if you do not give them a chance to return to it, they will become victims of wrong memory, just as surely as an addict does. The stomach will start pouring out gastric juice at the wrong times, the colon will go into spasms, and the smooth linkage between the whole gastrointestinal system will collapse. Hence the burning ulcers and chronic irritated colon experienced by many people under high stress.

In the case of the addict, one of the reactions that is blocked by drugs is the ability to think rationally and perceive clearly. As long as his receptors are full, the addict will feel euphoric and his perceptions will be a woozy blur, a condition that may be pleasant in the

short run but devastating over the long term—without clear perception, the brain cannot issue the most basic instructions for thinking,
eating, working, relating to other people, and so on. All of life requires clear thinking, clear thinking requires a host of different neurotransmitters, yet the addict has seized on only a few and clings to
them desperately.

Likewise, a strictly physical explanation for cancer is not convincing.
It must be tied in to a distortion that is more abstract; perhaps a
distorted memory can occur at the cellular level. Let us say that a
doctor takes a patient's X ray and discovers a malignant tumor, then
a year later another X ray is taken and the same tumor shows up.
The doctor is in fact not accurate in calling this the same cancer,
because the cells that showed up the year before have been entirely
replaced.

What he is really seeing is the result of a memory that has per-
sisted, reincarnating again and again in a new tumor. Cancer is not
so much a wild, runaway cell as the distorted blueprint of that cell, a
set of wrong instructions that turns normal cellular behavior into the
suicidal mania of cancer. When we are fortunate, the body deals with
this situation from a primary level. The DNA senses any deviation in
memory, including incipient tumors, and quickly eliminates it.

As yet, we do not know how to wipe out cancerous memories at
the cellular level, because we cannot penetrate the cell wall to "talk"
to the DNA. It is known, however, that a key step is taken when the
immune system secretes certain anti-cancer agents called interleukins, a class of proteins that resemble hormones. Our immune cells
produce interleukins in many situations—cuts, bruises, infections,
internal tissue damage, and allergies all call them forth. (The name
"interleukin" was chosen because researchers originally discovered
that these chemicals send signals between leukocytes, or white
cells.)

As they naturally occur, interleukins exist in minute quantity;
therefore, they are prohibitively expensive to duplicate commer-

cially. Despite this obstacle, researchers have recently extracted large amounts of interleukin-2 (IL-2) and transfused it into about 450 patients with advanced skin and kidney cancers (the current price runs as high as $80,000 for a single course of treatment). Some patients, from 5 percent to 10 percent, have had dramatic regressions of their tumors via this therapy, at the cost of severe side effects, which have killed several people. The question of the IL-2's long-term influence on the rest of the body remains unanswered.

Despite their drawbacks, interleukins are on the verge of becoming the next promising cancer cure, as interferon, a close chemical relation, was the cure of the 1970s. Already, teams of genetic engineers are racing to figure out how to manufacture interleukins on a marketable scale. With a sinking feeling, one senses that another false hope is being born. Why is the promise never fulfilled? Medicine knows hundreds of facts about interleukins, such as that "the alpha and beta strains of interleukin-1 are only 26 percent homologous at the amino-acid level of their genes"; or that both bind to receptors "with high affinity in the 10^{-10} molar range." When one penetrates the jargon, these are not insignificant facts.

Yet they say literally nothing about interleukin's intelligence, which is the salient point. If interleukins "know" when and where to fight cancer, then it is not their molecules that should interest us, but something invisible—the cell's ability to recognize that a cancerous memory is present and needs to be eradicated. This cannot be injected into the body. The body's war against cancer pits intelligence against intelligence. The physical manifestations—interferon, interleukin, hormones, peptides, et cetera—may be thought of as weapons if you like, but they must first be aimed.

In the deepest sense, that is why I have no faith in the "magic bullet" approach. Penicillin was an effective bullet because one's aim did not have to be at all accurate; once an antibiotic is in the bloodstream, it automatically attacks the cell walls of bacteria and destroys them. Similarly, early chemotherapy for cancer was a crude bullet, no different from the chemical warfare of World War I. (In fact, the most toxic drugs used against cancer, called alkylating agents, originated with nitrogen mustard, the infamous mustard gas that so terrified soldiers in that war.) Later classes of chemotherapy, such as the various adrenal hormones and estrogen, derived from the body itself, and therefore their aim was less approximate; but now we see that this advance in fact may be the last gasp of the magic-bullet theory.

At a certain point, the chemicals you want to use are so precise that their action is effective only within the narrowest possible limits. If you aim a hormone, you have to hit one receptor, not just the huge, broad avenues of the bloodstream where penicillin goes. If the receptor you want to hit is involved in a complex process, as the ones for interleukins are, then no aim may ever be accurate enough, for the life and death of the cell involves the precise attunement of every chemical it contains. By analogy, if you mistune one string inside a piano, you have thrown everything out of tune; a piano sonata will never be right if even one note is wrong.

I do not mean to make this sound like the logic of doom. Millions of patients have been successfully treated with cancer drugs. The toxicity of chemotherapy has been steadily reduced, and in many cases the dreaded side effects that have given the treatment its bad reputation are actually fairly mild, particularly considering the risk of leaving cancer untreated. But it still remains true that without very early detection, cancer is incurable. If a patient comes to me with lung cancer, even early detection is no help. I can give him radiation and call it a therapy, but in 95 percent of the cases it is little more than a short reprieve—perhaps he and I go through with it just to fend off the despair of having no treatment at all. Other common cancers, such as melanomas, belong in this category.

We desperately need a medicine without bullets. If you look at interleukins free of a material bias, their most important attributes are invisible. Interleukins are being produced by the immune cell's DNA in exact dosages, combinations, and timing, all of which are more important than the molecule itself.

A white cell engulfing an invader, such as a bacterium or cancer cell, looks deceptively simple under the microscope, like a drop of amber surrounding a fly. In actuality, there is no more intricate process in the human body. An interleukin arrives on the scene at a precisely determined point in a most exacting maneuver. We may call this the "hunt for cancer," but much of the immune process is highly abstract. It is conducted almost entirely by the exchange of information. Hitting the target is one of the more minor parts of the campaign.

Before a macrophage, or immune cell, ever secretes any anti-cancer agent, the immune system goes through many other steps. It must first detect that a problem exists and identify it exactly; a cancer cell is not a virus, and neither one is a bacterium. Using a class of message carriers called helper T-cells, the body notifies the rest of the immune system to become activated and starts to produce natural killer cells. To make sure that the killers do not destroy the wrong thing, the body hangs a chemical nametag on the macrophages inscribed with the enemy's identity, which they can show to other cells they meet. This is just the barest outline of the immune system's initial sequence of action, which has many branches, over-lappings, and unexplained convolutions.

Having just fathomed the full intricacy of the immune system in the last five years, researchers like to compare it to the brain in complexity. Like the brain, the immune system has a phenomenal capacity for absorbing new information, learning and memorizing the identity of any new disease organism, and sorting out billions of bits of knowledge. We could just as easily say that the brain and the immune system are not *like* each other—they *are* each other, because they operate within the same chemical network.

The only difference between an immune cell and a brain cell is that their DNA has selected to emphasize certain aspects of its total knowledge and suppress others. Interleukin comes very close in structure to being a neuropeptide (the research literature calls it a "hormonelike polypeptide"). This means that when our emotions join up with molecules, like riders on a horse, the mounts they choose are almost identical to interleukin. For all intents and purposes, to feel happy and to fight cancer are much the same thing at the molecular level. We could call both of them healing messages. It is false even to divide cells into senders and receivers of such messages; for although certain immune cells secrete interleukins as part of their specific role, virtually every cell in the body can receive them, implying an ability to produce them as well. Perhaps this "silent" ability is activated in spontaneous remissions.

Or are there levels of thought that fight the ghosts of memory hand to hand, and the physical molecules we see are just so many fired shells littering the battlefield? For this last possibility to be true, the mind would have to be directly aware that a cancerous memory is endangering us. Certainly the addict and the anorexic know that the ghost is there. And I have already mentioned certain tumors, such as tumor of the pancreas, that begin to make the patient moody and depressed long before the doctor can physically detect the malignancy. This early warning still depends on the actual presence of a cancer cell. However, that does not exclude a warning that is earlier still.

To find out where it might come from, we will have to go deeper into the whole issue of how intelligence and matter are paired. It is imperative to do this, I believe, before the magic-bullet theory collapses. Interleukin is not a bullet but a speck of life on the move, with intelligence the invisible rider. Life itself is intelligence riding everywhere on chemicals. We mustn't make the mistake of thinking that the rider and the horse are the same. Intelligence is free to go where it likes, even where molecules cannot.

EXPANDING THE TOPIC

By saying that a thought is always paired with a brain chemical and vice versa, this chapter took an important step. The wall that separates mind and body is thick and ancient. Only by going down to the molecular level and tagging the very chemicals that carry out the instructions of the mind can a new picture emerge.

But a nicely stated theory that comes wrapped in an intellectual bow doesn't carry much weight when a doctor reaches for his prescription pad. Patients want magic bullets; doctors have a holster full of them. To break the lockstep between physicians and pharmaceuticals, even a little bit, took some dramatic news. Since *Quantum Healing* first appeared, nothing has been more dramatic than the controversy stirred by a February 2010 cover article in *Newsweek* that proclaimed in stark terms, "Antidepressants Don't Work." The story made public what the psychiatric profession was already beginning to realize: The efficacy of the most popular drugs for fighting depression was no better than a placebo, according to the researches of psychologist Irving Kirsch.

Taking a sugar pill, in other words, is about as useful if you want to alleviate the symptoms of depression as taking the highly touted, expensive drugs promoted by Big Pharma. Protestors and supporters cried out on one side or the other. The protestors alleged that depressed patients who believed in medications like Zoloft and Lexapro were now being stripped of hope. The supporters pointed out that antidepressants never cured depression to begin with but only alleviated the symptoms, with an added risk of various side effects, up to and including outbreaks of violence and suicidal tendencies, not to mention the sharp rise in dependency on these drugs.

In June 2011 more fuel was added by Marcia Angell, the former editor in chief of the *New England Journal of Medicine,* who wrote two articles in *The New York Review of Books* about antidepressants and psychoactive drugs in general. Angell favorably reviewed several books that reached much the same conclusions about how badly and erratically these drugs work compared to the hyped-up claims made for them. Her mainstream colleagues were shocked. Psychoactive drugs, largely used for depression and anxiety, are taken by 1 in 10 Americans. Here was a Harvard Medical School authority casting them into serious doubt.

But as charges and countercharges filled the air, the average doctor still believed in the basic research behind these drugs, which held that mental illness was due to an imbalance in brain chemistry that could be restored to balance with drugs. This article of faith was shaken to the core by a 2013 headline in *Science News* magazine: "A massive effort to uncover genes involved in depression has largely failed."

I addressed the uproar in an online article coauthored by Dr. Rudy Tanzi of Massachusetts General Hospital, one of the world's leading genetics researchers, and Professor P. Murali Doraiswamy, M.D., of Duke University, who specializes in cognitive neuroscience and mental health. Since depression exists in epidemic proportions in this country, and since it serves so well to outline the mind-brain mystery, let me go into detail.

Before these challenges to antidepressants arose, the public perception was that depression is being handled pretty well. Everyone knows a friend or relation who feels better taking Zoloft. Informed medical opinion is very ambiguous, however, because the model for depression that has been accepted for decades considers it as a brain disorder, and brain disorders are rooted in genetics. The failure to find the genes involved in depression strongly suggests—as more than one prominent researcher now concedes—that the genes of depressed people are not damaged or distorted compared with the genes of people who aren't depressed.

Another false assumption is closely linked to this. The most popular antidepressants supposedly work by repairing chemical imbalances in the synapses—the gaps between two nerve endings—where the culprit was an imbalance of serotonin, one of the brain's most important neurotransmitters along with dopamine. But serotonin is directly regulated by genes, and some key research indicates either that drugs aimed at fixing the serotonin problem don't work that way or that there wasn't a serotonin problem in the first place.

The *Science News* report doesn't leave much wiggle room for a laissez-faire attitude on this point: "By combing through the DNA of 34,549 volunteers, an international team of 86 scientists hoped to uncover genetic influences that affect a person's vulnerability to depression. But the analysis turned up nothing." Nothing doesn't mean something.

If the chain of explanation running from genes to the synapses and finally to the pharmaceutical lab is broken, a host of doubts arises. Is depression a brain disease in the first place, or is it—as psychiatry assumed before the arrival of modern drug treatment—a disorder of the mind? The latest theories aren't black-and-white. Here's a list, by no means complete, of things that can make you depressed:

Outside stress
Personal crisis
Grief
Physical illness
Sudden life changes
Accidents and unforeseen setbacks
Loss of job or money
Personal insecurity
Failure
Bad parenting
Low self-esteem
Negative religious beliefs leading to guilt and shame
Other causes of guilt and shame
Rejection in love
Being around other depressed people, particularly family members
The X factor

This is a long list. Even if we discount some undiscovered cause (the X factor), the mind is faced with the complexity of life, and numerous experiences can engender depression. If I tell you that you've just been fired, it's not your brain that will make you depressed. It's a sudden jolt of devastating bad news. Nobody knows why some people convert bad experiences into depression while others don't. It is equally true, after all, that the glass is half empty and half full. In studies, when shown neutral photos of various people and situations, depressed people habitually see them as negative, disappointing, sad, and unlikely to lead to a positive outcome.

With so many variables in play, there are still a few general conclusions that seem reliable:

1. There are many kinds of depression.
2. Each depressed person displays his or her own mixture of causes and symptoms.
3. The mental component in depression includes upbringing, learned behavior, core beliefs, and judgment about the self.
4. The brain component includes wired-in neural pathways, suggesting weaknesses in certain areas of the brain whose causes aren't understood. But depression isn't localized in just a single region in the brain. The interaction of multiple regions is involved.

The genetic component may explain why depression runs in families, but no gene or group of genes seems to guarantee that a person will become depressed. We are talking instead about genes that make you susceptible to the disorder. What triggers these (unknown) genes remains a mystery. In any case, genes are not fixed but fluid in their output, so the genetic situation is changeable. As for the X factor, it could be a predisposition in young children that doesn't blossom into depression for years to come. It could be social interactions that create a sense of helplessness or victimization.

A skeptic could look at this list and say, "So anything and everything can make me depressed. That's the same as proving nothing." But finding the many variables that contribute to depression isn't the same as giving up. Instead, we are heading in the direction *Quantum Healing* points to, seeing mind and body as intimately, dynamically related at every moment of life. About 20 percent of people will experience a severe depression sometime in their lives. At the moment, there is a rash of depression among combat soldiers who served in Iraq and Afghanistan (this would be directly related to a sudden increase in suicides, which is generally linked to depression) and among laid-off workers who are enduring long-term unemployment. In both cases, an outside event led to the depression, but we do not know why, in the sense that only a certain proportion of people become depressed under the same stimulus (war and losing your job).

Another hidden issue is the failure of the disease model when it comes to depression. A cold is caused by a specific virus, just as AIDS is caused by the HIV retrovirus. One cause leads to one effect. That's the germ model in a nutshell, as applied to physical disorders. Extending the model to mental disorders, which is the whole basis of psychiatry, becomes very wobbly when so many factors, internal and external, genetic and environmental, fixed and changeable, exist. It's even difficult to define for research purposes who is clinically depressed and who is not. Depression "spreads" in families and among friends without the need for an inherited gene. Can someone be a "carrier" of depression, and if so, how do they infect one person and not another?

And what about treating depression through old-fashioned couch therapy, talking about the underlying issues that a person feels troubled about? Depressed patients respond about equally well, according to various studies, whether they talk about their depression or swallow a pill. But here's the truly mysterious part. It was found that the tranquilizer Prozac had an unexpected use in treating people with obsessive-compulsive disorder, or OCD. Typically, these are people who feel compelled to repeat a ritual like washing their hands or dusting the house many times a day, who can't stop even though they want to. Taking Prozac seems to reduce overactivity in a certain area of the brain associated with OCD; the patient's symptoms begin to improve. OCD can also be treated with couch therapy, and to everyone's surprise, the same brain areas, when scanned by fMRI, also improve, exactly as if a drug were administered.

The original study about the failure to find the genes responsible for depression, which was published in the January 3, 2013, issue of *Biological Psychiatry*, took an unusual approach by ignoring diagnoses of depression and going instead with symptoms. This wasn't necessarily better, only different. Asking people about symptoms results in a lower number of those who would be considered depressed. This could be because some people are in denial or don't know the difference between depression and ordinary sadness. But more important, symptoms change over a lifetime; there is a sliding scale for each sufferer and for the disorder as a whole.

From person to person, depression has a large circular component of response and habit. A person learns to respond to ordinary situations by being depressed, and once learned, this response becomes a habit that reinforces itself. The habit of depression is as hard to break as addiction. And in both cases one hears the cry, "I can't help it. I have to be this way. This is me." Telling someone that they are prisoners of their sick or damaged brain only reinforces this defeatist belief and the circle of depression.

In the end, the situation is too cloudy for anyone to offer either a pessimistic or optimistic prediction about where depression is heading. Drug treatment remains hugely popular, no matter what the basic science says. In cases of mild to moderate depression—the most common type—antidepressants "work," as long as you discount the fact that their rate of efficacy, around 30 percent, isn't an improvement over placebos. That's too much to discount. An effective drug must at the very least do better than taking sugar. Some symptoms of severe depression remain intractable, and yet in other cases, the chronically depressed perform the best with drug treatment. Hope is always better than giving up.

The point of this detailed discussion is that depression is joining other mental disorders, particularly schizophrenia, where no simple disease model works. There are too many variables, and patients follow highly individual paths as the disorder sets in. It would be naïve to believe that America is going to abandon a belief system that puts materialism ahead of everything else. But discounting the mind while constantly referring everything to the brain is folly. It defies common sense, and more important, it blinds us to the real possibilities of quantum healing.

6

THE QUANTUM MECHANICAL
HUMAN BODY

Ninety years after they began to emerge, the insights of quantum physics remain a total mystery to most people. Yet, once you understand what the discovery of neuropeptides means, then understanding the quantum is only a step further. The discovery of neuropeptides was so significant because it showed that the body is fluid enough to match the mind. Thanks to messenger molecules, events that seem totally unconnected—such as a thought and a bodily reaction—are now seen to be consistent. The neuropeptide isn't a thought, but it moves with thought, serving as a point of transformation. The quantum does exactly the same thing, except that the body in question is the universe, or nature as a whole.

We need to consult the quantum to really understand how the mind pivots on the turning point of a molecule. A neuropeptide springs into existence at the touch of a thought, but where does it spring from? A thought of fear and the neurochemical that it turns into are somehow connected in a hidden process, a transformation of nonmatter into matter.

The same thing happens everywhere in nature, except that we do not call it thinking. When you get to the level of atoms, the landscape is not one of solid objects moving around each other like partners in a dance, following predictable steps. Subatomic particles are separated by huge gaps, making every atom more than 99.999 percent empty space. This holds true for hydrogen atoms in the air and carbon atoms in the wood that tables are made of, as well as all the "solid" atoms in our cells. Therefore, everything solid, including our bodies, is proportionately as void as intergalactic space.

How could such vast reaches of emptiness, dotted at faraway intervals by specks of matter, turn into human beings? To answer that question requires a quantum perspective. By understanding the quantum, we enter into a vaster reality, spanning from quarks to galaxies. At the same time, the behavior of quantum reality turns out to be very intimate to us—indeed, the faintest shadow-line separates the human body from the cosmic body.

In his monumental project to make all of physics follow a few consistent, rational laws, Isaac Newton explained nature's workings in terms of solid bodies, straight-line motion, and fixed constants that ruled all physical events. This is the model of nature as a complex billiard game, with Newton as the master player. Because matter and energy stayed within set rules, there was no need to theorize about a hidden world; everything happened aboveboard. We can express this idea with a simple diagram:

A ⟹ B

Here, A is a cause and B is an effect. They are joined by a straight line, expressing that cause and effect are logically connected in the world we are familiar with, the world of the senses. If A and B are two billiard balls, making one hit the other is a predictable event.

However, if A is a thought and B is a neuropeptide, then the diagram would not apply. There is no straight-line connection between a nonmaterial thought and a material object, even one as small as a peptide molecule. Instead, one has to draw a different diagram with a detour in it:

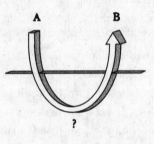

The U shape shows that a process has to take place that is not above the line, in Newton's rational, straight-line world. There is some hidden transformation happening that turns a thought into a molecule. The transformation doesn't take any time and doesn't happen in any place—it is carried out just by the presence of an impulse of the nervous system. When you think the word *rose,* a large number of brain cells have to fire (no one knows how many, but let us say 1 million, which is probably absurdly small), but these cells don't get in touch with one another by passing a message from A to B to C, and so on, until all 1 million get the message. The thought just appears, suddenly localized in time and space, and with it, the brain's cells all change in sync. The perfect coordination of this thought-event and 1 million brain cells making neurotransmitters must have happened below the line.

The whole area below the line is not a region to be visited in space and time; it just stands for wherever it is you go when you turn thoughts into molecules. One could also think of it as the control room that correlates any mental impulse with the body. At any one time, all 15 billion neurons in the nervous system are being coordinated with perfect precision from below the line.

The same change from straight-line causes to U-shaped detours occurred when quantum physics was born. Although everything in nature once appeared to happen above the table, according to classic Newtonian theory—obviously, physicists leave mental events out of the picture—a few things could not be explained without a detour. The most obvious was light. Light can behave like A, a wave, or B, a particle. These two are totally unalike in Newtonian physics, since waves are nonmaterial and particles are concrete. But light somehow can act like one or the other, depending on circumstances, and therefore it must have taken a detour under the line:

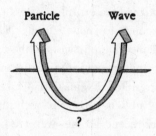

To see light as a wave, or vibration, is easy enough. A prism breaks white light down into the colors of a rainbow; the reason for this is that white light is composed of separate wavelengths of light, a fact that becomes apparent when they are broken apart into a spectrum. The light from an incandescent light bulb has its own spectrum of wavelengths, generated when electricity passes through the tungsten filament. But if you turn the light down with a dimmer switch until just the smallest amount of light can come out, it will come out not like a wave but like a particle. (No dimmer switch is this fine-tuned, but physicists have broadcast light so that it exposes its "graininess." Nature has also equipped our eyes to respond physically to light at its quantum level—if only a single photon falls on the retina, a flash is transmitted along the optic nerve. Our brains, however, do not process just one flash.)

The word *quantum*—from Latin for "how much?"—describes

the smallest unit that can be called particlelike. A photon is a quantum of light, because you cannot split it into finer particles. The photon manifests when a flow of electrons hits a tungsten atom; the moving electrons in the electricity collide with electrons whirling in orbit around the outside of the tungsten atom, and out of their collision jumps a photon, a quantum of light. This quantum is a very strange particle, because it has no mass, but for our purposes, what makes it important is that in order for a light wave to become a photon, it must take a detour beneath the table. In an unknown realm not covered by Newton's laws, the transformation takes place.

Since we are not trying to explain physics here, I won't go into elaborations. It is enough to know that after Einstein, when Max Planck and other pioneering physicists at the turn of the century were able to demonstrate the quantum nature of light, many, many curious conclusions resulted. Events that we take for granted in the world of the senses had to be reconciled with strange distortions of time and space—but reconciled they were. As with the neuropeptide, the quantum allowed nature to become flexible enough to permit the inexplicable transformation of nonmatter into matter, time into space, mass into energy.

Here is the pattern for a basic quantum event; it shows the detour that always takes place outside the reach of ordinary events:

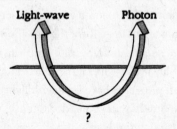

Like the thought and the neuropeptide, light cannot be a wave and a photon at the same time; it is either one or the other. Yet it is obvious that a tungsten light bulb doesn't enter another reality when you turn it down. Somehow, nature sets up its laws so that light can be either A or B, and both are kept inside the boundaries of the same reality by building in a transformation point. (People today still casually assume that Einstein overthrew Newton, when in fact he saved Newton's belief in perfect order by expanding it.)

A strikingly elegant view of mind and body can be formed from this basic quantum event, requiring only one diagram:

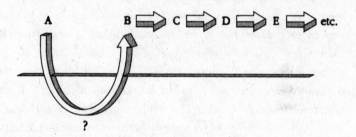

The mind and the body are both above the line. A is a mental event, or thought; all the other letters are physical processes that follow from A. If you feel afraid (A), then the other letters stand for signals to your adrenal glands, the production of adrenaline, the pounding of your heart, elevated blood pressure, and so on. These are B, C, D, et cetera. All the physical changes that take place in the body can be connected in a logical chain of cause and effect, except for the space after A. This is the point where the transformation from thought to matter first occurs—and it must occur, or the rest of the events will not happen.

At some point in the lineup, there must be a detour. At that point, the lineup breaks down, because mind does not touch matter above the table. If you want to lift your little finger (point A), a physiologist can trace the neurotransmitter (B) that activates an impulse that runs down the axon of the nerve (C), causing a muscle cell to respond (D), resulting in the lifting of your little finger (E). However, nothing a physiologist can describe will get him from A to B—it requires a detour. The whole picture is like a bucket brigade, where each fireman gets his bucket from the fireman before him, except for the first, who gets his from nowhere.

"Nowhere" is almost an exact term here, because you cannot subdivide the body to arrive at the precise junction where a thought turns into a molecule, any more than you can find the station house where photons are fashioned into light waves. What exactly happens in the ? zone is not known, either in physics or in medicine. Miraculous cures seem to be examples of dipping into the ? zone, because the cooperation of mind and matter takes an inexplicable quantum leap in such cases, but so are other mind-body dramas that play themselves out in mysterious ways.

Several years ago, a Boston fireman in his mid-forties came into the emergency room of a suburban hospital one night complaining of sudden, sharp chest pains. The resident on call examined him and could find no evidence of irregularity in his heart function. The patient went away without being reassured, and soon he returned with the same symptoms. He was turned over to me as senior physician, but I could find nothing wrong with his heart, either.

Despite his thorough examination, the fireman began to return to the ER repeatedly, usually late at night. Every time he came in, he told me with great trepidation that he was certain he had a heart condition, but no test, including the most sophisticated echocardiograms and angiograms, detected the slightest defect. Finally, in the face of the man's mounting anxiety, I recommended that he be retired with full disability purely for psychological reasons. The fire department's medical examining board refused, on the grounds that no physical evidence had been offered. Two months later, the man showed up one last time at the emergency room, this time on a stretcher, the victim of a massive heart attack. Within ten minutes of his coronary, which destroyed 90 percent of his heart muscle, he died, but he had enough strength to turn to me and whisper, "Now do you believe I have a heart condition?"

What this case so dramatically attests is that the detour into the ? zone is powerful—it can change any physical reality in the body. I feel I must call what happened here a quantum event, because it did not follow the cause-and-effect rules that have been observed and set down by medicine as the body's normal state of affairs. Many people entertain fears that they might have a heart condition, but they don't die from them; conversely, many heart attacks occur without the slightest forewarning from the mind. Even if we say, in keeping with mind-body medicine, that a thought caused the heart attack, how did this thought find a way to carry out its fatal intention?

If you program the concept of "heart attack" into a computer, you know exactly what you have done. If you want to retrieve it, the circuits can be activated to bring it up to the screen, and once it is there, you can use software to manipulate it. But the thought "heart attack" didn't act like this at all in my patient. He didn't know where the thought came from; once it came, he was powerless to escape it; and far short of staying in one place, the thought invaded his body, with disastrous results.

This is only half of the mystery of a quantum event—the negative half; the journey into the ? zone can have amazingly positive results, too. Another patient of mine, a quiet woman in her fifties, came to me about ten years ago complaining of severe abdominal pains and jaundice. Believing that she was suffering from gallstones, I had her admitted for immediate surgery, but when she was opened up, it was found that she had a large malignant tumor that had spread to her liver, with scattered pockets of cancer throughout her abdominal cavity.

Judging the case inoperable, her surgeons closed the incision without taking further action. Because the woman's daughter pleaded with me not to tell her mother the truth, I informed my patient that the gallstones had been successfully removed. I rationalized that her family would break the news to her in time, and that in all likelihood she had only a few months to live—at least she could spend them with peace of mind.

Eight months later I was astonished to see the same woman back in my office. She had returned for a routine physical exam, which revealed no jaundice, no pain, and no detectable signs of cancer. Only after another year passed did she confess anything unusual to me. She said, "Doctor, I was so sure I had cancer two years ago that when it turned out to be just gallstones, I told myself I would never be sick another day in my life." Her cancer never recurred.

This woman used no technique; she got well, it appears, through her deep-seated resolve, and that was good enough. This case, too, I must call a quantum event, because of the fundamental transformation that went deeper than organs, tissues, cells, or even DNA, directly to the source of the body's existence in time and space. Both of my patients—one with positive thoughts, the other with negative—managed to dip into the ? realm, and from there they dictated their own reality.

As mysterious as these two cases are, are they really examples of quantum events? A physicist could object that we are just making metaphors here, that the hidden world of elementary particles and fundamental forces explored by quantum physics is very different from the mind's hidden world. Yet, one can argue that the inconceivable region from which we fetch the thought of a rose is the same as that from which a photon emerges—or the cosmos. Intelligence, we will discover, has many quantum properties. To make this clear, we start with the familiar textbook scheme that arranges the body vertically, as a hierarchy of systems, organs, tissues, and cells:

System
Organ
Tissues
Cell
DNA

?

In this picture, each level of the body is logically related to the next—as long as you remain above the line, the processes that appear as life unfolds happen in a definite sequence. This is exhibited by a fetus in the womb: a baby begins as a speck of DNA sitting in the middle of one fertilized egg cell; over time, that cell multiplies until a ball of cells is formed, large enough to begin to sort itself out into the be-ginnings of tissues and eventually organs, such as the heart, stomach, spinal cord, and so on; then the entire nervous system, digestive system, respiratory system, and so on emerge; and finally, at the moment of birth, the trillions of cells in the newborn are precisely coordinated to sustain the life of the whole organism without the mother's help.

But if DNA is the bottom rung of this neat stepladder, what makes DNA unfold in the first place? Why does it initially divide on the second day after conception and begin to make a nervous system on day eighteen? As with all quantum events, something inexplicable happens beneath the surface to form the all-knowing intelligence of DNA. The point is not that DNA is too complex to understand, being a super-genius molecule; what makes DNA mysterious is that it lives right at the point of transformation, just like the quantum. Its whole life is spent creating more life, which we have defined as "intelligence tied up in chemicals." DNA is constantly transferring messages from the quantum world to ours, tying new bits of intelligence to new bits of matter.

Sitting by itself in the middle of every cell, completely offstage, DNA manages to choreograph all that happens onstage. It can spin out parts of itself to travel through the bloodstream as neuropeptides, hormones, and enzymes, while at the same time attaching other bits of itself to the cell wall as receptors, setting up antennae to listen for answers to a flood of questions. How does DNA manage to be the question, the answer, and the silent observer of the whole process at the same time?

The answer is not at the level of matter. Molecular biologists

long ago broke DNA down into its finer components, but the whole
operation still remains above the line in the Newtonian world:

DNA
Organic submolecules
Atoms
Subatomic particles

?

As we saw before, DNA is not made out of anything special. Its
strands of genetic material can be subdivided into simpler molecules like sugars and amines, and these into atoms of carbon, hydrogen, oxygen, and so on. When it is not tied into DNA, a hydrogen or
carbon atom doesn't have anything like timing built into it. In billions of other combinations, hydrogen and carbon simply exist; yet
in DNA, they contribute to a mastery over time, an ability to produce something new every day, which lasts, in a human being, more
than seventy years—every stage of life develops according to DNA's
timetable. (In a bristlecone pine, DNA is timed for more than two
thousand years.)

No matter how closely you look, the ground for the stepladder is
not very firm. When you get beyond atoms and start subdividing
DNA into electrons, protons, and smaller particles, a quantum
event must take place. Otherwise, you are left in the embarrassing
position of claiming that life is made out of nothingness—empty
space devoid of matter and energy—which is all you *get* if you divide solid particles beyond a certain point.

At the quantum level, matter and energy come into being out of
something that is neither matter nor energy. Physicists sometimes

refer to this primordial state as a "singularity," an abstract construct that is not limited in time and space but is a compression of all the expanded dimensions of the universe. In the Big Bang, the whole universe jumped out of a singularity—so it is theorized—which we can think of by analogy as a point smaller than the smallest thing in existence. Yet, that stupendous event of creation happens on another scale every time you think the word *rose*.

There is no piece of matter existing in a definite place that holds this word for you—it springs into existence from a region that simply knows how to organize matter and intelligence, mind and form. The atoms in your brain come and go, but the word *rose* does not disappear. Now we are at a very exciting point. The singularity is quite explorable today: it did not exist *before* the Big Bang, since it is outside time and space; therefore, it must be here now—in fact, it is everywhere and has no confines in past, present, or future. Quantum physics uses mammoth particle accelerators and other arcane equipment to wrest from the ? zone even one minute glimpse of this hidden world. The track of a new elementary particle whizzing by for a millionth of a second is a major finding, because it means that the unknown zone has been reached and a bit of its reality brought into ours. Can it really be that we are doing the same thing just by thinking, feeling, dreaming, and wishing?

What would the quantum level inside us be like? It would simply be the logical extension of something we are very familiar with by now, the neuropeptide. The neuropeptide's great ability is that it can respond with lightning speed to the mind's commands. It does this, I believe, by sitting on the borderline of the quantum zone. Science has already discovered that hundreds of neuropeptides exist and are manufactured all over the body. It is just another step to find that every one of our cells can make every one of these substances. If that turns out to be true, then the whole body is a "thinking body," the creation and expression of intelligence. Here is another diagram that sketches the situation:

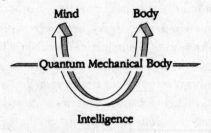

We already know that intelligence can take the form of a thought or a molecule; this is represented in the diagram by having "mind" and "body" as the two choices that intelligence can make. The two are always matched to each other, even when they appear to be separate. To coordinate them, I have inserted a quantum level, called the "quantum mechanical body." This is not a physical artifact but a layer of intelligence, the layer where the body as a whole is organized and correlated. This is where the know-how comes from that makes molecules "smart" instead of inert.

We should not assume that thoughts turn into messenger chemicals one at a time. It is well known that in many ways all the billions of bits of DNA in our systems act like one big DNA molecule, as when the incredibly complex development of a fetus is coordinated in the mother's womb—from the first day to the ninth month, all the DNA in an unborn child acts as one. The same holds true for us today.

Perhaps quantum events are not exclusively "out there" in space, but "in here" as well. Do we have "black holes" into which matter and energy disappear forever? Yes—we call it forgetting. Do we speed up time and slow it down, as a space traveler does in the event that his rocket can accelerate to near the speed of light? Yes again, for a writer can think up in an instant a story that may take hours of normal time to set down on paper; conversely, you can spend half an hour trying to retrieve someone's first name, which comes instantly once you find the timeless zone, called memory, from which it must be retrieved.

Whenever any mental event needs to find a physical counterpart, it works through the quantum mechanical human body. That is the secret of how the two universes of mind and matter associate with each other without mistakes. No matter how different they appear, mind and body are both soaked through with intelligence. Science tends to be skeptical in the face of any claim that intelligence is at work in nature (this is a strange historical anomaly, since every generation before us has accepted without question some kind of universal order). However, if there is nothing outside ordinary reality to hold things and events together, then one is led to a set of impossibilities.

We can see this in the law of gravity. Common sense says that two objects separated by empty space should have no connection with each other; in the jargon of physics, they occupy their own "local reality." But the Earth revolves around the sun, held in its orbit by gravity, even though the two bodies are separated by a void of 93 million miles. When he discovered this violation of local reality, Newton was shocked and refused to speculate on how it happens. Since then, local reality has taken one beating after another. Light, radio waves, lasers, and all other electromagnetic forces travel through empty space; matter and antimatter seem to exist in coordinated universes that have no physical contact; subatomic particles have spins that are matched to one another, and it doesn't matter how far apart in time and space the particles are—their spins can be matched at opposite ends of the universe.

What this implies is that the commonsense idea of local reality is true only at a certain level. The whole of reality, as explained by quantum physics, lies deeper. A famous mathematical formula, known as Bell's theorem (after its author, the Irish physicist John Bell), holds that the reality of the universe must be nonlocal; in other words, all objects and events in the cosmos are inter-connected with one another and respond to one another's changes of state. Bell's theorem was formulated in 1964, but decades earlier, the great English astronomer Sir Arthur Eddington had anticipated inter-connectedness by saying, "When the electron vibrates, the universe shakes." Physicists now accept inter-connectedness as a ruling principle, along with many forms of symmetry that extend across the universe—for example, it is theorized that every black hole may be matched up somewhere with a corresponding "white hole," though none has actually been observed.

What kind of explanation would satisfy Bell's requirement for a totally inter-connected, nonlocal reality? It would have to be a quantum explanation, because if gravity is present everywhere at the same time, if black holes know what white holes are doing, and if a change of spin in one particle causes an equal but opposite change instantly in its partner somewhere in outer space, it is obvious that the information going from one place to the other is traveling faster than the speed of light. This is not permitted in ordinary reality, either by Newton or Einstein.

Contemporary theorists such as British physicist, David Bohm, who has worked extensively with the implications of Bell's theorem, have had to suppose that there is an "invisible field" that holds all of reality together, a field that possesses the property of knowing what is happening everywhere at once. (The word *invisible* here means not just invisible to the eye but undetectable by any measuring instrument.) Without going deeper into these speculations, you can see that the invisible field sounds very much like the underlying intelligence in DNA, and both behave very much like the mind. The mind has the property of holding all our ideas in place, in a silent reservoir so to speak, where they are precisely organized into concepts and categories.

Without calling it "thinking," we may be watching nature think through many different channels, of which our minds are one of the most privileged, because the mind can create its quantum reality and experience it at the same time. Witnessing a quantum event in the field of light waves may seem completely objective, but what if quantum reality was just as present in our own thoughts, emotions, and desires? Eddington once flatly stated his belief as a physicist that "the stuff of the world is mind-stuff." So the quantum mechanical body, as a formation of intelligence, has a plausible place in nonlocal reality.

The beauty of such a simple picture is that intelligence *is* simple; the complications arise when one tries to track down the incredibly complex machinery of the mind-body system. The brain-wave patterns of a psychotic and a poet look the same on a roll of EEG paper as it comes off the electroencephalograph, no matter how sophisticated the analysis. Thinking about the thousands of hours it would take to scientifically describe the chemical consequences of one cell's daily life, a neuroscientist friend of mine remarked, "You have to conclude that nature is intelligent because it's too complicated to be called anything else."

He could just as easily have said "too simple." A human brain that changes its thoughts into thousands of chemicals every second is, after all, not so much complicated as inconceivable. In ancient India, it was supposed that intelligence existed everywhere; it was called Brahman, from the Sanskrit word for "big," and was just like an invisible field. A saying from thousands of years ago holds that a man who has not found Brahman is like a thirsty fish who has not found water.

Our whole physiology can be transformed as quickly as a neuropeptide, which is an integral part of the quantum mechanical body. Because we can change like quicksilver, the flowing quality of life is natural to us. The material body is a river of atoms, the mind is a river of thought, and what holds them together is a river of intelligence.

It may seem that the quantum mechanical body is involved only in life-or-death situations, but that isn't so. We live in it, casually and without thinking, just as we live in the body as a whole. I have a patient who glimpsed this fact while sitting on the grass eating French bread and listening to Mozart. She had been a frustrating case for more than two years. She suffered from a combination of nagging symptoms, including irritable bowel, headaches, fatigue, insomnia, and depression, that humbled every attempt to cure her. None of these conditions was fatal, but they made her life miserable nonetheless. Conventional treatment with anti-depressants and tranquilizers had done her little good; neither had anything I did using Ayurveda.

Then one day she went to Tanglewood, the summer home of the Boston Symphony and an idyllic place to have a picnic. She spread out a checkered cloth, lay in the sun listening to music, and peacefully ate her lunch. These things made her very happy, and that night she slept soundly for the first time in years. However, she was so used to being sick that this new event did not register on her. Another year of misery passed, until it was time for her to go to Tanglewood again, and the same thing happened—all her symptoms disappeared for the day, and she slept beautifully that night.

This time it registered. She came to see me jubilantly waving a sheaf of reprints from medical journals on the SAD syndrome. The initials stand for "seasonal affective disorder," referring to a condition in which patients become seriously depressed every winter without apparent cause. Now we know that the cause has to do with the pineal organ, deep inside the skull; this small, flat, oval endocrine gland, although surrounded by brain matter, responds to changes in sunlight, being the source of the "third eye" that everyone wants to look through in the New Age (some lower animals such as the lamprey do possess a literal third eye). In certain people, insufficient exposure to sunlight in the winter throws off their pineal secretions; the gland starts to produce too much of a hormone called melatonin, giving rise to depression.

"See," she said, "I've had SAD all along, and by sitting in the sun, I've got a normal pineal gland again."

"I'm sorry," I said, "but that disorder occurs in winter." Her face started to fall, and I quickly added, "You've put your finger on something important, though. Now we have a deficiency we can treat."

"What's that?" she asked.

"Picnic deficiency," I said. For the first time since I'd known her, she flashed me a genuine smile.

Her self-treatment continues to work. She regularly escapes the gray confines of her office building to sit in the sun at lunch, talk to friends, and listen to lots of Mozart. This may not sound like advanced medicine, and in a sense it isn't, but the reason it works is that we need Nature to free up our nature. We are surrounded by the best of all healing influences—fresh air, sunlight, and beauty. In India, the Hippocrates of Ayurveda, a great physician and sage named Charaka, prescribed some sunlight for all diseases, along with a walk in the early morning, and his advice will never grow stale.

If I find a green meadow splashed with daisies and sit down beside a clear-running brook, I have found medicine. It soothes my hurts as well as when I sat in my mother's lap in infancy, because the Earth really is my mother, and the green meadow is her lap. You and I are strangers, but the internal rhythm of our bodies listens to the same ocean tides that cradled us in a time beyond memory.

Nature is man's healer, because Nature is man. When Ayurveda says that the sun is our right eye and the moon our left eye, we mustn't sneer. By bathing us in the moon, the sun, and the sea, Nature fashioned the bodies we inhabit. These were the ingredients that provided us each with our piece of Nature—a shelter, life-support system, intimate companion, and home for seven decades or more.

The discovery of the quantum realm opened a way to follow the influence of the sun, moon, and sea down deeper into ourselves. I am taking you there only in the hope that there is even more healing to be found there. We already know that a human fetus develops by remembering and imitating the shapes of fish, amphibians, and early mammals. Quantum discoveries enable us to go into our very atoms and remember the early universe itself. Aeons ago, light and heat came into being in the universe, to last for 20 billion years; yet, every human being strikes the spark again, lighting the fire that kindles life. In Vedic India, the same sacred fire that was in the hearth shared the name *Agni* with the digestive fire in the belly and the solar fire in the sky.

Sir Arthur Eddington once affirmed that there were two realities that had to be known on their own terms, one of which was trivial, the other all-important. The trivial one was the mechanistic reality investigated by science; the all-important one was the human reality of ordinary experience. In the scientific reality, Eddington said, Earth is a speck of matter whirling around a mediocre star, both of them cast adrift among billions of more important stellar objects. But in the human reality, Earth remains the center of the universe, because the life it harbors is the only important thing that exists, at least for us.

The most poignant expression of this idea came to me from a patient who had many health problems, including cancer. To regain her perspective, she wrote down certain important experiences from her past. One of these occurred when she was a girl of 16; she entitled it, "But How Can I Be the Moon?—Age 16:"

> Lying alone in the pasture, dark except for the magnetic full moon. There is an overwhelming sense of quietness. My being is part of the earth and part of the pure white light of the moon at the same time. Nothing else is significant. For a second I wonder, "Am I dead?" It isn't important—I am spending an hour in God's hands, and it will become part of me.

A surprising number of people have had such experiences, which Eddington called "the mystic contact with the earth." My patient later slipped away from her experience, gradually becoming used to the grind of work and family worries that disconnects all of us from Nature; in her case, the accumulated stress led to frequent sickness. (She wryly titled her later life, "Going Against Nature— This Is Adulthood?")

What is so unusual is that when she stopped going against Nature, the old feeling of contact came back with undiminished freshness. In her late twenties she visited the Pacific shore and wrote this:

> For about two hours on the beach alone, I was with God again. I was the surf, its sound and strength. I was the sand, warm, vibrating, alive. I was the breeze, soft and free. I was the sky, endless and pure . . . I felt only great love. I was more than my body and knew it. This moment was absolutely cleansing and beautiful.

What she expresses I also believe as a doctor. The healing mechanism inside us perfectly matches the one outside. The human body does not look like the green meadow, but its breezes, its laughing water, sunlight, and earth were merely transformed into us, not forgotten. (There is good reason for all the ancient medicines to say that man is made of earth, air, fire, and water.) Because the body is intelligent, it knows this fact, and when it returns home to Nature, it feels free. With overflowing joy it knows its mother. That feeling of freedom and joy is vital—it allows inner and outer nature to blend. The same is true of the quantum mechanical body; it is just a doorway back to Nature. One does not even need to explain it, except for the sad fact that the intellect, going against Nature, has done such a good job of blocking the door.

There is a lot more to say about the quantum mechanical body. I can think of nothing we need to know more about. Today, medicine wants to make the leap beyond its present dilemmas, but the wanting has turned into waiting. A fellow student from my medical-school days in New Delhi has risen meteorically as a research physician in the United States, becoming a professor at Harvard Medical School before he turned 45. Recently we sat after dinner in a Boston restaurant and he predicted the future. "All the top researchers met quietly in Washington," he said glumly, "and we agreed that by the year 2010, no major cancer would be cured, and there would be no breakthrough in understanding AIDS."

This gloomy prognostication must be avoided at all costs. It may be impeccable science, but it makes no sense from the quantum perspective. We are all expert navigators in the realm of ? zone, where science gropes with one small light. Doesn't this suggest a solution? The mysterious breakdowns of the body's intelligence that occur in cancer and AIDS may all be traceable to a single distortion—a wrong detour into the hidden regions of DNA's intelligence. To see how the mind-body problem can be solved, we need to look more closely at these detours and their invisible origin.

EXPANDING THE TOPIC

Reading this chapter almost three decades after I wrote it, two impressions strike me, one theoretical, the other medical. The theoretical part refers to a knowledge explosion in all the sciences. The medical part has to do with applying this new knowledge to healing diseases and moving human evolution forward. There is a huge mismatch between the two.

By 2003, the Human Genome Project, considered the greatest scientific triumph at the end of the twentieth century, had mapped the three billion base pairs that constitute human DNA. Yet the promise of quick major advances in genetic medical treatments never materialized. Except for treating a handful of quite specific cancers (for example, those where a single genetic mutation can be targeted using a specialized "designer drug"), the general medical applications have been nil. The vast majority of designer drugs are also exorbitantly expensive.

In physics, the rise of superstring theory from its roots in the 1980s has been the main "advance" in understanding the quantum domain since *Quantum Healing* appeared. The quotation marks refer to the fact that not a single experiment has validated string theory, a purely mathematical construct that so far doesn't have practical applications except to employ more physicists to invent new variations on the theory.

A third mismatch, which is in neuroscience, revolves around the baffling dilemma known as the "hard problem," a term coined by the Australian philosopher David Chalmers and which quickly took hold. The hard problem is how to explain the mind as it relates to the brain. Despite a flood of new knowledge about how the brain works, none of this fascinating data comes close to solving the hard problem—the mind remains as elusive as ever. There isn't even a basic explanation for where thoughts come from. The definition of life offered in this chapter, "intelligence wrapped up in chemicals," puts the dilemma in a nutshell. How did intelligence ever get associated with inert physical lumps built from atoms, molecules, and subatomic particles?

I've put the whole state of mismatch in simple terms, but I haven't distorted it. Biology, genetics, physics, and medicine are at once roaring successes and under threat of reaching a dead end. The successes get a lot of publicity, the dead end almost none. Most people will shrug off the news that despite decades of deep thinking and billions of dollars spent on high-speed particle accelerators, physics is no closer to a Theory of Everything and may actually have moved backward. The discovery of so-called dark energy and matter ("dark" means both invisible and outside the parameters of accepted natural laws) has shaken physics to the core.

The public can also shrug off the frustratingly slow progress of genetic medicine, although on the medical front there is increasing awareness that highly touted drugs either don't work well or fail to produce any of the advertised results (a recent example being the revelation that statin drugs, widely prescribed to lower cholesterol, in fact don't reduce the risk of having a heart attack).

To actually grasp the devastating mismatch between theory and application, you have to stand far, far back. Every single scientific fact has its source in the emergence of matter and energy, space and time, from a hidden state in the quantum domain. This is where reality comes from. A gene, a molecule of serotonin, the World Series, a rose, the Andromeda galaxy, and your next thought all arise from a pre-created state. So-called quantum foam is the bubbling up of the universe from a source that gives rise to space and time without being in space and time. It serves as the womb for matter and energy without itself being material or exhibiting the traits of the four forces that "glue" the universe together (gravity, electromagnetism, and the weak and strong forces).

Standing this far back, close to the source, all mysteries converge. But the one mystery that would impact every person's life, the riddle that cannot be shrugged off as an arcane scientific quest, is the hard problem. We must discover whether mind or matter comes first in creation. The other mysteries will all be answered once this one is answered. Here is what's at stake, depending on whether "mind first" or "matter first" is correct.

If mind is primary and matter is secondary, then we live in an intelligent universe. All the aspects of human intelligence are invisibly wrapped up in every atom. We are creative because the universe is creative. Our lives have purpose and meaning because we emerged in a meaningful cosmos. Matter arises, then, because cosmic intelligence needed a way to express itself. Nothing about the unfolding universe from the instant of the Big Bang has been random, then. Randomness is a mere appearance, like the stirring of water and flour when a baker kneads his dough. Flour and water molecules whirl around with no discernible order as the kneading proceeds, yet we know that a completely purposeful outcome—a loaf of bread—is being produced.

On the other hand, if matter is primary in creation, then mind arrived much later, after billions of years of random interactions between atoms and molecules. There is no underlying purpose or meaning to the emergence of mind. It just happened that the first three atoms that coalesced after the Big Bang—hydrogen, helium, and lithium—started a journey on the way to becoming interstellar dust. The dust randomly formed stars; some of these stars exploded as supernovas, and the heavy atoms of iron and other metals went on to gather into planets.

On one planet, Earth, the same random process continued to produce the chemicals necessary for life. From these primitive organic molecules DNA eventually formed, and if we jump ahead three billion years, living cells created a nervous system that evolved into the human brain. Only at the end of this incredibly complex but always random chain of events did mind emerge.

I've skewed the choices in favor of the first one, "mind first." The second narrative, "matter first," seems unbelievable to me. The chance that human DNA evolved from random processes over ten billion years is like the chance that a hurricane can blow through a junkyard and create a Boeing 747, to use a famous metaphor from the British physicist Fred Hoyle. But by backing the "mind first" explanation, *Quantum Healing* angered as many people as it inspired, because "matter first" is the basis of every natural science. Since science continues to produce newer and better technologies (*Quantum Healing* was written in a world without iPhones, tablets, Google, Wikipedia, etc.), how dare anyone suggest that science is headed for a dead end?

Time has proved the skeptics and defenders of the status quo wrong. Across the spectrum of science new thinking arose to close the gap between theory and application by returning to the fundamental mystery of the mind and where it came from. The hard problem has led, directly or indirectly, to new fields like quantum biology, undreamed of thirty years ago. Consciousness has become an area of serious scientific inquiry where it was arrogantly dismissed when I was writing the book—consciousness was simply a given, like the air we breathe. You can build a car without knowing how respiration works. You can't explain the cosmos, life, the brain, or evolution without understanding consciousness. This realization overturned the applecart.

The apples are still scattered. Angry divisions exist between total materialists at one end of the spectrum and proponents of panpsychism (the notion that everything in existence is conscious) at the other end. Religion has been hauled into the discussion, usually by militant atheists, because claiming that intelligence is woven into the universe implies a cosmic mind. A cosmic mind sounds a lot like God, and God raises the unholy specter of Intelligent Design. People are now wrapping their minds around how design and intelligence can both exist without a Creator God. (The dilemma is less painful in the East, since the philosophies derived from ancient India didn't automatically connect cosmic mind with a God in human form. India has always been comfortable with abstractions, especially when it comes to higher consciousness.)

It's poignant to look around at a scene so filled with confusion, divisiveness, and ill will. But the waters aren't actually muddy. The hard problem has forced amazing creativity to emerge. Especially among the younger generation, "mind first" is being seen as the only viable option.

When *Quantum Healing* was written, you risked your scientific reputation to say that mind creates matter (even though the brain performs this act of transformation every time a thought creates a shift in the chemistry inside a neuron). According to the prevailing worldview back then, the body is a machine, the brain a "computer made of meat," the mind a secondary effect, like the heat given off by a bonfire. Now the tide has turned. None of those beliefs hold water, even if they stick around as tenets of rigid materialism. The reality, that we are thoughts that learned to create a body, is far more miraculous, and it's also the truth.

7

NOWHERE AND EVERYWHERE

No one will ever see the quantum mechanical body. For many people, this will be a problem. Not just scientists but all of us are comfortable with things we can see and touch. The history of modern medicine consists largely of tracking down solid objects that cause disease, although almost all of them dwell in the realm of the invisible, beyond anything the naked eye can perceive.

A canny observer in fourteenth-century Europe might have conjectured that a rat in the house portended the danger of bubonic plague (in actuality, rats were so common that the connection was never made); spotting a flea on the rat's pelt gets one closer to the actual cause, but only when you investigate the rat's blood under a microscope and find the bacterium *Pasteurella pestis* have you actually solved the riddle of the Black Death, a nemesis of mankind so ancient that it is credited with decimating the Persian army when it marched against Greece in the fifth century B.C.

Without a microscope, what would a bacterium be? Something invisible to the eye and yet as big as the world, since it reaches every locale on Earth, even the poles. It would come and go like smoke, penetrating the tightest sealed doors and windows—if you believed only in your senses, the ability of such an organism to be nowhere and everywhere at the same time would seem fantastic. In essence, the quantum world is but another step down on the scale of invisibility. Unlike the tiniest bacteria or viruses, a single photon, electron, or any other object in the quantum world can never be seen using any extension of sight and touch. They are truly everywhere and nowhere at the same time.

This fact hardly concerned medicine until very recently, because the smallest virus is still many millions of times larger than an elementary particle. Also, germs are quite stable in time and space, while quantum objects wink in and out of existence unpredictably. If *Pasteurella pestis* lurks in your blood, it is there, absolutely and definitely, unlike the ghostly mesons that leave faint flashes on a photographic plate for a few millionths of a second, only to vanish out of material existence, and most unlike the neutrino, which can pass undetected through the entire Earth as though nothing stood in the way.

The vast difference in scale between medicine and quantum physics safely kept the two sciences on separate ground until 1987, when a French immunologist, Jacques Benveniste, performed an experiment that is outrageous to all nonquantum views of the world. On the surface, the experiment began innocuously. Dr. Benveniste took a common antibody called IgE (standing for immunoglobulin E type) and exposed it to certain white cells in the blood called basophils. It is well known what happens when these two interact— the IgE antibody clamps on firmly to specific receptor sites and waits. What it is waiting for is an invading molecule floating by in the bloodstream that needs to be defended against. In this case, the invader is not a germ but an antigen, a substance that causes allergies.

If you are allergic to bee sting, the molecules of bee venom would not be in your body more than a few seconds before they triggered the IgE antibody. It in turn would set off a complex chain reaction in the cell that throws the body's allergic response into high gear; the basophil would release a chemical called histamine, which causes the swelling, redness, itching, and shortness of breath typical of an allergy attack. The mystery in allergies is that the antigens, the offending substances entering the body, are generally harmless—wool, pollen, dust—and yet the immune system treats them like the deadliest enemy. To find their cause, allergies have been thoroughly studied at the molecular level, and one of the results is a firm grasp of IgE.

This sets the stage for Dr. Benveniste's dramatic experiment. He took some human blood serum full of white cells and IgE and mixed it with a solution prepared from goat's blood that was certain to trigger the release of histamine. This second solution contained an anti-IgE antibody, which represents bee venom, pollen, or other antigen. When the IgE and the anti-IgE hit, the reaction in the test tube went off exactly as it would in a person with a bad allergy, and large amounts of histamine were produced.

Benveniste then diluted the anti-IgE tenfold and added it again—still the same reaction. He kept on diluting, time after time, and as before, about half of the IgE (40 to 60 percent) continued to react. This was extremely surprising, because he was well past the limit where the solution should be chemically active. He decided to dilute the anti-IgE even more, making it a hundred times weaker each time, until he knew that there was no anti-IgE at all. His last dilution contained 1 part antibody to 10^{120} parts water; if written out, this number would be expressed as 10 followed by 120 zeroes. Using a constant called Avogadro's number, he confirmed mathematically that it was impossible for the water to contain a single molecule of antibody. When he added this "solution," which was now just distilled water, the histamine reaction was set off with the same power as before. (The classic Humphrey Bogart movie, *To Have and Have Not*, contains the quirky line, "Have you ever been stung by a dead bee?" In this case, the bee is also invisible.)

Although his result was an absurdity, Benveniste duplicated it seventy times, and asked other research teams to repeat it in Israel, Canada, and Italy—all came up with the same result. They all discovered that you can trigger the immune system with an antibody that isn't there. In our terms, Benveniste had uncovered the ghost of memory—he himself speculates whether water contains the phantom imprint of the molecules that were once in it. His results were reluctantly published in the June 1988 issue of the prestigious British journal *Nature*. Its editors frankly declared their repugnance at the result, stating quite rightly that "there is no physical basis" for it. The human white cells were acting as if the anti-IgE was attacking them from everywhere when in fact it was nowhere.

Medicine is reluctant to walk through the quantum door, even though this experiment clearly opens it.° It was widely held that Benveniste was lending credence to the methods of homeopathy, a medical system invented two hundred years ago by a German physician, Samuel Hahnemann, and still popular throughout Europe. The term *homeopathy* comes from two Greek roots that mean "similar suffering"; this points to the fundamental homeopathic principle that "like treats like." Homeopathy approaches all diseases using Benveniste's method: tiny amounts of antagonistic substances are taken by the patient to build up immunity or to drive out a disease if it is already present.

When conventional medicine administers a smallpox vaccine, it appears that homeopathic logic is at work—the dead virus in the vaccine stimulates anti-smallpox antibodies in the body. (This

---

° In July 1988, a month after publishing his findings, *Nature* sent a team of investigators to France to view Benveniste's experiment and clear up their disbelief. Unfortunately, he was unable to consistently duplicate his results in their presence; some trials worked, others didn't. Subsequently, *Nature* repudiated his work, calling his results a "delusion." A heated controversy arose that has not been settled to date. Benveniste still stands behind his work (his original paper was signed by twelve other researchers in four countries). Since the ability of water to remember is inexplicable, its ability to forget can hardly be held against it! These may be two sides of the same coin.

method of fighting smallpox goes back to ancient China, where doctors knew to take scabs from the sores of smallpox victims and rub them on small cuts in the arms of those they wanted to protect from the disease.) Unlike vaccination, however, homeopathy is based on symptoms rather than on the actual organisms that cause a disease.

Using an elaborate system of poisons and toxic herbs that mimic the symptoms of true disease, the homeopath gives the body a taste of what he wants to cure. Ground-up *Nux vomica* seeds, for example, which contain strychnine, would be given to counteract chronic fatigue and irritability, because they produce these symptoms themselves. Benveniste's experiment in fact did not endorse homeopathic logic as a whole but only a corner of it, by showing that the body can react to a microdose of a foreign substance. The rest of homeopathy remains ambiguous. (The principle of "like treats like" is accepted in Ayurveda, and even broadened to say that every part of the body is matched by herbs, minerals, and even colors and sounds that can be used to treat it. However, Ayurveda does not follow the homeopathic logic that the body should be made sick in order to make it well.)

The deeper import of Benveniste's experiment, I believe, is brought out by one of the quantum diagrams from the last chapter:

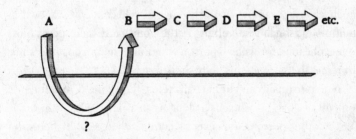

A bodily process, we noted, is like a bucket brigade, a chain of events passing from one step to another, with the exception of the first bucket (B). This bucket appears as if out of nowhere, even though we can obviously see that it is triggered by some initial impulse (A). What Benveniste did so beautifully was to strip this model down to its barest essentials:

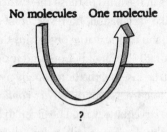

No molecules   One molecule

?

We continually cross over from the state of no molecules to one. If you try to remember the first time you ever drove a car, the brain chemicals present on that occasion have by now vanished. (Most of them disappeared before the drive was over.) When you re-create that memory today, seeing the car and feeling the steering wheel in your hands, you are triggering cellular reactions that begin "no-where," since your brain cells are as empty of the old molecules as Benveniste's water.

If you can explain how the bodymind gets from no molecules to one, then a great many mysteries about the brain will be cleared up. After that first tiny bit of matter, the rest of the sequence follows laws of nature that are well known. Aside from homeopathy, I see a much clearer example in the strange psychiatric cases known as multiple personalities. Nothing in the mind-body field seems quite so inexplicable, for when a person with multiple personalities shifts from one to the other, his body shifts too.

One personality might have diabetes, for example, and the person will be insulin-deficient as long as that personality is in force. Yet the other personalities may be completely free of diabetes, recording the same blood sugar levels as a normal person. Daniel Goleman, a psychologist and frequent reporter on mind-body topics, describes a child named Timmy who adopts nearly a dozen separate personalities.

One of these breaks out into hives if he drinks orange juice.

"The hives will occur," Goleman writes, "even if Timmy drinks orange juice and another personality appears while the juice is still being digested. What is more, if Timmy comes back while the allergic reaction is present, the itching of the hives will cease immediately, and the water-filled blisters will begin to subside."

When I first read these words, I felt very excited. Medical texts do not say that allergic reactions can be turned off and on at will. How could they? The white cells of the immune system, coated with antibodies like IgE, merely wait for the contact of an antigen. When contact occurs, they are automatically triggered to react. Yet, in Timmy's body, one has to envision the orange-juice molecules approaching the white cell, and then a *decision* is made whether to react. This implies that the cell itself is intelligent, just as I have been arguing. Moreover, its intelligence is wrapped up in every molecule, not doled out to a special one like DNA, for the antibody and the orange juice meet end to end with very ordinary atoms of carbon, hydrogen, and oxygen.

To say that molecules make decisions defies current physical science—it is as if salt sometimes feels like being salty and sometimes not. But to cross over from one event in the bodymind to another is always a projection of intelligence; it is only the remarkable swiftness and intensity of Timmy's case that stuns us. Once we absorb the fact that he is choosing to be allergic—for how else could he turn his hives off and on?—then we confront the possibility that we, too, are choosing our own diseases. We are not aware of this choice, because it takes place below the level of our conscious thoughts. But if it is present, we should be able to change it.

All of us can shift the biology of our bodies from one extreme to the other. When you are wildly happy, you are not the same person, physiologically speaking, as when you are deeply depressed. The multiple personalities demonstrate that this ability to change from the inside is under precise control. I'd like to relate a bit of Chopra family lore that relates to this and also, curiously enough, to the IgE antibody.

My father is a cardiologist in India. For many years he served as an army doctor, which required us to move from post to post throughout the country. While I was an infant, he was sent to Jammu, far away to the north in the state of Kashmir. I remember nothing of our stay there, but for years I heard about the terrible allergies my mother suffered in that place. Her tormentor was the pollen of a native flower that covered the ground when it blossomed every spring. It caused her to have severe asthma attacks; her body swelled, and on her skin appeared large red welts and blisters (her condition is known as angioneurotic edema).

My father is very devoted to my mother, and out of compassion he drove her every spring to Srinigar, the capital of Kashmir. The air in Srinigar is free of this particular pollen, and she was delighted to find herself in a mountain valley that is one of the most beautiful places on Earth.

One spring the heavy rains had made the road impassable, and my father decided that they should fly back home early. They boarded the plane, and after an hour it touched down. He put his hand reassuringly on my mother's arm, but he could already see the red spots on her skin and the effort it took for her just to breathe. My mother's allergy was so severe that the steward ran up and asked what was wrong.

"There's nothing you can do," my father said. "It's the pollen in Jammu."

"Jammu?" The steward looked puzzled. "We haven't landed there yet—this is Udhampur, our first stop. Didn't they tell you?"

My father was quite startled. When he looked at my mother, her wheezing had subsided and her sores were vanishing on the spot. For years afterward he would shake his head and mutter, "All you have to do is say the word *Jammu* and your mother breaks out." When I told him about the IgE experiment, he was very relieved—now he had a scientific answer, of sorts, to our family mystery. My mother has only one personality, but this shift was both extreme and swift.

Many multiple-personality cases have been studied and verified, particularly by Dr. Bennett Braun, a research psychiatrist and specialist in the field. When the patient's personality shifts, warts, scars, and rashes have been seen to appear and disappear, along with hypertension and epilepsy. A specific personality can be color blind, only to return to normal sight when the personality changes back. Almost as a rule, such patients have at least one personality that is a child, and when it emerges, their bodies respond to lower doses of drugs. In one case, 5 milligrams of a tranquilizer made the patient relaxed and sleepy when he was a child, while a dose twenty times stronger had no effect on the adult.

Mystified researchers are looking for a mechanism to explain these seemingly impossible occurrences; it will be found, I believe, only by seeing that a quantum shift has taken place. A personality has no molecules in it, being composed only of memories and psychological tendencies; yet these are more permanent than the cells being affected. This is not a huge mystery—every molecule in your own body is wrapped up, as we saw, with a bit of invisible intelligence.

Memory is not a term used by physicists, and yet it is easy to find it in the quantum world—particles that are separated by immense distances of space-time know what one another are doing. When an electron jumps into a new orbit on the outside of an atom, the anti-electron (or positron) paired with it must react, no matter where it lives in the cosmos. In fact, the entire universe is knitted together by this kind of memory network.

To a physicist, the only puzzle in Benveniste's experiment is that no one has ever believed that quantum events take place at the level of molecules. A photon sits on the quantum threshold, where faint, random vibrations are the rule. Some of these vibrations die off into nothingness; others wake up and enter material reality as matter or energy. Because the photon is almost nothing to begin with, it can wink in and out of existence. A molecule like IgE, however, is tremendously more substantial than these fluctuating vibrations. If it weren't, molecules might jump in and out of existence without warning—along with things made out of molecules, like blue whales and skyscrapers. Since this does not happen, it has not been deemed necessary to invest molecules with memory.

To understand how such memory works, one has to know more about the quantum level of nature. Its peculiarity, setting it aside from all other states of matter and energy, is its emptiness. We have already seen that at its heart, an atom is almost totally empty, being proportionately as void as intergalactic space. The same must hold true for us, since obviously we are made of atoms. That means we are made out of a void; more than anything else, it is our raw material.

Instead of seeing the space among the stars as bleak, cold, and lifeless, one should look through a physicist's eyes and see it packed with unseen energy waiting to coalesce into atoms. Every cubic centimeter of space teems with energy, nearly infinite amounts of it, although much of this energy is in "virtual" form, meaning that it is locked up and plays no active part in material reality. (A wonderful line from an ancient Indian Upanishad declares, "The power penetrating the universe is much more than what, shines through." In terms of quantum objects, most of which are locked up in virtual form, this is true literally.)

Our senses are not prepared to see emptiness as the womb of reality, being tuned in to a grosser level of nature populated with flowers, rocks, trees, and our families. It is said that the human eye can distinguish 2 million shades of color, each of which occupies a narrow band of light energy, but our optical mechanism nevertheless doesn't register these energy vibrations as vibrations. Much less do we register a chunk of solid marble as vibrations, although at bottom that is what it is, just the same as color.

As light shifts from color to color, each small gradation exerts an enormous influence. Visible light, for example, gives the world shape and definition as perceived by our eyes. If you shift down just slightly to the infrared band, the human eye would feel warm from the light but be blind; if you shift up to X rays, the eye would be destroyed. Every quantum gradation is slight, but it implies a completely new reality at the grosser level of molecules and living things. The spectrum of light is like a long, continuous string, vibrating slower at one spot and faster at another. We make our home on a tiny part of the spectrum, but it takes the entire length for us to exist. Beginning at zero vibration, shakes of the string are responsible for the light, heat, magnetism, and countless other discrete energy forms that fill the universe. It is just a few steps on the ladder of creation from empty space to intergalactic dust to a sun and finally the living Earth. What this shows is that emptiness, the point of zero vibration, is not a void but the starting point for everything that exists. And this starting point is always in contact with every other point—there are no breaks in continuity.

The reason for discussing the subatomic void is that we experience the void every time we think. Just as in the universe at large, something material—the neuropeptide—springs out of nowhere. In this case it is not the atoms of the neuropeptide that are created, because the necessary hydrogen, carbon, oxygen, and so forth are already present in the glucose that the brain uses as fuel. What is created out of nowhere is the configuration of the neuropeptide, but that is magical enough.

At the very instant that you think, "I am happy," a chemical messenger translates your emotion, which has no solid existence whatever in the material world, into a bit of matter so perfectly attuned to your desire that literally every cell in your body learns of your happiness and joins in. The fact that you can instantly talk to 50 trillion cells in their own language is just as inexplicable as the moment when nature created the first photon out of empty space.

These brain chemicals are so small that it has taken science several centuries to identify them. Yet if we look at the messenger molecules as being the finest material expression of intelligence the brain can produce, we have to admit that they are still not quite fine enough to build a secure bridge between mind and body. In fact, nothing could be fine enough, because one shore we want to bridge, the mind, is not small in any physical sense—to think that a thought has a size is absurd. Mind is not "hanging out" in space taking up room, even the infinitesimal room needed for an electron. The obvious nonsense of putting mind into a box was one of the chief reasons why science separated mind and matter to begin with, since all matter can fit into a box. Fortunately, quantum physics comes to the bridge builder's rescue. It was born to explore these nonsensical-seeming regions on the fringes of space-time.

Quantum physics has taken responsibility for measuring things that are as small as possible. The atom, although very small, was found around 1900 to have a nucleus, and when that was sliced apart, its smallest unit seemed to be the proton, until further atom-smashing revealed, at the edge of material existence, still finer particles called quarks. Beyond the quark, however, the smashing seems to stop.

One would think that there has to be something material out there that the quark is built from. Strangely enough, this does not seem to be true. In ancient Greece, the philosopher Democritus first proposed that the material world was composed of minute, invisible particles, which he named atoms, from the Greek word for "not divisible." When Plato heard of this theory (which of course could not be tested experimentally), he offered an objection that uncannily predicts quantum physics. If we think of an atom as a thing, Plato argued, then it must take up some space; therefore, it can be cut in half to occupy a smaller space. Anything that can be cut in half is not the smallest constituent of the material world.

By this impeccable reasoning, Plato demolished all solid particles as contenders for nature's basic building block, not just the atom, but the proton, electron, and quark. All of these can be cut in half, even if we can't actually do it, without end. Whatever it is that builds the world, it must be something so tiny that it occupies no space. Plato contended that the world was born out of invisible, perfect forms, similar to geometric shapes. In its turn, modern physics has turned to somewhat more tangible alternatives, such as invisible matter called "Virtual" particles, as well as to energy fields. Einstein's famous equation $E = mc^2$ proved that energy could be transformed into matter, and this allowed physics to go beyond the barrier that is "smaller than small."

No one can confidently say what builds a quark, but it is certainly not a piece of matter in solid form—the quark is already outside the limit of anything that one can "see" or "touch," even using scientific instruments to extend our senses; its building block may well be merely a vibration that has the potential to turn into matter. Therefore, it is smaller than small. To a physicist, all size stops at a specific number, 10^{-33} cubic centimeters, an inconceivable fraction that can be written out as $\frac{1}{10}$ followed by 32 zeros; this is known as Planck's limit, a kind of absolute zero for space, just as there is an absolute zero for temperature.

Once this barrier is reached, however, what lies beyond? Here physical science stands mute. But it is fascinating to discover that all the founders of quantum physics were basically Platonists. That is, they believed that the world of things is a shadowy projection of a vaster, invisible reality that is nonmaterial. Some, like Einstein, stood in awe at the orderliness of nature without ascribing intelligence to it. Others, like Eddington, flatly declared that the raw material of the whole universe is "mind-stuff." Eddington defends his position with a logical argument as elegant as Plato's. Our picture of the world, he points out, is basically a formation of brain impulses. This is formed in turn out of impulses traveling up and down the nerves. These in turn come from vibrations of energy at the ends of the nerves. At the basis of the energy is emptiness, the quantum void. Which part is real? The answer is none, because every step along the way, from energy vibrations to nerve impulses to brain formation, is just a code.

No matter where you look, the visible universe is fundamentally a set of signals. Yet these signals all hold together, turning totally meaningless vibrations into full-blown experiences that have human meaning. The love between man and wife can be broken down into raw physical data, but to do that is to lose its reality. Therefore, Eddington says, all these codes must stand for something more real, something beyond our senses. At the same time, this something is very intimate to us, for all of us can read the code, turning random quantum vibrations into an orderly reality.

A good image for this would be a pianist playing a Chopin etude. Where is the music? You can find it at many levels—in the vibrating strings, the trip of the hammers, the fingers striking the keys, the black marks on the paper, or the nerve impulses produced in the player's brain. But all of these are just codes; the reality of music is the shimmering, beautiful, invisible form that haunts our memories without ever being present in the physical world.

To be like the quantum, the body does not have to banish its molecules to another dimension; it has only to learn to re-form them into new chemical patterns. It is these patterns that jump in and out of existence, paralleling what happened in Benveniste's test tubes. If you think hard about leaping off a cliff and your heart starts to pound, you have generated adrenaline using a stimulus that is just as invisible as the anti-IgE in the experiment. Similarly, one of Timmy's personalities remembers how to be allergic to orange juice, even though that personality may hide in some invisible realm for days at a time. As soon as it returns, the body must obey its commands.

I have tried to make all of this sound reasonable, contrary to one of the editors at *Nature,* who said that the IgE experiment, if true, throws out two hundred years of rational thought in biology. But biology will have to change now, and medicine with it. Contrary to what physicians currently suppose, the abnormal pancreas of a diabetic is not as real as the distorted memory that has wrapped itself inside the pancreatic cells.

This realization opens the door for quantum healing. The mental techniques used by Ayurveda depend on being able to control the invisible patterns that order the body. Recently I saw a patient, an elderly woman, who was suffering from dull chest pains; they had previously been diagnosed as angina pectoris, one of the most common symptoms of advanced heart disease. Between January and May of that year, she had recorded sixty attacks of angina, which were relieved by taking a nitroglycerine tablet. I instructed her in the "primordial sound technique" for heart disease, and she left to practice it on her own.

In July, about two months later, my patient wrote me a letter stating that her attacks had stopped on the day she received the technique and have never recurred. She feels comfortable in activity now—most angina sufferers are extremely anxious about exerting themselves, even slightly. On her own she has discontinued the use of her medication, and she recently enrolled as a full-time college student. She was very proud to write this last piece of news, since she is 88 years old.

In my own mind, I explain this result by saying that the mind-body connection is coming under control. I would also say that the Ayurvedic technique is not magical; it is only imitating nature. Is there any difference between my patient making her angina disappear and a multiple personality doing the same thing?

A skeptical doctor might object that angina usually has two causes. One is spasm of the coronary arteries, the blood vessels that feed oxygen to the heart. If these go into spasm and squeeze shut, then the oxygen-deprived heart muscle screams out in pain. My patient must have had this kind of angina, a skeptic would say. The other kind is caused by fatty blockages in the coronary arteries and couldn't possibly be cured by a mental technique. I would have to answer that both examples involve memory. The fatty blockages are not as substantial as they appear. If you perform a heart-bypass graft and replace the old clogged arteries with open ones, the new replacements will often clog up in a matter of months. This is because the vessel has changed but the ghost of memory has not—it still wants to load fatty plaque into that artery.

On the reverse side, many bypass patients don't feel the return of their agonizing, frightening chest pain, even with clogged arteries, because they are sure that their surgery cured them. Surgeons have even experimented with placebo operations, doing nothing more than opening the chest and closing it again—a good percentage of those patients felt relief from their angina. In fact, my patient did not have blocked coronary arteries, but the mechanism behind her angina was physically real nonetheless; her brain did not X-ray her blood vessels before reacting with pain.

If I have a patient who is afraid, I can grasp his hand reassuringly and he will feel better; this happens even under anesthesia. You can grasp the patient's hand at a difficult moment in surgery and see the monitors for blood pressure and heartbeat register the calming effect. The heart and the brain, it seems, are connected much deeper than where molecules are. One sees the truth of this whenever a baby is cradled in its mother's arms. Within a few minutes, the two of them will be breathing together, even if the baby is asleep, and their heartbeats will start to synchronize (they will not match beat for beat, since the child's heart rate is faster than the mother's). This bodymind connection is invisible, but who would call it unreal? It has been passed on silently from generation to generation. Perhaps it still wraps us all in a bond of sympathy. Out of separate beings, trapped in their own concerns, it helps to mold one human race.

Once science recovers from its shock over the IgE experiment, a new domain will need to be explored, the domain of emptiness. Quantum physics has discovered something mysteriously rich about empty space. Now we are on the verge of extending this richness into the human dimension.

The universe in its primordial state has been likened to energy soup that turned into particles of matter. I would liken us, then, to intelligence soup—except that we aren't soup at all but intelligence that has learned to crystallize into beautiful, precise, powerful, organic particles we call thoughts. This makes the void inside us far more fascinating than the one that gave birth to the universe.

EXPANDING THE TOPIC

Revealing the strangeness of "nowhere and everywhere" was important when getting at the true nature of reality. But it probably left readers wondering how to navigate such bizarre territory. The temptation is to fall back on a default position that takes the world of the five senses as is. Even physicists who understand that physical objects are reducible to invisible clouds of energy in an infinite quantum field still drive their Honda or bicycle to work, not an energy cloud. Since this chapter was written, experiments about water having memory seem to be largely discredited, yet the debate about homeopathy hasn't been settled.

It's inevitable that studies showing that homeopathic treatments for the flu actually work are balanced by studies showing that they don't. The prestigious British medical journal *The Lancet* has weighed in several times on the issue, endorsing homeopathy as being only as effective as a placebo, while generally dismissing the whole approach. And yet *The Lancet* also reviewed studies of flu vaccines in elderly people and found no effectiveness either in preventing the disease or lowering hospital admissions due to complications. Going further, after analyzing "every study published in any language," *The Lancet* "could not find a single study that showed a flu vaccine led to the reduction in mortality or serious complications from the flu." Disease, it seems, keeps pushing the mystery of mind and body into our lives.

But my mind always returns to the practical side—how can we learn to navigate quantum reality when it's invisible and totally counterintuitive, where everything solid, tangible, fixed, and reliable dissolves in our hands? The answer isn't to return to school and get an advanced degree in physics. Either the quantum domain makes a difference in daily life, here and now, or it's irrelevant.

I actually did find two physicists who helped guide me through the morass: Amit Goswami, then at the University of Oregon, and Menas Kafatos at Chapman University in Orange, California. They became close colleagues, a source of far-reaching ideas, and sometime coauthors. (The skeptical assault is relentless, and it was necessary to present highly credentialed scientists as allies and defenders.) It was Kafatos who first showed me the breakthrough I was seeking when it came to navigating the quantum domain.

To see where our thinking led us, stop the clock this very minute. What are you doing? You are participating in reality. In what way? By perceiving what's around you. Your eyes see this page, but out of the corner of your eyes you are aware of the room you're sitting in. Smells and sounds are floating your way. The air brushing past your skin is warm or cool. These are the qualities of life. Thanks to Newton's theory of optics, sunlight can be broken down into the colors that compose it, but this analysis isn't the same as seeing a rainbow in the sky, and very far from how you feel while gazing at it.

We participate in the world through experience. Winnowing the experience of a rainbow down to wavelengths of light, weather conditions, time of day, the refractive power of raindrops—all of that is nonparticipatory. The mind has to stand apart to collect data and make measurements leading to more data. By standing apart, science can reveal a host of facts, but as the poet William Wordsworth astutely observed, "we murder to dissect." Once you cut an experience up into measurements, data, and facts, the life has gone out of it. The dissecting mind is as deadly as a scalpel.

In the name of objectivity, science excludes subjective experience, on the grounds that subjectivity is fickle, unpredictable, prone to biases, etc. But this attitude, pure as its motives may be, forgets that life is what we live. The universe is what we participate in. Experience is what we have. Even doing science is another kind of experience.

So it follows that to explain the universe, it's just as viable to begin with our experience of it. More viable, actually, because attempting to be totally objective about the world is a chimera. Too much is happening "under the table," to use a phrase in earlier chapters. The domain of fixed physical objects that can be measured and cut like a tailor making a suit excludes most of what makes life worth living—love, beauty, creativity, insight, gratitude, reverence, art, music, and intuition. These, too, are the fits we gain by participating in the universe rather than staring at it with our noses pressed up against the glass, like children pressing up to a bakery window.

The building blocks of experience are known as *qualia,* related to the Latin word for quality. An apple has the qualities of sweet, red, crunchy, and tart. Those qualia are what the brain processes in order for an apple to exist. My inner response to eating an apple is also qualia. "Out there" the apple's qualia seem to be physical and beyond my influence. "In here" my response to eating an apple—whether I like apples or not, finding this one too sweet or overripe, and so on—is also a world of qualia. Both kinds of experience, inner and outer, are created in consciousness. For that reason, subjectivity is no longer the elephant in the room. A science based on qualia can have the best of objectivity and subjectivity.

Let's translate these points into personal terms. How do you experience your body? You have external experiences—looking at yourself in the mirror, jogging around the park, ordering dessert in a restaurant. You also have inner experiences—feeling your muscles grow tired while you jog, thinking you look old when you see yourself in the mirror, wrestling with your conscience about ordering dessert in a restaurant. Clearly all of these experiences are linked, and they begin "in here."

"In here" is the source of sensations, images, feelings, and thoughts, reducible to the acronym SIFT, devised by Daniel J. Siegel, professor of psychiatry at the University of California, Los Angeles School of Medicine. In his clinical work, Dr. Siegel has made important breakthroughs matching subjective states with areas of the brain in a healing relationship. A patient who claims to have no emotions, for example, is subjectively describing a state of numbness that won't be purely subjective. In the amygdala, the area of the brain devoted to emotions, there will be a parallel—the objective and subjective domains merge.

Materialists claim that the amygdala creates emotions, putting the objective evidence first and foremost. No doubt a brain scan will show increased or decreased activity in areas of the amygdala that correlate with what a patient feels. But neurons don't laugh and cry; people do. Medicine isn't out to make the amygdala feel better; it aims to make the patient feel better. What Dr. Siegel perceived is that he could work from both ends of the spectrum—and this leads to an extraordinary conclusion.

We don't have to say that the brain creates the mind or that the mind creates the brain. In a continuous feedback loop, emotions are always creating molecules in the brain, and these chemicals influence the next emotion. Nature crosses the mind-body barrier all the time, revealing that it was constructed arbitrarily to fit a certain worldview. With a shift in worldview, everything changes. The redness of an apple doesn't have to be "out there" while its sweetness is "in here." In fact, there is no such thing as "out there" and "in here." There is only the quantum field producing different aspects of experience.

In the Bhagavad-Gita (the Song of the Lord from ancient India), Lord Krishna declares, "I am the field and the knower of the field." This carries us deeper into reality. Instead of talking about the quantum field, we can simply refer to "the" field—reality itself. Here, knower and known are not separate. They are fused into a holistic experience.

To bring this back to your body, you experience your hand as a thing, a pink, fleshy appendage you can wave in front of your face. You also experience it as a tool when you hammer in a nail, a source of Eros when you stroke the skin of your beloved, the extension of your imagination when you pick up a paintbrush, a calculating instrument when you count on your fingers, and much more. Life flows through this pink fleshy appendage according to what the mind desires.

Therefore, to say that you exist inside your body is entirely untrue. The truth is that your body exists in you, inside your consciousness. Nothing about your hand—movement, touch, pain, dexterity, et cetera—exists anywhere except in consciousness. And since every quality you experience comes from the field, you can echo Lord Krishna: *You are the field and the knower of the field*.

Now you no longer have to travel under the assumed identity of "I," the limited ego trapped inside a package of skin and bone. Your actual identity takes you to the level of the quantum mechanical human body. From there no one can predict the kind of power, creativity, and control that's available. Particularly in the West, getting past the boundary of the ego is new territory. We are conditioned by materialism and the scientific attachment to facts, data, and objectivity.

Fortunately, participating in the universe isn't Eastern or Western. I've come to believe that it's more reliable to feel one's way through life than to try to figure everything out mentally. Bringing medicine back to a patient's personal reality, filled with unique experiences, memories, likes and dislikes, core beliefs, and expectations—that will be the key to quantum healing on a scale my book only hinted at.

8

SILENT WITNESS

The pressing need for a quantum medicine is well illustrated, I think, by the following case study.

A young Israeli named Aaron, 24 years old, called me at my office and said, "I feel perfectly healthy, but my doctor has given me ninety days to live. He took some tests which showed that I have an incurable blood disorder—that was exactly twenty-three days ago."

Barely managing to suppress his emotions, he told me a story that had taken several strange turns. His diagnosis had come about entirely by accident. Because of an old soccer injury, he had a deviated septum, which made it difficult for him to breathe. He visited a surgeon in Chicago who could repair his nose—Aaron had moved to the United States several years earlier to attend business school—and the surgeon asked him to have a routine blood test.

When the results came back from the lab, the doctor was very disturbed. They showed that Aaron was severely anemic: his hemoglobin count had fallen from a normal of 14 to 6 (a count of 12 would be considered borderline anemic); hemoglobin is the chemical component of the blood that carries oxygen throughout the body. His hematocrit had plummeted to 16; this means that when his blood was spun in a centrifuge to separate the red blood cells from the plasma, the red cells occupied only 16 percent of the total volume. In normal blood, this should be closer to 40 percent.

Aaron was immediately referred to a blood specialist, a hematologist, who asked him a standard series of questions.

"Have you been feeling short of breath lately?"

"No," Aaron answered.

"Do you wake up in the middle of the night feeling suffocated?"

"No."

"Have your ankles been swelling up?"

"No."

The hematologist looked at him very hard. "Look," he said, "you're pretty tired all the time, aren't you?" Aaron shook his head. "That's amazing!" the doctor exclaimed. "With your hemoglobin counts, you should be in congestive heart failure by now."

Aaron was shocked. Looking at the blood tests, however, his doctor had a right to be amazed. In severe anemia, the heart has to work much harder than normal to supply enough oxygen to the rest of the body. This, combined with its own oxygen deprivation, causes the heart muscle to swell, leading to congestive heart failure. The patient begins to wake up at night feeling that he is suffocating to death, and eventually that is what happens.

Mystified, the hematologist took a sample of Aaron's bone marrow. The body typically contains only 9 ounces of bone marrow, but that is enough to manufacture our total supply of red blood corpuscles, at a rate of 200 billion new cells per day. Under examination, Aaron's marrow showed no signs of the red-cell precursors that should have been present. The hematologist now knew that at the root of Aaron's condition was a shutdown of the bone marrow (called aplastic anemia), but he could not determine any cause for it. Even without symptoms, Aaron was very sick.

"No one knows for sure how long a red blood cell lives," the doctor said. "The accepted figure is one hundred twenty days, but it could be as short as a month. Since you are not replacing your current red cells, I'm afraid you cannot live much longer than ninety days."

As Aaron listened numbly, the doctor told him that medicine could do very little for him—the suggested treatment was a bone marrow transplant, a major operation that he might not survive and that probably would not save him. He could be given a blood transfusion to raise his red-cell count, but the sudden incursion of another person's blood would further dampen his bone marrow function; moreover, when the marrow detected that the blood count was up again, it might interpret that as a sign to roll back even further.

Because he felt no symptoms, Aaron hesitated to undergo the transplant. The hematologist gave him two weeks to decide. He also said that it was his legal duty to advise the young man to settle his affairs as quickly as possible. (Aaron was not exactly treated with compassion at any step of the way. At one point, he divulged to his doctor that his older sister had died suddenly and tragically in law school. The cause of death, though vague, was thought to be a rare blood disorder, perhaps inherited. On hearing this, the hematologist enthusiastically asked Aaron to try to find out precisely what his sister had died of, since together he and she would make an excellent article for the journals. When Aaron later recounted this incident, I found myself growing extremely angry.)

Within a day of his diagnosis, Aaron began to feel short of breath and found himself unable to sleep. He sought in desperation for a way to cure himself. Almost by chance he took up meditation and heard about our Ayurvedic clinic. Within a month, he had become my patient in Lancaster.

"The most hopeful thing," I said, "is that you felt healthy before you found out what was wrong with you. Let's go on the assumption that you are controlling this disorder and do everything we can to allow your body to heal itself."

Without knowing what caused his disease, I found as I was interviewing Aaron that there were many points of concern. The first was the frightening diagnosis itself, which had thrown him into a panic. In such a condition, it is difficult to see how the bodymind could begin to find a route toward healing. In addition, Aaron seemed a tense and driven person. He had worked four jobs at a time while he was in school, pushing himself to the limit in order to buy a car and keep ahead of school debts. The pressure of school itself was enormous. He routinely took huge doses of vitamins, plus an anti-ulcer medication to soothe his chronic stomach pain. A few months earlier he'd had tendonitis from playing tennis too hard and had taken an anti-inflammatory agent to bring down the swelling—such drugs are known to suppress bone marrow function. I asked him to discontinue all medication.

He stayed two weeks at the clinic and for the first time lived in an environment free of "normal" stress. He continued to meditate, ate a simple vegetarian diet suited to his particular body type, and received a course of massage treatments that Ayurveda prescribes to purify the physiology. I also instructed him in the primordial sound technique suitable for his condition. One night a nurse caught him walking down the hall with wet hair, and he sheepishly confessed that he had sneaked off the property to go swimming. When I heard this, I was very happy—another patient with Aaron's blood count could easily have been on oxygen and blood transfusions. The signs were more than encouraging.

On the day he left, I asked Aaron not to have any more blood tests for at least two weeks. A blood sample drawn at Lancaster had disclosed that his supply of immature red blood cells, called reticulocytes, was four times higher than when he entered. Since these are the cells that later mature into red corpuscles, I felt that his condition had turned around. As I write, Aaron has just outlived his original prognosis. He is still severely anemic, but on the other hand he has not gone into the serious decline expected of someone whose blood count is heading toward zero. In fact, his anemia has slightly improved.

In my mind, Aaron stands on the dividing line between two kinds of medicine. The first is standard scientific medicine, whose methods are deeply ingrained in me, but which I can no longer trust absolutely. It is not that standard medicine has failed. Aaron's doctors expertly tracked down his disease at every level of the body, from tissues to cells to molecules—in Aaron's case, the tissue was bone marrow, the cells were red blood corpuscles, and the molecule was hemoglobin. To a doctor trained in conventional medicine, this is the end of the route, a route that has taken two centuries of painstakingly rational investigation to find. Once you know what is wrong with a person's very molecules, what else can be known?

This logic is impeccable science, but it is dangerously divorced from the ordinary input of life. By "ordinary input" I mean what a person eats and how he sleeps, the thoughts that go through his head, and all the sights, smells, sounds, and textures that enter through his senses. You can say that the body is made out of molecules, but with equal justice you could say that it is made out of experiences. That definition matches our own self-image, which is not scientific but fluid, changeable, and alive. Out of ordinary experiences, the second medicine, which is quantum, takes its origin.

We might casually think that everyday life is too commonplace and simple for science to bother with. In truth, it is far too complex. Although a molecule of hemoglobin is structured out of 10,000 separate atoms, it can be isolated and mapped—a feat that has led to several Nobel prizes. However, to trace what hemoglobin is doing when you take in a single breath would be impossible, because each red blood cell contains 280 million molecules of hemoglobin, each of which picks up 8 atoms of oxygen. Considering that the lungs expose about one quart of blood to the air per breath, containing 5 trillion red cells, the total number of chemical exchanges is astronomical. The whole process quickly disintegrates into a swirling chaos of activity.

When you open the human body during surgery, what confronts you is not the well-defined map of textbook anatomy, with the nerves in blue, blood vessels in red, and a green liver neatly set apart from a yellow gallbladder. Instead, an uneducated eye sees a jumble of tissue that is mostly undifferentiated—almost all of it is pink and moist; one organ slides imperceptibly into another. The great wonder is that scientific medicine has learned as much as it has about this pulsating chaos. But in return for its knowledge, science has paid a high price by having to abandon ordinary experience. A breath of air, after all, is not chaos, except to a molecular biologist. Breathing is the basic rhythm of life, upon which all other rhythms are based.

Eric Cassell, a professor of physiology at Cornell, astutely points out that when a doctor asks his patient questions, he is not trying to find out what is wrong with him; he is trying to find out what symptoms he might have that match a known, classified disease. This is a subtle but very important distinction. It reminds us that the whole system of organs, tissues, and so on was set up intellectually to make the body easier to classify. There must be other views that are truer to nature, in that they rely on ordinary experience, defying nature's disorderly exterior in order to understand its real meaning.

Chaos is just an appearance, a mask, and with a different eye it metamorphoses into pure order. Until its code was cracked, a honeybee's dance looked like chaos, a random display of twitches and turns. Now we see it as a precise set of directions leading the other bees in the hive to a source of nectar. This does not mean that the dance changed from chaos to order, only that its appearance changed in our eyes. Similarly, if you take a few blood pressure readings from a heart patient, it is unlikely that they will form any pattern, but if you monitor him constantly, a definite wave pattern emerges, with peaks and valleys that occur over the space of one or two days. This fact, which was only recently uncovered, has allowed cardiologists to detect hypertension in patients who have deceptively normal pressure in a doctor's office because their peaks occur only at night. Clearly some kind of tidal swing is at work, but no one yet knows its significance. The mask of chaos is too freshly broken.

The two medicines do not have to be antagonists, but for the moment they clearly face in opposite directions. To a hematologist, it is largely irrelevant if Aaron is tense, driven, full of dubious substances, and panicked at the thought of dying. To an Ayurvedic doctor, these are primary inputs to his sickness—they have entered on the quantum level, where he turns into the person he is. The hematologist is not being heartless; he may care very deeply about Aaron, but he cannot prove a connection between bone marrow dysfunction and working four jobs at a time. That is the limit where the Newtonian notion of cause and effect, the basis of standard scientific medicine, breaks down.

You cannot possibly ask enough questions to find out what really makes a patient sick. In Aaron's case, I would want to know how he felt about his sister's death, what he eats for breakfast, who his friends are, how he feels when he loses at tennis—in effect, I want to know every relevant experience. This is virtually impossible. So many influences press in on us every day that the idea of causation disappears. I would think it absurd to dissect a poet's brain to find the cause of his sonnets; his cortex undeniably had to exhibit specific brain-wave patterns to produce a sonnet, but they have evaporated and been carried to a realm hidden by time. It begins to seem just as absurd to claim that an isolated physical cause lies behind Aaron's bone marrow dysfunction. His life is swept along by time, too, and what I want to find has evaporated.

I know this sounds shocking, because without a cause, how can we find a cure? But all physical causes are partial at best. If you try to give someone a cold, for example, it takes more than a virus. Experimenters have incubated cold viruses, placed them directly on the mucous lining of the nose, and found that their subjects came down with colds only 12 percent of the time. These odds could not be increased by exposing the subjects to cold drafts, putting their feet in ice water to give them chills, or anything else that was purely physical. Ordinary experience, a complex play of inner and outer forces, defies the rules of causation that work for billiard balls.

Conventional medicine already recognizes that ordinary experience can play a complex role in disease. For example, statistics show that single people and widows living alone are more likely to get cancer than people who are married. Their loneliness is called a risk factor—one could just as truly call it a carcinogen. Then why isn't curing loneliness a cure for cancer? It may well be, but in a different kind of medicine than we now practice. An Ayurvedic physician is more interested in the patient he sees before him than in his disease. He recognizes that what makes up the person is experience—sorrows, joys, fleeting seconds of trauma, long hours of nothing special at all. The minutes of life silently accumulate, and like grains of sand deposited by a river, the minutes can eventually pile up into a hidden formation that crops above the surface as a disease.

The process of accumulation is impossible to see or to stop. I may sit in a traffic jam and think, "Well, nothing is happening to me now," but in fact I am taking in, or ingesting, the world around me. My body is metabolizing everything I see, hear, smell, and touch and turning it into *me*, just as surely as it ingests my orange juice.

The input that is turning into me is constant, and by my participation I shape it into final form. Science will not be able to measure this process, because it cannot put my senses or my emotions on a scale. How much loneliness does it take to turn into cancer? This is a meaningless question. The carcinogen is invisible. I remember one night when I stood in the emergency room of a suburban hospital after attending to an overflow of patients. A late commuter train had crashed, and with one other doctor I had to work in a near frenzy seeing dozens of passengers who might be in shock, bandaging their wounds, calming their nerves, setting bones, and performing minor surgeries. Our job seemed endless, but after five hours it was done, and we felt like heroes.

Then the ambulance radio came on again, and the driver said, "We're coming in with a two-month-old infant, female, who is unconscious. No signs of respiration or pulse, and she's turning blue." All at once I went cold, and I saw a look of despair on the other doctor's face. We knew what was ahead of us. The ambulance unloaded its stretcher, bearing a tiny infant who looked lost on the big, white sheet. To put an endotracheal tube down her throat and begin cardiac massage was a horrible travesty, but we went through with it. From the first moment, we knew this must be a "crib death," which medicine calls sudden infant death syndrome. It affects seemingly normal babies, there is no known cause, and even the fastest emergency treatment is usually of no avail.

As soon as we decently could, we took away our apparatus and closed the baby's eyes. I went out to talk to the parents, young and well-to-do, who were devastated. All I could do was tell them about a support group of other parents whose children had died this way. They left, still in shock, and I never saw them again. Who can measure what happened to me? I don't recall the face of a single victim from the train wreck, people whose bodies I worked on for hours. But the blond hair and blue eyes of the baby are as vivid in my mind as the first second I saw her. She has entered into me. I do not know where she lives inside me—is it really some bit of gray matter in my cortex? It would seem ridiculous to look for the location. What is important is that my whole being is made up of such experiences. I have metabolized a hundred thousand such things every day, and if you want to see them in detail, just look at me.

As long as you are surrounded by the input of life, there is no stopping the rush of events that makes me what I am. On the other hand, my nature may go deeper than the things I see and hear. There may be a zero point in me, like the point of zero vibration which gives rise to the entire spectrum of light.

If you stepped outside my thoughts, senses, and emotions, you would be left with the equivalent of empty space. But like the empty space of quantum physics, my "inner space" may not be empty at all.

I would argue that our inner space is a rich field of silent intelligence, and that it exerts a powerful influence on us.

Intelligence is easily located and yet impossible to find. The body's know-how seems to be the result of a complexity of parts, broken down according to functions—digestion, respiration, metabolism, and so on. Although this division of labor is real enough, intelligence remains everywhere the same despite it, just as a drop of sea water shares the saltiness of the whole ocean. Sea water gives us a perfect example, in fact. The fluid in the body tastes as salty as the ocean and is equally rich in magnesium, gold, and other trace elements. Life began in the sea, and we are alive outside it only because we carry an internal ocean around with us. When you are thirsty and take a drink of water, you are actually rebalancing the fluid chemistry everywhere in your inner ocean.

The feeling of being thirsty is stimulated by the hypothalamus, a piece of the brain about the size of a finger joint, which in turn is connected by both nerves and chemical messengers to the kidneys. The kidneys constantly monitor the body's need for water by "listening in" to signals from the blood. The signals are chemical, as with the neuro-peptides, but in this case the molecules involved are salts, proteins, and blood sugar, as well as specific messengers. The blood in turn is picking up these signals from every cell in the body, each of which is constantly monitoring its own need for water. In other words, when you want a drink of water, you are not just obeying an impulse from your brain—you are listening to a request from every cell in your body.

If you drink one small glass of water, you will replace only $\frac{1}{400}$ of your total bodily fluid, yet that will satisfy the precise needs of 50 trillion different cells. Such exact monitoring is often attributed to the kidneys alone, but as we have just seen, the kidneys never make decisions alone; they work in constant consultation with the quantum mechanical body—the whole field of intelligence. The evenness of intelligence is not apparent from the physical makeup of the cells; it coexists with the body's extreme specialization. The neuron, which is outfitted on its cell wall with a million sodium-potassium pumps, is not at all like a heart cell or stomach cell. Yet, the integrity of the message "time for some water" is constant everywhere.

In physics, a field is what propagates an influence over a large, or even infinite, expanse of space. A magnet creates a magnetic field around itself; small magnets have a weak field that extends a few inches, while the Earth's magnetic poles are powerful enough to cover the entire globe. Anything that falls within a field feels its effect; that is why the magnetic needle of a compass automatically aligns itself with the Earth's magnetic polarity. Sitting in the body's field of intelligence, each cell is aligned with the brain, which stands as the north magnetic pole.

A cell is a small outcropping in the field, while the brain is a huge one. But the cell, when it "talks" to the rest of the body, is not inferior to the brain in the quality of what it says. Like the brain, it must correlate its message with trillions of others; it must participate in thousands of chemical exchanges every second; and most important of all, its DNA is the equal of any neuron's. Therefore, the smallest impulse of intelligence is as intelligent as the largest. In fact, it is meaningless to speak of important pieces of intelligence or insignificant ones. We need only to remember the chain that builds dopamine; the inability to turn the humble protein serine into the equally humble metabolite called glycine leads to a minutely higher level of dopamine, with the catastrophic outcome of schizophrenia, overwhelming the entire mind.

Every cell is a little sentient being. Sitting in the liver or heart or kidney, it "knows" everything you know, but in its own fashion. We are of course used to the idea that we are smarter than our kidneys. The very concept of a "building block" implies that the brick is simpler than the building. That is true of a nonliving structure, but not of us. The nerve impulse for worry, for example, may show up in the stomach as an ulcer, in the colon as a spasm, or in the mind as an obsession, but they are various manifestations of the same impulse.

Worry transforms itself from organ to organ, yet each point in the body knows that there is worrying going on, and every cell remembers. You may consciously forget that you are worrying, but then all at once the feeling is there to remind you, and it seems to be everywhere.

Earlier, we noted that if you could see the body as it really is, you would see it as constant change mixed with complete non-change. It is like a house whose bricks are constantly being replaced, or a sculpture that at the same time is a river. The obstacle confronting medicine so far is that one side of our nature—the flowing and changing—has been sacrificed for the sake of the other—the stable and fixed. Now, having looked at the quantum level, perhaps we can package both into one unit that captures our real double essence— the impulse of intelligence. An impulse of intelligence is the smallest unit that preserves itself intact (non-change) while undergoing transformation (change). If impulses of intelligence did not have this one general property, then they could not be the basic building block of the body; either some purely mental impulse or some purely physical particle would have that distinction.

But neither of these can survive change. The molecules forming your brain on the day that you first thought the word *rose* are not there anymore, and yet the concept is. At the same time, you do not have to think the word *rose* all the time to retain it; you can think literally millions of other thoughts without ever referring to this word. The next time you want it back, there it is, without confusion. It has retained its integrity through thick and thin because the impulse of intelligence contains mind, matter, and the silence that glues them together.

The physical structure of the body mirrors intelligence and gives it a projected form, but intelligence is not trapped inside this framework of flesh and bones. A startling confirmation of this fact appears in the brain. Karl Lashley, a pioneer in neurophysiology, tried to discover where memory was located in the brain by performing a simple experiment with lab rats. He taught them to run a maze, a skill that is remembered and stored in their brains, just as we acquire skills. Then he systematically removed a small amount of cerebral tissue. Lashley supposed that if the rats still remembered how to run the maze (as measured by their speed and accuracy), then the brain's memory center must still be intact.

Little by little, he took out more brain matter, but the rats, curiously enough, still remembered how to run the maze. Finally, more than 90 percent of the entire cortex was gone, leaving only a speck of brain tissue, and still the rats remembered the maze, with a slight fall-off in accuracy and speed. This experiment, among others, suggested a revolutionary idea, that every cell of the brain must store the whole brain while at the same time storing its own specific task. This is exactly what we have found: every impulse of intelligence is equally intelligent, opening up endless possible projections of mind into body.

John Lorber, a British neurologist, specialized in examining patients who were hydrocephalic—in place of cerebral tissue, their brain cavities were filled with fluid. Generally, this condition, popularly called "water on the brain," can be quite dangerous and lead to serious mental impairment.

However, one of Lorber's patients was a gifted college student, majoring in mathematics, whose IQ was measured near 130. Referred to Lorber by his family doctor, who thought his patient had an enlarged head, the student was given a brain scan, which revealed that his cortex was only 1 millimeter thick, compared to the usual 4.5 centimeters. In other words, fluid had replaced about 98 percent of the neurons needed for thinking, remembering, and all the other higher functions centered in the cerebral cortex. With 2 percent of a normal cortex, this man was in the same position as Lashley's rats, physiologically, and yet infinitely more capable—he was in fact normal or above average in all respects.

We are being driven closer and closer to the silent field of intelligence as our fundamental reality. But once again, there is the problem that a silent mind seems to contain nothing at all. If we go back nearly a hundred years, a similar dilemma was very much in the air. A new science called psychology was trying to be born, but it was having a hard time because to qualify as a science, psychology needed an object to study. It was obvious that every person had a psyche, but no one had ever seen or touched one. The most basic questions about the psyche had remained unsettled for centuries. Was it the soul, the mind, the personality, or all three? No one was going to be able to set up the first experiment in psychology until these matters were settled.

The turning point came when William James, a brilliant philosopher at Harvard who also held a medical degree, asserted that psychology did indeed have a proper object to study. Or rather, thousands of objects—all the thoughts, emotions, desires, and impressions that swirled through the mind. James called these the "stream of consciousness." If there was a mental essence or soul, as pre-psychologists back to Plato had affirmed, then science could not find it. James did not say that such an invisible essence did not exist, but he saw no way to experiment upon it scientifically.

James defended the stream of consciousness on purely pragmatic grounds, reasoning that nothing in the mind could be considered tangible except the objects (thoughts) that passed through it. If one is always thinking or dreaming—no one knows what he does mentally in deep, nondream sleep—then the reality of the mind must be simply a continuous flow of thoughts and dreams. James was a very astute observer; he had to be when you consider that he basically founded the field of psychology on the data he saw in his own head (as Freud did, extending the data into the field of dreams and unconscious motives). But James missed a tiny aspect of the mind that might have seemed completely trivial. The stream of consciousness is not made up solely of objects floating downriver; in between every thought there is a fleeting gap of silence.

It may be very tiny and all but unnoticeable, but the gap is always there and absolutely necessary. Without it, we would be think-

ing like this: "IlikethislunchanddessertbutifleattoomuchohthereisSid
Ineedtowhereismywallet . . ." and so on. The silent gap between
thoughts, being intangible, still plays no part in modern psychology,
which is oriented completely to the mind's contents or the brain's
mechanics. The gap turns out to be the central player, however, if
you are interested in what lies beyond thought. Every fraction of a
second we are permitted a glimpse into another world, one that is
inside us and yet obscurely out of reach. A verse from an ancient
Indian Upanishad describes this beautifully: "A man is like two
doves sitting in a cherry tree. One bird is eating of the fruit while the
other silently looks on." The bird who is the silent witness stands for
that deep silence in everyone, which appears to be nothing at all
when in reality it is the origin of intelligence.

The fascinating thing about intelligence is that it is like a one-
way arrow: you can use intelligence to shape a molecule, but if you
look at the molecule, you cannot take the intelligence back out of it.
When the poet Keats wrote his beautiful sonnet "To Sleep," he
began with the haunting line, "O soft embalmer of the still mid-
night." If he had been hooked up to an EEG while he was writing,
the readout of brain waves would have formed a unique pattern, yet
no amount of examination of those brain waves could ever yield a
line of poetry.

In the same way, all of our molecules are hitched up with a bit of
intelligence, which influences everything they do, but you cannot
see it by looking at them. DNA provides a good example. Sitting in
the nucleus of each cell, DNA is constantly bathed in a swirl of free-
floating organic molecules, the basic building blocks of the material
body. Whenever it wants to be active, DNA attracts these chemicals
and uses them to form new DNA. This is an essential part of cell
division—one double strand of DNA must divide in half, splitting
right down the middle like a zipper, and then each half turns into
new, complete DNA by attracting the appropriate molecules to itself. The bath of swirling, aimless source molecules surrounding
DNA provides it with "letters" to combine—there are just four of

them, labeled A, T, C, and G, for adenine, thymine, cytosine, and guanine. DNA spins these four letters out into an infinite variety of combinations, some of which are short (it takes three letters to code a basic amino acid), others of which are very long, like the polypeptide chains that can be seen streaming away from DNA like tendrils.

The DNA knows exactly what information to pick out and how it all goes together for each thing it wants to "say" chemically. Besides building itself, DNA knows how to build RNA, or ribonucleic acid, which is its nearly identical twin and active counterpart. RNA's mission is to travel away from the DNA in order to produce the proteins, more than 2 million in number, that actually build and repair the body. RNA is like active knowledge, in comparison to DNA's silent intelligence.

DNA does not work just from rote memory. It can invent new chemicals at will (such as a new antibody after you catch a strain of flu you have never been exposed to before). Exactly how this is accomplished is not known, although molecular biologists have found the spacers that separate different genetic words, or genomes. It is also well established that only 1 percent of the genetic material in DNA is used for its complicated coding, self-repair, and manufacture of RNA, leaving 99 percent doing nothing that science can account for.

This puzzling silence has stimulated a great deal of curiosity, especially among people who believe that humans do not use their full intelligence. William James ventured to guess that we use only 5 percent of our intelligence—he meant mental capacity—with an Einstein utilizing up to 15 percent or 20 percent. How this percentage translates into usable DNA is unknown, but we can venture to say that DNA is keeping a large vocabulary in silent storage—one geneticist has calculated that the number of molecular "words" produced in a single cell, if translated into English, would fill a thousand-volume library. And that is the product of just the active 1 percent we have managed to understand. Thanks to the discovery of recombinant DNA (pieces of genetic material that can be shuffled in and out of sequence on the DNA strands), the potential vocabulary may be infinitely larger than we suspect; already the combinations of "letters" encoded on DNA are sufficient to create every life form on Earth, from bacteria and molds to all plants, insects, mammals, and people.

One might suppose that the more complex the organism, the greater its share of DNA, but in fact a lily contains about a hundred times more DNA than a human being. Counting genes does not give very much of a meaningful picture: the difference between man's DNA and that of chimpanzees or gorillas is about 1.1 percent. This seems like a surprisingly small divergence, and a highly suspicious one. Can all the structural differences between a jungle primate and *Homo sapiens*, as well as our vastly superior brains, be packed into such a tiny fractional difference? Evolutionists, having inherited Darwin's faith in materialism, insist that it can. The issue is somewhat blunted when you realize, once again, that a gene count is not very significant—two different kinds of fruit flies (*Drosophila*) are much more closely related than man and chimpanzees, yet their DNA differs by considerably more.

Another way to show that our inner silence is alive and intelligent is to compare it to a machine's. When a computer approaches a problem, it uses electrical impulses that must be separated from one another by gaps, forming a complex series of coded data out of 1 and 0. This enables the computer to handle any problem that can be broken down into information, since all information can be coded into 1 and 0, just as any message in English can be broken down into the dots and dashes of Morse code. The human brain also takes advantage of mechanically coded information, but the gaps in between are not just empty; they are the pivots that allow the mind to swing any way it wants. In other words, a computer has finite gaps made of emptiness; we have infinite gaps full of intelligence.

We can pull anything out of the gap. Mozart pulled whole symphonies at a time, not just note by note, but—as he recounted the experience—with every orchestral line already composed and orchestrated. Mathematics, like music, has many such mysteries. A woman in India named Shakuntala Devi multiplied two 13-digit numbers together in her head, arriving at the 23-digit answer in 26 seconds. (It takes more time than that to read the numbers out loud: $7,686,369,774,870 \times 2,465,099,745,779 = 18,947,668,177,995,426,773,730$.)

If you tell a computer to add 2 plus 2, it comes up with either a right or a wrong answer. If you ask a 5-year-old boy to do the same, he may come up with an arithmetical answer, but he just as well might say, "I want some vanilla ice cream." We can assume that he is bored; perhaps he is too tired for an arithmetic lesson. So it is not correct to say that his response is a computational error; his mind is simply not under our control—you cannot come up with a program to include all the possible reactions a human being can display as he interacts with the world.

What this all amounts to, in my mind, is a vindication of how complex ordinary experience really is, and how far away from life a scientific model is when it tries to describe it. The old view that the brain is a computer, stable in time and space, localized into various functions, and restricted in its flexibility, is unjustified. A Nobel Prize–winning neuroscientist, Dr. Gerald Edelman, has pointed out that the brain is much more like a process than a thing, and this process is continually evolving. It is true, for example, that memory depends on two small pieces of "hardware" on either side of the brain called the hippocampus; if both sites become damaged (through loss of blood flow or disease), the ability to recollect is destroyed.

Yet, within this physical limitation, each person's brain is unique, both in structure and content. No two people have the same neuronal connections, and each person is constantly growing new ones from the moment of birth onward, giving rise to all the memories that make you and me totally different. (A connection does not have to be physical; the flashing signals in the brain are constantly making patterns and reforming them into new patterns.)

Edelman holds that no one literally repeats a memory. When you recollect a familiar face, something will be different about it, if not the face itself, then the context that caused you to remember, which may be sad now instead of happy. Memory is a creative act, then. It creates new images and new brain at the same time. Edelman theorizes that *every* experience one has in life changes the brain's anatomy. Therefore, it is not wholly true to say that the hippocampus is the seat of memory, for any one memory—the first day you saw a field of daffodils—shifts and shimmers across your entire cortex, touching other memories here and there, passing into new interpretations, and having to be re-created every time you need to recollect it. Unlike any computer, we remember, reconsider, and change our minds. The universe was created once, but we re-create ourselves with every thought.

Everything, in short, depends upon how well you can build in silence. Whatever can be experienced on the surface of life—love or hate, disease or health—wells up from a deeper level and floats above it as little more than a bubble. One can try to prick the bubbles one by one, but they float up from below unendingly. If we want to navigate the field of intelligence, we must learn about it to the very depths, where the silent witness inside us waits. That is our next step, to map the inner silence and master its secret places.

EXPANDING THE TOPIC

Only doctors are licensed to practice medicine, but everyone practices Ayurveda, only not systematically. The "science of life" pertains to everyday experiences of pain and pleasure, likes and dislikes, comfort and discomfort. This goes back to a term introduced at the end of the last chapter, *qualia*. A qualia is any quality of experience.

Consider pain, a qualia no one likes to experience. If you X-ray the spine of any older person, there will be compression in the resilient fibrous disks that provide a cushion between each vertebra. Yet only a certain percentage of older people experience lower back pain.

Obviously the ones who experience no pain shouldn't be treated medically. The patients who complain of severe or acute pain should be treated immediately, while most people, who experience inter-mittent pain that goes away on its own, fall somewhere in between. We should look at pain, then, very personally.

Ayurveda takes the personal approach to every situation. By consulting a person's level of discomfort, the diagnosis can be any of the following:

1. There is no imbalance. The person is healthy.
2. There are early signs of imbalance. The person needs to make a lifestyle change to bring the system back into balance.
3. The imbalance has reached the stage of exhibiting physical symptoms. Medical intervention is called for.
4. The symptoms are so severe that chronic illness has set in, with the possibility in extreme cases of imminent death. Intense medical intervention is called for.

In the mid-1980s I was struck by how sensible and natural this way of looking at disease was. It gave me a prime motivation for writing *Quantum Healing*. Asking people to possess medical school knowledge about their bodies is unreasonable. Asking them to be in touch with their experience isn't. How else can we live?

Recently I heard about a case where a man in his seventies had a stiff shoulder that over time became quite painful. Suspecting the onset of arthritis, his doctor took X rays, and indeed, the rotator cuff had turned dry and pitted because the slick membrane that keeps joints moving smoothly had worn down. The doctor explained that this deterioration was irreversible and would only grow worse. He recommended immediate replacement, a procedure that has become standard for millions of older people once a shoulder, hip, or knee gives out.

What if I go to physical therapy instead? his patient asked.

The doctor, who was an experienced orthopedist, shrugged. Physical therapy would deliver some short-term relief, but replacement surgery was a certainty down the road, probably sooner than later.

The man went for a second opinion, which concurred with the first. But something inside resisted the trauma of major surgery, and he decided to pursue physical therapy. Today, seven years later, his pain remains intermittent. It hasn't grown worse, and the man himself feels that his shoulder is flexible enough for normal tasks like driving. Since he hasn't returned to an orthopedist for regular X rays, no one knows if the underlying arthritic condition has worsened. But it doesn't matter right now. If the patient's quality of life hasn't deteriorated, that's the main thing.

The fact that Ayurveda is based on personal experience makes it something unique: a qualia medicine. To someone just discovering Ayurveda, its diagnostic powers can seem mysterious. The most basic diagnosis is body type, or more specifically a person's *prakriti*, which determines the fundamental qualia that have been dominant since birth. One of these is Vata, associated with air. If you meet someone with prominent Vata, one glance will allow you to say, "I imagine you have irregular habits. You often aren't hungry at mealtimes. You find it hard to get regular sleep and often wake up at night. Under stress you become anxious and nervous. But your disposition is cheerful, and even though you suffer from inexplicable aches and pains that come and go, your attitude toward them isn't gloomy."

Not many people are such pure Vata types that this entire description will apply, but when it does, they are frequently amazed. (It should be emphasized immediately that Ayurvedic diagnosis consists of several procedures, not simply laying eyes on the patient.) Searching for an explanation in Western terms is often quite difficult, because the qualia that Ayurveda is based on sound totally nonmedical. Besides Vata (air) there is Pitta (fire), Kapha (water and earth), and most mysterious of all, Akasha, or space. The combination of these qualities leads to a highly sophisticated system of diagnosis, because they interact and go out of balance in hundreds of ways.

A Western-trained physician is also dependent on qualia, because treatment always begins with how a patient feels. But from there two paths diverge. Western allopathic medicine searches for objective underlying causes with scientific precision, essentially leaving qualia behind. Ayurveda continues on the road of qualia, seeking to bring them back into balance. And here is where a needless source of confusion and difficulty arises.

Being a "science of life," Ayurveda prescribes a way of life. Its advice about diet, for example, varies from person to person, because a Vata type benefits, for example, from heavy, sweet, oily foods that are not necessarily good—and may be bad—for other types. Balance is dynamic. It changes from day to day. Therefore, someone who has grown up in an Ayurvedic lifestyle (which means growing up in India before the modern era) will be constantly monitoring their qualia. This is a form of self-care that requires each person to know exactly how he or she feels when going out of balance, long before symptoms arise.

Hence the confusion, because modern people—including modern Indians—go to the doctor when they feel bad, by which time symptoms have already appeared. They are at the second or third stage of imbalance described above. At this point, after years of ignoring the easily treatable signs of imbalance, Ayurveda may be helpless compared with Western scientific medicine. It's like bringing a car in for its first tune-up after 150,000 miles.

When *Quantum Healing* was written, I constantly encountered skepticism from other physicians, accompanied by hostile remarks like, "If I got into a car accident, a bunch of herbs isn't going to help me." Of course not. Nobody said it would. Today one doesn't meet as much skepticism, yet it's clear that qualia medicine, the kind based on personal quality of life, cannot simply be a replay of Ayurveda. Knowledge evolves, and we find ourselves equipped with knowledge from science and knowledge from centuries of human experience.

They don't have to oppose each other. In the expanding field of integrated medicine, the doctor utilizes both. For example, the majority of patients seek a doctor's care because they suffer from a cold, headaches, insomnia, or anxiety and depression. These are endemic, usually low-level side effects of modern life itself. They also happen to be Vata disorders. If the doctor knows this, he has more tools at his disposal to cure the most common ills. But that won't rule out the usual pills, if that's what he and the patient prefer.

Such a preference shouldn't come from blind allegiance to science or a rigid belief that one size fits all. The whole point of integrated medicine isn't to find alternatives to standard medical practice just for the sake of doing so. The point is to personalize medical care based on the patient's quality of life. It's frustrating that every medical school student isn't taught this principle on the first day of class.

Quantum Healing set out a workable theory of Ayurveda for the Western mind. Realizing that readers would ask, "But what do I do?" I wrote a practical handbook on the Ayurvedic lifestyle called *Perfect Health*. The title wasn't meant to be hyperbole. Every healthy cell exists in perfect health. It's our personal choices over a long period of time that create the imbalances that eventually start to damage our cells. Therefore, positing perfect health as a starting point is medically sound.

As things stand today, I practice integrated medicine solidly established on Ayurveda and the Ayurvedic lifestyle. I realize, with a touch of chagrin, that my being Indian makes the medicine go down more easily for my patients. This bias has led me to talk much less about Ayurveda and much more about qualia. For the average person, Ayurveda is a narrow, exotic, specialized interest. But everyone is interested in their quality of life. Self-care based on qualia provides the best results, because it makes the whole project intimate and personal. The fact that thousands of years of wisdom lies in the background is just one more reason to pursue optimal wellbeing.

9

THE MYSTERY OF THE GAP

Recently I saw a patient who had been diagnosed in 1983 with a malignant tumor in her right breast. For reasons of her own, she had refused any form of conventional treatment, including radiation, chemotherapy, and hormones. She told me that the tumor was quite large but had not spread to any lymph nodes under her arm.

"I think I'd better examine it," I said, and she hesitated.

"I should warn you," she said, "that most doctors are very frightened when they see this, because of its size. I generally don't even let a doctor touch me, because the fear in their eyes makes me scared. On my own I'm not scared. You may not believe this, but I have never felt that I was in any danger. I can be shaken, though, when I see a doctor's fear. They even say things like, 'How dare you be so cruel to your husband by not having surgery.'

"I thought that maybe a woman doctor would be more understanding, but when I went to one, she was more horrified than the rest. She asked me, 'Why did you come to see me if you aren't going to let me remove that thing?' And I said, 'Because I just want you to monitor it—it has grown slightly in the past five years, and I want it followed. Almost shaking, she stood up and told me, 'Don't come back to see me unless you want that thing removed. I can't stand the sight of it.'"

I had no idea what my reaction would be. About half of the women diagnosed with breast cancer have localized tumors confined to the breast. The standard treatment has been either to remove the breast or to remove the lump and radiate the site to kill any remaining cancer cells. In both cases, when there is no further follow-up treatment, 70 percent of patients do not have a recurrence in the next three years. With some sort of chemotherapy, ranging from mild to quite heavy, the proportion of long-term survivors can be raised to 90 percent. This woman had decided to defy odds that were very much in the patient's favor—and yet she would not be the first to ignore doctors and survive.

When she lay on the examining table and I saw the tumor, I understood why her previous doctors had been shocked—it distended a large portion of her breast. I controlled my automatic reaction, and I hope no fear showed in my eyes. I sat down and held her hand, thinking. "Look," I said softly, "I don't believe you are in danger here. You have said that you don't feel any danger, and that is good enough for me. But this tumor is a nuisance. You are denying yourself a more beautiful life by having to look after this. Why not go to a surgeon and have the nuisance removed?"

Apparently this struck her as an entirely new angle. She readily agreed that there was no advantage to keeping the tumor, and I referred her to a sympathetic surgeon.

One of her parting comments stays with me. "I don't identify myself with this tumor," she said serenely, "I know I am much more than it. It will come and go like the rest of me, but inside, I am not really touched by it." When she left the office, she looked extremely happy.

I felt that this woman had reason on her side. The fear in a doctor's eyes is a terrible stroke of condemnation, and in her position I would not have believed much in my chances of recovery. The impulses from my brain would not be saying, "I'm definitely going to recover." Instead, they would be saying, "They tell me I'll probably recover," which is quite a different thing.

When a doctor looks at a patient and says, "You have breast cancer, but you're going to get well," what is he really saying? The answer is by no means certain. At one extreme, his reassuring words, if they are believable, may be enough to make the difference in the patient's case. At the other extreme, if he actually thinks the patient is doomed, something in his voice will give that message, and from it a destructive confusion may set in.

Recently the term *placebo* was inverted into a new term, *nocebo*, to describe the negative effects of a doctor's opinion. With placebo, you give a dummy drug and the patient responds because the doctor has told him that the drug will work. With nocebo, you give a viable drug, but the patient doesn't respond, because the doctor has signaled that the drug isn't going to work.

If you take a completely materialistic view, there seems no difference between the surgery this woman refused before and the one she agreed to now. Yet, now she identifies surgery with healing, whereas before it was violence. If a patient regards any treatment as violence, then his body will be flooded with negative emotions and the chemicals associated with them. It is well documented that in a climate of negativity, the ability to heal is greatly reduced— depressed people not only lower their immune response, for example, but even weaken their DNA's ability to repair itself. So my patient had reasonable cause, I think, to wait until her emotions told her to go ahead.

This case reminds me that there are always two centers of action within people, the head and the heart. Medical statistics appeal to the head, but the heart keeps its own counsel. In recent years, alternative medicine has won much of its appeal on the basis of bringing back the heart, using love and caring to heal. Without these ingredients, the nocebo effect can run wild, for the surroundings of modern hospitals inject a powerful dose of it. The psychotic episodes that sometimes strike out of the blue in intensive care units show how unhealthy it is to hold people in sterile, confined spaces. (As a young child, my son showed an almost equal fascination with hospitals and prisons, which I trace to a fear he could not express. If he saw either institution from the car, he would invariably ask, "Daddy, are people dying in there?")

The great drawback of proclaiming that we need to bring the heart back into medicine is that it punishes people for their emotional weaknesses. The heart can be very frail; it can be hardened by suffering, or just by life. Books on holistic healing like to say that sick people "need" their sickness. Mainstream psychiatry points its own finger when it says that chronic diseases can stand symbolically for self-punishment, revenge, or a deep feeling of worthlessness. I will not argue these insights, except to suggest that they may be harmful to the healing process rather than helpful. It is hard enough for any of us to face up to our emotional fallibility even at the best of times. Can we really be expected to reform when we are ill?

The deeper issue is that *anything* can function as a nocebo, just as anything can function as a placebo. It is not the dummy drug, the doctor's bedside manner, or the antiseptic smell of a hospital that does harm or good; it is the patient's interpretation of it. Therefore, the real war is not between the head and the heart. Something deeper, in the realm of silence, creates our view of reality.

The basic understanding most of us have about ourselves comes from thinking and feeling, which seems only natural. But we know very little about the field of silence and how it exercises control over us. The head and the heart, it seems, are not the whole person. The stream of consciousness, which is constantly full of thoughts, acts as a screen to keep silence hidden. The solid appearance of the physical body is another kind of screen, since we cannot see the molecules that are being constantly shuffled around inside us, much less their blueprint, which is what we would like to change.

The blueprint of reality is an important concept. Every impulse of intelligence gives rise to a thought or a molecule, which spends a certain time in the relative world—the world of the senses—before the next impulse follows. In that sense, every thought is like a piece of the future when it is created, a piece of the present when it is experienced, and a piece of the past after it has gone. As long as each impulse is healthy, the future is not unknown—it will flow naturally from the present, moment by moment. (This accounts for why people who make the most of every day tend to retain their mental faculties intact into old age; the stream of intelligence is never allowed to dry up.)

Thinking A ➡ B ➡ C ➡ D ➡ etc.

———————— Quantum Mechanical Body ————————

Intelligence

Above the line is a flow of thoughts that never ends, at least while we are awake. Thought is linked to thought without end. Our normal experience keeps within this range of ongoing events, which may be infinite on the horizontal axis yet quite shallow on the vertical. It is possible to spend a lifetime listening to the inventory of the mind without ever dipping into its source. Yet, touching the source is how the mind creates its patterns of intelligence. These patterns are at first only blueprints, but whatever they inscribe will hold—they will form our ideas and beliefs about reality.

The field of intelligence is extremely sensitive to change, however, both for good and ill. Two years ago I saw a woman in her thirties who came to Lancaster to be treated for breast cancer. Her condition was extremely serious, since the malignancy had metasta- sized to the bone marrow everywhere in her body. She suffered from constant pain in her bones as a result. After receiving the nor- mal, and quite drastic, courses of radiation and chemotherapy from her doctor at home in Denver, she came to Boston for Ayurvedic treatments. She responded very well. After spending a week as an inpatient, her bone pain disappeared. She was not offered any promises about her cancer, but she went home in a state of renewed hope and optimism. Unfortunately, when she reported to her doctor that she had improved, he told her that it was all in her head—she had received no orthodox therapy that could have relieved her symptoms. Within a day her bone pain returned. She called me, feeling panicky, and I asked if she could return to Boston immedi- ately. She did, and fortunately after another week her bone pain again receded.

Without intending to harm his patient—I am sure he wanted to be realistic in his appraisal—this woman's doctor made a cruel mis- take. He assumed that what is "in your head" is not real, or at least very inferior to the reality of cancer. Being trained in scientific methods, he knew the predictable outcomes of various kinds of ma- lignancy, and when he saw an unexpected result, he tried to push it back into the range of the predictable. Doctors push patients into predictable results all the time, because medical-school training is focused entirely on the horizontal axis.

Making the links of cause and effect tighter and tighter is the whole motivation behind medical research. Our great-grandfathers vaguely knew that germs existed; we can anatomize thousands of specific viruses and bacteria, down to the tiniest amino-acid groups and beyond. Unfortunately, this leaves very little opening for any journey along the vertical axis, which might take one to a deeper reality.

A recent patient listed on his medical questionnaire that he "once had a brain tumor." I asked him what that meant, and he told me this story: About five years ago, while living in Michigan, he began to have sudden dizzy spells. These quickly grew worse, and in a few weeks he was vomiting and had double vision, with increasing loss of balance and motor coordination. He went to a hospital, where a CAT scan was taken of his brain. The doctors informed him that the test had disclosed a shadowy mass in his forebrain larger than a lemon; in their opinion, he had a brain tumor. A tissue sample taken from the tumor revealed that indeed it was a deadly, rapidly growing cancer.

Because the tumor was so large and delicately placed, it was considered inoperable. The doctors recommended high doses of radiation and chemotherapy, without which the man would be dead in six months. The therapy would have severe side effects, nearly as bad as his present symptoms. Certain of these, such as nausea, headaches, and skin irritation, would be uncomfortable; others, such as the weakening of his immune system, could be deadly, since he would become prone to contracting other types of cancer in the future. There was also the definite possibility that he would be prey to anxiety and depression, which could be lasting. Even with maximum treatment to shrink the tumor, the prognosis for full recovery was not good, but it was better than nothing.

The patient could not accept this reasoning (although it is statistically quite sound). He moved to California and joined a meditation group; he practiced a whole series of diets, mental techniques, exercises, and visualizations. He encouraged in himself a totally positive attitude toward his condition. Thousands of cancer patients, as a rule from the best-educated groups, turn to such measures, which conventional medicine looks on as trying to buy false hope. In this case, however, the man began to feel better, and within six months his symptoms were almost completely gone. Hopeful but also anxious, he returned to Michigan and underwent another CAT scan. This one showed no traces of cancer and no sign that any had ever been present.

In response to this, his doctors informed him that he had not recovered from cancer, because they had never heard of such a recovery. In fact, they said, the original CAT scan was not his but another patient's. They were sorry for the mistake, but from that moment on, they disavowed any involvement with his case. The patient was immensely relieved that his symptoms were gone, and he believes in the original CAT scan, which has his name and Social Security number on it. When I contacted the hospital to ask for his records, I was informed that he had never been treated there for cancer but had been mixed up with another brain-tumor patient.

All I can assume is that even with X rays and a biopsy, these doctors could not accept that a remission had occurred, for the simple reason that their experience told them it was impossible. One should never underestimate the power of indoctrination. Medical training is highly technical, specialized, and rigorous, but it came about just like any other human activity—by people collecting experiences and using those experiences to form explanations and patterns. These patterns in turn serve to indoctrinate the pattern makers, and within a very short period of time the indoctrination becomes law.

It is fascinating that a major study of four hundred spontaneous remissions of cancer, later interpreted by Elmer and Alyce Green of the Menninger Clinic, found that all the patients had only one thing in common—every person had changed his attitudes before the remission occurred, finding some way to become hopeful, courageous, and positive. In other words, they broke down their indoctrination (even if the doctors did not break down theirs). The mystery that clouds this otherwise clear finding has to do with causation. Did the remissions occur because of the new attitudes or parallel to them? Perhaps causation is too delicate to pinpoint in this case, being replaced by a general, holistic process of getting well in mind and body at the same time. The mind-body system, about to throw off the cancer, should know that the process is under way and may begin to generate much more positive thoughts simultaneously.

However it works, the key seems to be spontaneity. Channeling positive attitudes into oneself as a planned therapy has proved only haphazardly successful as a means of fighting disease. The positive

input does not tend to go very deep. Consciousness is more perva-
sive than medicine gives it credit for. Even when it is ignored, however, the silent field of intelligence knows what is happening. It is,
after all, intelligent. Its knowledge reaches beyond buffers and
screens, going farther than we expect.

To illustrate: for decades, surgeons safely assumed that an anes-
thetized patient was unconscious and therefore not influenced by
what happened in the operating room. Then it was discovered (by
hypnotizing postoperative patients) that in fact the "unconscious"
mind heard every word that was uttered during the procedure.
When the surgeons said aloud that a condition was more serious
than they had thought or had little chance of cure, the patients
tended to play out those gloomy predictions by not recovering. As a
result of these findings, which validate the idea of nocebo, it is now
standard practice not to make negative remarks during surgery. The
more positive the surgeon's expressed opinions, in fact, the more
positive the outcome for the patient.

It would be even better to use this highly sensitive, extremely
powerful intelligence for the patient's cure. The point of diving into
the region of the quantum body is to change the blueprint itself,
rather than to wait for symptoms on the surface, which will then
have to be manipulated using medicine. The case of the woman
with bone pain is a reminder that the buffer that keeps us so se-
curely above the line, away from our deeper selves, is always made
by us. It is therefore subject to revision at any time. We constantly
build patterns of intelligence and look through them to tell us what
is real. If we see pain, there is pain, but if we don't, the pain will be
gone.

Nature did not make us ignorant of our deeper selves. Anesthe-
tized patients have known what was going on all along, presumably
since the beginnings of modern surgery in the 1850s. The silent
field of intelligence is out of reach by our choice, reinforced through
generations of cultural bias. Sometimes a new reality forces itself to
be recognized, and then things can shift. New patterns of intelli-

gence arise; a deep transformation can then take place, but it is not essentially different from the mind-body transformations we have already been talking about.

Normal reality is like a spell—a very necessary one, since we must live by habits, routines, and codes that we take for granted. The problem arises when you can make the spell but not break it. If you could dive, this very minute, below your everyday reality to its source, you would certainly have a remarkable experience. The psychologist Abraham Maslow, who was a pioneer in studying the positive aspects of the human personality, gave a classic description of the experience of the deep self: "These moments were of pure, positive happiness, when all doubts, all fears, all inhibitions, all tensions, all weaknesses, were left behind. Now self-consciousness was lost. All separateness and distance from the world disappeared. . . ."

Although such experiences are rare—Maslow termed them "peak experiences" for that reason—they have a curative power that goes far beyond their brief duration, which may be a few days or just a few hours. Maslow records that two of his patients, one a long-term depressive who had often considered suicide, the other a person who suffered from severe anxiety attacks, were both immediately and permanently cured after spontaneously falling into such experiences (for each it happened only once).

Maslow also talks about the reconciliation with life that people have realized through these moments: "They felt one with the world, fused with it, really belonging to it instead of being outside looking in. (One subject said, for instance, 'I felt like a member of a family, not like an orphan.')"

Any sudden revelation of a deeper reality carries enormous power with it—one taste alone can make life undeniably worthwhile. Maslow's patients recognized this inner power as something quite outside the ordinary. It is not energy or strength, genius or insight, but it underlies all of these. It is life power in its purest form. Maslow's understanding stopped short at the critical moment—he was never able actually to give anyone a peak experience—yet he was fascinated by these events that transcend normal life. In 1961, after several decades of writing and thinking about the subject, he concluded that it was indeed normal life and not the mystical that he had been observing:

"The little that I had ever read about mystic experiences tied them in with religion, with visions of the supernatural. And, like most scientists, I had sniffed at them in disbelief and considered it all nonsense, maybe hallucinations, maybe hysteria—almost surely pathological. But the people telling me about these experiences were not such people—they were the healthiest people!"

Because he detected these experiences in fewer than 1 percent of the population, Maslow viewed them as accidents or as moments of grace. I believe that they were glimpses into a field that underlies everyone's life, but which has remained elusive. The implication is that we should dive very deep if we want to transcend normal reality. We are in search of an experience that will reshape the world.

Finding the silent gap that flashes in between our thoughts seems relatively easy, but because it flashes by, a tiny gap is not a doorway. The quantum body is not separate from us—it *is* us—yet we are not experiencing it right now. Sitting here, we are thinking, reading, talking, breathing, digesting, and so on, all of which happens above the line.

Here is an analogy that brings the quantum mechanical body into focus: Take a bar magnet and place a piece of paper over it. Next, sprinkle iron filings on the paper and jostle it slightly. What will emerge is a pattern of curving lines, one inside the other, that arch from the magnet's north to south pole and back again. The overall design you have made represents a map of the magnetic lines of force that otherwise would be invisible, except that the iron particles automatically align themselves to bring out the image.

In this analogy, we see all mind-body activity above the paper and the hidden field of intelligence below. The iron filings moving around are mind-body activity, automatically aligning with the magnetic field, which is intelligence. The field is completely invisible and unknowable until it shows its hand by moving some bits of matter around. And the piece of paper? It is the quantum mechanical body, a thin screen that shows exactly what patterns of intelligence are being manifested at the moment.

There is more to this simple comparison than you might at first suppose. Without the paper to separate the two, the magnet and the iron could not interact in any orderly way. Try bringing a magnet close to some iron filings. Instead of forming regularly spaced lines, the filings simply clump shapelessly onto the magnet's surface. With the paper in place, not only do you have an image of the magnetic field, but if you rotate the magnet you can watch the iron filings move to mirror the new field that has been created. If you didn't know that there was a magnet, you would swear that the iron was alive, because it seems to move by itself. But it is really the hidden field that is generating these lifelike appearances.

There you have a true picture of how the bodymind actually relates to the field of intelligence. The two remain separated, but the division is invisible and has no thickness whatever. It is just a gap. The only way one knows that the quantum level even exists is that images and patterns keep cropping up everywhere in the body. Mysterious furrows run across the surface of the brain; beautiful swirls, exactly like the center of a sunflower, show up in molecules of DNA; the inside of the femur contains marvelous webs of bone tissue, like the intricate supports of a cantilever bridge.

Wherever you look, there is no chaos, and that is the strongest proof of all that there really is a hidden physiology. Intelligence turns chaos into patterns. There is incredible chaos implied in the idea of having to process billions of chemical messages every minute, yet in reality, the complexity of the mind-body system is misleading: what emerges from our brains are coherent images, just as a coherent newspaper photograph emerges from thousands of scattered dots. The matter in our bodies never disintegrates into a shapeless, mindless pile—until the moment of death. In answer to the obvious question, "Where is this quantum mechanical body, anyway?" one can now confidently answer that it lies in a gap that unfortunately is rather difficult to picture, since it is silent, has no thickness, and exists everywhere.

To dive into the field of intelligence appears easy now: it requires only a trip across a gap. But even though the gap has no thickness, it forms a barrier no steel door could possibly match. We can simplify our diagram to show what has happened to make the journey so difficult:

Active Intelligence

—————— **Gap** ——————

Silent Intelligence

The whole story is contained in the difference between active and silent intelligence. We have confirmed that this difference is very real. DNA can be active or silent; our thoughts can be expressed or stored away in drawers of silence; we can be awake or asleep. All these changes require a journey across the gap, but not a conscious journey. To see what sleep is like, you would have to stay awake, which is impossible. If you want to see the difference between active and dormant DNA, you cannot find it in any chemical bond, since the two DNAs are physically identical. And so on and on for all the transformations of mind and body.

The same difficulty holds true in physics—a photon is a form of light, as is a light wave, but both arise from a hidden field. On the surface of reality we see either photons or light waves, but the reason why both can exist in one reality is that they preexist as mere possibilities in the quantum field. Who has ever photographed a possibility? Yet, that is all the quantum world is made of. If you say a word or make a molecule, you have chosen to act. A little wave laps up from the ocean's surface, becoming an incident in the space-time world. The whole ocean remains behind, a vast, silent reservoir of possibilities, of waves that have yet to be born.

As they dance around on the paper, the iron filings might look at one another and say, "Well, this is life, let's look into its mysteries." Deciding to do that, they can begin a thought-adventure of the kind we call science. No matter how adventurous their thoughts become, they will never cross the gap. The gap is a one-way door, as far as thinking goes, and that is its true mystery.

From a certain perspective, the whole idea that we are outcroppings from an invisible, infinite field seems ridiculous. A man's body is a packet of flesh and bones occupying a few cubic feet of space; his mind is an amazingly intricate but finite mechanism filled with a set number of conceptions; his society is a grossly imperfect organization bound to a history of ignorance and conflict.

These obvious facts have never settled the issue, strangely enough. We trust our finite everyday experiences, which are good enough for driving a car, earning a living, and going to the beach, but they are not quite convincing enough compared to the overwhelming experience of the infinite. That experience, repeated throughout the centuries, causes some people to suspect that reality is very different, and far vaster, than what the mind, the body, and society generally accept.

Einstein himself experienced this reality. He has testified to moments when "one feels free from one's own identification with human limitation":

"At such moments one imagines that one stands on some spot of a small planet gazing in amazement at the cold and yet profoundly moving beauty of the eternal, the unfathomable. Life and death flow into one, and there is neither evolution nor destiny, only Being."

Although this sounds like a spiritual insight (and Einstein considered himself deeply spiritual), it is really a glimpse into a level of our own consciousness that can be mapped and explored. Without having any control over their awareness or any cogent explanation for what is happening, people sense that the state of rapt silence is not simply emptiness. The great traditions of wisdom have largely been founded by one or a few individuals who realized the universe through themselves. To solve the mystery of the gap, we need to consult the ones who have been there; if they have found a real world, then there will be new Einsteins to follow, and they will be Einsteins of consciousness.

EXPANDING THE TOPIC

The wisdom of the body comes from two places—active intelligence and silent intelligence. Self-care is an example of active intelligence. You listen to your body. You heed its signals of pain and discomfort. You take steps to maintain a state of wellbeing. Active intelligence stretches no one's imagination. Silent intelligence is different, because being invisible, it can only be located in the gap. Yet of the two kinds of intelligence, the kind that works in silence is infinitely wiser.

When *Quantum Healing* first appeared, it was almost impossible to get mainstream doctors even to entertain such a notion as "the wisdom of the body." I found refuge in the mystical poets, who became almost constant companions. They knew about the hidden dimensions of existence. Here is a verse from Rumi, the illuminated Persian poet:

> What do I long for?
> Something that is felt in the night
> But not seen in the day.

In a rational age, poetic intimations aren't enough. Yet poets can think, too, as when Rabindranath Tagore, the great Bengali poet, contemplates how a full-blown rose opens from a bud. He sees at work the same silent intelligence I was describing in the human body.

> He who can open a bud does it simply
> One glance, and the sap must stir,
> One breath, and a flower flutters in the wind,
> Colors flash out like longings of the heart,
> And perfume betrays sweet secrets.
> He who can open a bud does it simply.

Who could put it more beautifully? Instead of saying "He who can open a bud," why not "She who can bring a child into the world"? Silent intelligence is simple, spontaneous, and a part of us.

As it turned out, I was lucky to be writing when I was. Hard research was just uncovering the receptor sites on the cell membrane, the "plug-ins" for messages from the brain. One found exactly the same receptor sites everywhere. The immune system therefore became known as a floating brain, and science had an explanation for gut instincts—tissues remote from the brain were thinking, too, in a chemical language.

Yet the lifestyle advice that looks so promising for healing the mind-body connection doesn't really penetrate into the quantum domain. It remains in the domain of active intelligence. We have to be a bit careful here. If you change your diet, new messages will be sent to the cells of the digestive tract, and from there the messaging throughout the body is altered (which is why, for example, you fall asleep after eating too much at Thanksgiving). Because all messages are produced in the gap, there is a quantum dimension to every process in the body.

What's lacking is a direct telephone line, so that you can speak to your own silent intelligence and hear what it says in return. A direct line is opened through "second attention." With first attention you live your life in the world—working, eating, sleeping, relating. With second attention you peer into the invisible domain that creates, governs, and regulates the flow of life. Let's call silent intelligence X, because it cannot be labeled or named. Labels belong to things, not to processes. What is X doing from its invisible station behind the scene? Its range of activity is quite astonishing:

It takes each tiny event and weaves it into the tapestry of life.
It gives meaning and purpose to everything you experience.
It guides every action to its highest and best use.
It breathes love into being.
It favors evolution and progress.
It promotes those outcomes that are the most life supporting.

If this sounds like a mystical laundry list, consider the beating of a single heart cell. It meshes with every other heart cell in perfect sync. It registers love, pain, hope, fear, and every other emotion. It tells you without a doubt that you are in love. It settles into wise contentment as you mature. It looks out for the health of the entire body. I've used slightly metaphorical language, but a cell biologist could identify the receptor sites and messaging paths that connect brain and heart so completely that every function I've mentioned has a physiological basis.

The deeper point, however, is that every cell, all five trillion or so, depends upon silent intelligence to keep itself—and you—together. Intelligence is what prevents the living structures in the body from flying apart into a cloud of atoms. Such intelligence is far from incidental. As in the piano metaphor I find myself returning to, a piano doesn't make the music that comes out of it; a mind does. When a cell communicates with other cells, there is no message in the chemicals that carry the message until the mind puts one inside.

Second attention opens the lines of communication so that any impulse—love, compassion, empathy, appreciation, insight, intuition, imagination—is evolutionary and life supporting. Here we must look beyond science, because to a cell biologist, chemicals are chemicals. They are value neutral. An impulse of hatred can be encoded as easily as an impulse of love. But if you stand back and examine your life from the perspective of second attention, you can see value everywhere in the body. Cells cooperate with one another. They understand that the good of the whole body is paramount. They live in the present moment and base their lives on trusting that nourishment will always come to them. They know how to self-heal.

Second attention promotes these values, not by analyzing the activity of cells but by going to the source, from which life is sustained. Since writing *Quantum Healing,* I've become even more convinced that consciousness holds the key to the flow of life whether you define life scientifically, mystically, or through any other label. While we argue over labels, we are missing the opportunity to promote the silent intelligence that is crucial to everything.

A practical-minded reader will say, "Fine, but what do I do?" Beyond making the positive lifestyle changes that have become well-known, there are more subtle actions to perform. These are mental actions, but they aren't the same as positive thinking, therapy, or even self-awareness. They focus instead on attention and intention. When you have an intention to move your hand, there are no steps to go through. The instant you want to move your hand, it moves. But what about the intention to heal yourself or the intention to promote peace in your surroundings?

Science finds itself skeptical and largely baffled when such questions come up—they are barely considered legitimate. Yet on the fringes of respectability there are mounting research studies on the power of prayer to help the sick. Since *Quantum Healing* appeared, other studies have gone even deeper into the effectiveness of intention. Especially intriguing is a pioneering study of native Hawaiian healers led by the late Dr. Jeanne Achterberg, a physiologist of the mind-body connection who was fascinated by anecdotes that native healers often did their work from a distance. Here's how the Achterberg study worked, as described in *Super Brain,* which I wrote with Rudolph E. Tanzi.

In 2005, after a two-year search, she and her colleagues gathered eleven Hawaiian healers. Each had pursued their native healing tradition for an average of 23 years. The healers were asked to select a person with whom they had successfully worked in the past and with whom they felt an empathic connection. This person would be the recipient of healing in a controlled setting. The healers described their methods in a variety of ways—as prayer, sending energy, good intentions, or simply thinking and wishing the highest good for their subjects. Achterberg simply called these efforts distant intentionality (DI).

Each recipient was isolated from the healer while undergoing an fMRI of their brain activity. The healers were asked to randomly send DI at two-minute intervals; the recipients could not have anticipated when the DI was being sent. Yet their brains did. Significant differences were found between the experimental (send) periods and control (no-send) periods in ten out of eleven cases. For the send periods, specific areas within the subjects' brains "lit up" on the fMRI scan, indicating increased metabolic activity. This did not occur during the no-send periods.

Skeptics dismiss such studies without actually trying to duplicate them or to understand the hidden mechanics of intention. However, in the Vedic tradition, there has been a sophisticated description of the mechanics of intention going back centuries. It was divided into three parts. First, an effective intention must arise in a deep level of the mind, below the stream of constant activity. The very deepest state of awareness, which is calm, still, unmoved, and all-wise, is known in Sanskrit as *samadhi*.

What Helps *Samadhi*

- Meditation
- Calm, peaceful surroundings

- Lack of mental agitation
- Absence of stress
- Minimal distractions
- Self-acceptance
- Self-awareness

What Hurts *Samadhi*

The opposite of the above: anything that jangles the mind, making it restless, overactive, stressed, and outward gazing

The second part of the mechanics of intention is to have the intention be as clear and focused as possible. This gives awareness a specific direction. The term for this in Sanskrit is *dharana*.

What Helps *Dharana*

- Clear thinking
- Acting purposefully
- Not losing sight of the goal
- Confidence
- The ability to stick with a mental task
- Follow-through
- Diligence

What Hurts *Dharana*

- Multitasking
- Mental confusion
- Conflicted desires
- Lack of self-knowledge
- Fantasy and daydreaming
- Short attention span
- A craving to escape the self

The third part of the mechanics of intention is a state of flexibility where your mind is steady and active at the same time. You can see this state when a child is totally engrossed in playing with a toy. His attention is on nothing else, and yet inside the play, he does all kinds of things (pushing a toy truck, throwing finger paint on the walls). When you have an intention, your focus is sharp, but then you let go and allow silent intelligence to take care of the outcome. This isn't the same as passive indifference. You are open and alert, because there can be any response at all. The term in Sanskrit for this is *dhyana*.

What Helps *Dhyana*

- Being relaxed and easy
- Mindfulness
- Acceptance of things as they are
- Putting a value on being
- Trust
- Believing in the wisdom of uncertainty
- Allegiance to a higher level of intelligence that organizes reality

What Hurts *Dhyana*

- Tension
- Anticipation
- Controlling yourself and others
- Rigidity
- Insistence on rules and routines
- Obsession
- Compulsive behavior
- Inability to believe that the universe supports you

I've gone into detail here because at the time of *Quantum Healing*, there were few action steps that pertained to silent intelligence other than meditation, which remains the most powerful and direct means to connect with the mind's deeper levels. But meditation too often lacks a purposeful component. The toolbox is opened and the tools just lie there. That's why it's important to master the mechanics of intention. The paradox is that there's nothing really to do and yet everything to do. There's nothing to do as far as first attention is concerned. You live your life, dealing with its challenges as best you can.

At the level of second attention, however, there's everything to do, because you are calling upon the universe, to use a popular phrase, and activating hidden forces unknown to the outward-looking mind. A now-obscure Scottish writer and mountaineer, W. H. Murray, hit upon the mechanics of intention with uncanny precision, intuiting the same things that the Vedic sages described.

> There is one elementary truth, the ignorance of which kills countless ideas and splendid plans; that the moment one definitely commits oneself, then providence moves too.

Having discovered the connection between what happens "in here" (intention) and what happens "out there" (the forces that an intention can move), Murray saw that these awakened forces exist to support human aspirations.

> All sorts of things occur to help one that would never otherwise have occurred. A whole stream of events issues from the decision raising in one's favor all manner of unforeseen events, meetings and material assistance which no one could have dreamed would have come their way.

For quantum healing to be completely viable, the power of intention must be harnessed, calling not upon "providence," which many people don't accept, but upon the inner intelligence that more and more scientific evidence supports. That the mind can move molecules is just as wondrous as faith moving mountains.

PART II

BODY OF BLISS

In every atom, there are worlds within worlds.

—YOGA VASISHTHA

10

IN THE RISHI'S WORLD

A boy in India never has to wish for a time machine. When I was seven, a two-minute walk took me from Daddy's army hospital to the Poona grand bazaar. There the old smells hung in the air—saffron, dust, sandalwood, and cooking fires (not that I noticed them then, being glued to the snake charmers). In the hospital, the only smell was of Dettol, an all-purpose cleanser that stung your nose like straight formaldehyde. Physicists compare time to an arrow; in India, the arrow got bent and meets itself going backward. We adjusted to it. If a soldier came in with a puncture wound in his foot, my father gave him a tetanus shot, but if the man wanted to hobble out and make an offering to Shiva, my father understood.

Now when I go back home, I look out the airplane window and see bullocks plowing within sight of the tarmac. In the cities, it is not uncommon for businessmen dressed in impeccable copies of English wool suits to step around the bodies of sadhus, or holy men, who sit calmly in the middle of the sidewalks clothed in loincloths and orange robes. The daily scene is like an archaeological dig whose layers are hopelessly mixed up, or better yet, where the layers have jumped out of the ground and come to life.

Every dig has to have a bottom layer, though. In this case, it is the sadhus. India's holy men date from at least three thousand years before the birth of Christ. Their words have been recorded and passed on in the original Sanskrit, which lays good claim to being man's first language. Their traditional home is still the Himalayas, where they go to sit in *samadhi*, or deep meditation, for days or weeks at a time. For them, life is totally dedicated to inner silence. Very occasionally, the thought might enter their heads that they should go on a pilgrimage. Picking up their begging bowls, they then set off to the south, trusting to nature to provide them with the necessary food and shelter. In modern times, they can usually board any train or bus without a ticket.

As a child what I knew of sadhus came from one of my uncles, my father's older brother, who traveled all over the country selling sports equipment. We called him Bara Uncle, or "big uncle," a name that set him apart from our lesser relations. He inevitably arrived at our door with field hockey sticks (India traditionally used to beat the rest of the world in this minor sport), soccer balls, or badminton shuttles as presents. Naturally, we couldn't wait to see him.

Bara Uncle was hugely affable and gregarious. He spun fabulous tales about the wonders he met on his way. The most vivid happened in Calcutta. Bara Uncle was pushing his way through the crowds when he almost stumbled over an old sadhu sitting near the curb. Absentmindedly, my uncle reached into his pocket, found two annas (about two cents), and put them in the sadhu's bowl. The sadhu shot him a glance and said, "Make a wish for anything you want."

Taken aback, my uncle blurted, "I want some *burfi*." Burfi is an Indian candy, like fudge, that is usually made from almonds or coconut. Very calmly the sadhu reached his right hand into the air, materialized two pieces of fresh burfi, and gave them to Bara Uncle. Astounded, he stood transfixed for a few seconds, just enough time for the sadhu to rise and melt like a shadow into the crowd. My uncle never saw him again. In a way, he got a fair exchange, since his two annas would have bought him two pieces of burfi from a sweet-meat vendor on the street. But every time he told the story, my uncle would shake his head and mourn, "I am still thinking of all the things I could have wished for."

As a boy, I firmly believed Bara Uncle's story, but in contemporary India, people are more likely to see a sadhu and skeptically wonder if he is real. Starting in the 1920s, scientists from Europe and America began to visit India to observe the various swamis, yogis, and sadhus of every description. Some had attained remarkable degrees of control over their bodies—they could apparently stop breathing for minutes at a time or bring their heartbeats down almost to zero. A typical procedure would consist of taking one of those "saints," as holy men are commonly called in India, and burying him in a box six feet underground. This was supposedly a scientific experiment, but of a very crude sort. After a few days, when the box was unearthed, you either had a result or you didn't. The desired result would be that the saint was still alive. Almost all the physiological studies from the early days are very shallow in their approach, and many reflect this weird combination of science and sideshow.

A sadhu's control over his body, however, is still physical and misses the point of his existence. Such people are out to break through the mask of physical appearances; in our terms, they want to leave the world "above the line" to find out what lies beneath. Indian life, in fact, has traditionally been arranged to make this quest possible. After a man has been educated, raised a family, and enjoyed the rewards of material existence, he is expected to take *sanyasa*—that is, he renounces the householder life, takes up the begging bowl, and goes off in search of something else. If you say that he is searching for God, for truth, for reality, or for himself, all of these would not be quite right, because the essence of the quest is that the goal is unknown. He is setting off into another world that cannot be tracked from this one. To use our terms again, he is setting out across the gap.

I grew up to put on a Western-style suit and step around saints on the sidewalk, but as I looked deeper into the issues of mind-body medicine, I kept returning to India's ancient traditions. The second part of this book centers on what I have found. The known world of our senses, of atoms and molecules, does not just break off abruptly; it shades imperceptibly into a different reality. At some point, however, one reality flips into another. Time and space acquire a different meaning; the neat divisions between inner and outer reality disappear. We find ourselves in a world that has never been explored as well as in India. In his purest form, the sadhu is an investigator into the transcendental reality lying beyond the gap—that is the tradition he upholds, one of the longest and wisest on our planet. To understand his findings will take us on a new road, away from physics, but still on much the same track, in search of ourselves.

In the West, before the advent of the theory of relativity, there was no question that time, space, matter, and energy occupied separate compartments of reality. Our senses detect a tree as entirely different from a beam of light or a spark of electricity; we may feel that time is a more mysterious entity, capable of slowing down, speeding up, or even standing still, but we would never say, "I like New York better than Monday." It seems self-evident that time and space, matter and energy, are opposite pairs, for the simple reason that none can be turned into the others. The normal world of the senses can be diagrammed in our familiar manner:

Time/Space/Matter/Energy

—————— **Gap** ——————

?

After Einstein published the equation $E=mc^2$, this simple, commonsense view had to change, for it was now possible (as the atomic bomb proved) for matter to be transformed into huge amounts of energy. The general theory of relativity did the same thing for the separation between time and space. Now physics deals in a fused entity called space-time, which can be bent to fit certain circumstances (whenever an object travels near the speed of light, for example). After proving that nature was much less compartmentalized than science had previously thought, relativity opened another, even more surprising possibility. Einstein suggested that one underlying field exists as the background for all transformations of space-time and mass-energy. This implies a level of nature that is totally fused; in other words, there is a region of space-time-matter-energy.

Einstein was intuitively convinced of this possibility—the ultimate demolition of the world of the senses—at a time when no one else had the vision to consider it seriously. Beginning in the 1920s, he spent the last thirty years of his life, isolated from the other physicists of his generation and largely ignored, trying to compute the mathematics for a "unified field theory." His theory would unite all the basic forces in creation and thereby explain the universe as a whole. Instead of four compartments, there would be one.

"To unite," in the sense that physicists use the word, means to prove that two things that appear to be totally different can transform into each other at a deeper level of nature. The photon and the light wave are classic examples of this: they appear to be entirely different, yet at an infinitesimal level of nature, called the Planck scale, which is more than a billion billion times smaller than the smallest atom, the photon and the light wave can be united. No one has yet solved the mathematics for a unified field. That would be as much as solving the entire hidden zone we have labeled with a ?. (A new theory, however, called the superstring may have cracked the problem at last, thirty years after Einstein's death.)

In the face of a problem that rational thought cannot solve, science necessarily stops, but other routes may be open. Thousands of years ago, the ancient *rishis*, or seers, of India also contemplated this question of whether nature is ultimately unified. A rishi is like a sadhu in that his life is devoted to silence and the inner life, but rishis lived much further in the past—they were responsible for writing the most ancient texts of Veda, or revealed truth, such as Rig Veda, which may predate the Egyptian pyramids by several thousand years.

If you ask a modern Indian what the Veda is, he will point to the books that contain the rishis' words, but in truth Veda is the content of the rishis' consciousness, which is alive. A rishi has seen deep enough into the nature of things that even God sits at his feet to learn—the lesson can be found in the Yoga Vasishtha, in which the young Lord Rama, a divine incarnation, begs the sage Vasishtha for instruction.

I am not emphasizing the spiritual value of the rishi and his knowledge here. Until very recently in human history, all cultures freely blended religion, psychology, philosophy, and art into one homogeneous whole. But individual strands can be pulled out; in this case, I am interested in what the rishis had to say about the fundamental nature of reality (in the Yoga Vasishtha, God also showed a lively interest in this subject). The rishis were just as capable as we are of dividing nature up into space, time, matter, and energy, but they turned their backs on such an approach, which so totally dominates our way of seeing and thinking about the world.

They chose instead to solve the problem in the most practical way imaginable. They decided to cross the gap and actually enter the ? zone, where thinking cannot go. They used a simple twist in their awareness, but one that has profound consequences—it was like turning the objective world inside out. To do that, the rishis had to analyze nature in an unexpected way, which can be represented by another diagram:

Waking/Sleeping/Dreaming

————————— Gap ————————

?

This diagram is just as valid as the one on page 206, but it looks on the world from a purely subjective viewpoint. Rather than seeing time, space, matter, and energy "out there," the rishis observed that reality begins "in here," with our conscious awareness. At any particular time, they reasoned, a person must be in one of three states of subjective awareness—waking, sleeping, or dreaming. What he perceives in these states constitutes his reality. The ancients assumed that reality was thus different in different states of consciousness— a tiger in the dream state is not a tiger in the waking state. It obeys entirely different laws, and similarly, the laws of the sleep state, although not known to the conscious mind, must be distinct from those of the waking and dreaming states.

The rishis looked closer and detected between each of these states a gap that acts like a pivot as one reality turns into another. For example, just before falling asleep, the mind gradually leaves the waking state, withdrawing the senses, shutting out the waking world, but at the junction point before the mind actually falls asleep, a brief gap is opened, identical to the one that flashes by between each thought: it is like a little window into the field that is beyond either wakefulness or sleep. This realization opened the possibility for leaving behind the usual boundaries of the five senses by diving through the gap.

Considering that the West is supposed to be practical and the East mystical, it is fascinating to find that the rishis were much more avid for direct experience than any quantum physicist. Their subjective approach was called Yoga, the Sanskrit word for "union." (The various exercises taught in yoga classes belong to just one of its branches, called Hatha Yoga; we will be looking at Yoga's most powerful approach, which is mental.) Because both are looking for an underlying layer of unity in nature, one can immediately see the resemblance between Yoga and Einstein's quest for a unified field theory. The major difference between the two is that the rishis, not being theoretical, declared that the unified field exists in the real world—it is an experience and not merely a mental construct.

From the rishis' subjective viewpoint, the only thing that the unified field could be is another state of consciousness. They called it simply *turiya*, or the fourth, to denote that it was not part of the three states of waking, sleeping, and dreaming. They also referred to it as *para*, or beyond, meaning that it transcended ordinary experience. But how could a fourth state even exist? The answer was twofold. First, the seers said that the fourth state exists everywhere but is hidden by the other three states as if by a screen. (Some ancient texts declare that the fourth state has been mixed into the other three like milk into water, and finding it is as difficult as separating milk from water.) Second, they said that the fourth state can be directly experienced only after the mind has transcended its normal activity, which requires the special technique of meditation.

The word *rishi* itself stands for a person who has learned to enter the fourth state at will and observe what is there. This ability is not "thinking" as we use the term—the whole phenomenon is an immediate experience, like recognizing the fragrance of lilacs or the sound of a friend's voice. It is immediate, nonverbal, and, unlike a flower's fragrance, totally transforming. As they sat in meditation, deeply absorbed in their own subjective awareness, the rishis explored turiya the way we would look at the Grand Canyon. As individuals, these seers have names, but going into the transcendent blurred the edges of what we consider personal identity. Vasishtha, for example, is not just the name of one of the greatest of the ancient rishis; it stands for an integral part of Veda—transcendental knowledge—which the man Vasishtha first cognized; to truly know that part of Veda, one would have to be in "Vasishtha consciousness." In short, these sages observed existence in its purest form.

For all intents and purposes, there was no way for the West to systematically test the existence of the fourth state. Lacking the right technique, the scientific community has ignored turiya. In fact, many scientists would consider it irrelevant or threatening. The very notion of "union" brings undesirable images to mind: dissolving into a state of nothingness, or losing one's identity like a drop of water disappearing into the ocean. Despite occasional bursts of enthusiasm for Eastern ideas, the progress of knowledge in the West has overwhelmingly depended on outward observation, not inner.

But if there is a state that transcends the usual three, then it seems likely that it would show up from time to time, if only by accident. For example, Charles Lindbergh reported one experience that took place in 1927, during the most critical moments of his life. When he was into the second day of his historic solo flight across the Atlantic, Lindbergh found that he had passed the limits of physical exhaustion. Fearing that he would lose control of his craft, he skirted disaster by fitfully dozing off and hoping that he remained on course. Then, as Lindbergh recounts in his autobiography, a remarkable change of awareness took place:

> Over and over again on the second day of my flight, I would return to mental alertness sufficiently to realize that I had been flying while I was neither asleep nor awake. My eyes had been open. I had responded to my instruments' indications and held generally to compass course, but I had lost sense of circumstance and time. During immeasurable periods, I seemed to extend outside my plane and body, independent of worldly values, appreciative of beauty, form, and color without depending upon my eyes.

As a child, Lindbergh had lain in the cornfields on his father's farm and felt a similar sense of being "beyond mortality" as he gazed into the sky. But the episode over the North Atlantic went further. What Lindbergh concluded about it was this: "It was an experience in which both the intellect and senses were replaced by what might be termed a matterless awareness. . . . I recognized that vision and reality interchange, like energy and matter."

Doctors to whom I mention meditation generally assure me, whether they "believe" in it or not, that meditation is for relaxation. It is only in the light of Veda that one can understand why this view is so shortsighted.

Veda represents an immense expansion of the human mind. The best way to describe it is that Veda is the total content of the cosmic computer. All the input of nature is channeled into it, and out of it flows all natural phenomena. The control over this computer is located in the human brain, whose billions of neural connections give it enough complexity to mirror the complexity of the universe.

The brain is not important as an object, the rishis contend. It is important because our own subjectivity shines through it; when our brains show us the world, they are really showing us ourselves. By analogy, when an image falls upon a mirror, a blending takes place. The mirror is the reflection; the reflection is the mirror. In the same way, the only reality we can know anything about is the one that is being mirrored in the brain—everything that exists is therefore inside our subjectivity.

A physicist would not normally agree with this, since he cherishes the objective method and looks on subjectivity as virtually his enemy. A physicist says, "This is a proton," not, "This is my feeling for what a proton is." Actually, Veda is not devoid of objective knowledge—it gave rise to its own sciences of botany, physiology, astronomy, medicine, et cetera—but the rishis did not feel that objectivity was the most reliable way to know things, particularly once you investigate deeper than nature's surface. The truth, they said, is that subjectivity can be either narrow or expanded. Nature is like a radio band. When you pay attention to an isolated object—a rock, a star, or an entire galaxy—you select one channel on the band. The rest obviously has to be excluded—but only for that level of consciousness.

It may be that other levels of consciousness receive more bands, or more than one band at a time. Right now, physicists estimate that our senses choose less than one-billionth of the energy waves and particles that surround us. We live in an "energy soup" incredibly larger than the world we see. The visible universe itself is now thought to be but a minuscule version of the original creation, the residue of a much larger reality that collapsed somewhere before time began, reducing its original ten dimensions to our four. (I apologize for using the phrase "before time began," which is a blatant paradox, but there is no way to state verbally how pre–Big Bang events occurred.) Also, it appears that at the moment of creation our universe was filled with a billion times more energy than we now observe with radio telescopes; the remainder was reabsorbed into the same hidden field where the other six dimensions went.

The rishis declared that through expanded consciousness, even this inconceivable lost reality could be made available to us. Theoretical physics agrees that the lost dimensions and invisible energy fields have not actually gone anywhere; they have only sunk back to "sleep" in the primordial field. Similarly, the transcendental level of awareness is available everywhere; you need not go anywhere special to find it. It only needs to wake up. William James expressed this idea in a famous passage:

Our normal waking consciousness, rational consciousness as we call it, is but one special type of consciousness, whilst all around it, parted from it by the flimsiest of screens, there lie potential forms of consciousness entirely different. We may go through life without suspecting their existence; but apply the requisite stimulus, and at a touch they are there in all their completeness.

If so much more reality is nearby, why can't we touch it? Researchers found a clue to the answer, curiously enough, by experimenting with newborn kittens. Kittens are born with their eyes shut and their optic nerves undeveloped. When they open their eyes, the mechanism for sight matures at the same time; these two events always go hand in hand. However, it was found in the mid-1970s that if you blindfold a kitten during the two or three days when it first opens its eyes, the animal will be blind for life. During thus brief but critical period, the experience of seeing actually shapes the inter-neuronal connections in the brain that make sight possible.

This was an important finding, for biologists continue to disagree over whether genetics or experience is more important in behavior. This is the old question of whether a trait is innate or acquired. Does a robin learn to sing from its mother, or will it sing if raised in isolation? The experiment with the blind kittens showed that both "nature" and "nurture" are essential; the kitten's brain is programmed for sight, yet it requires seeing for the programming to unfold properly. There is a deeper implication to all this, however. Our own brains could be limited in just this way. Many things "out there" don't exist for us, not because they are unreal, but because "in here" we have not shaped the brain to perceive them. We are like radios that appear to have all the channels when actually they are stuck on three—waking, sleeping, and dreaming.

Because your brain is the only radio you have, you can never know whether the fourth state exists unless your nervous system is prepared for it. It is entirely possible that we are literally bathed and surrounded by the transcendent and yet have not tuned it in.

The Veda gives a supporting analogy: thoughts are like ocean waves. Rising and falling, they see only their own motion. They say, "I am a wave," but the greater truth, which they do not see, is, "I am ocean." There is no separation between the two, whatever the wave might suppose. When a wave settles down, then it instantly recognizes that its source in ocean—infinite, silent, and unchanging—was always there.

The same holds true for the mind. When it is thinking, it is all activity; when it stops thinking, it returns to its source in silence. Only then, when the mind touches pure awareness, will the real storehouse of Veda be located. The experience of Veda therefore is not ancient or even particularly Indian. It is universal and can be had at any moment by any person. The whole trick is not to move horizontally, which is how the stream of consciousness normally moves, but to sink vertically. This vertical descent is transcending, meditation, dhyan, "going beyond"—all manifestations of a mind that ceases to identify with waves and begins to identify with ocean.

If this argument is right, then the nature of the mind and the mind-body connection have to be reconsidered. The point that Archimedes was looking for—a place to stand on and move the world—actually exists. It is inside us, covered up by the fascinating but misleading moving-picture show of the waking state.

This may explain why mind-body medicine has proved so inconsistent. We casually assume that a person who survives cancer or can cure himself of a fatal disease operates with the same mental machinery as anyone else, but this is not true: mental processes can be deep or shallow. To go deep means to contact the hidden blueprint of intelligence and change it—only then can visualization of fighting cancer, for example, be strong enough to defeat the disease. But most people cannot do that; their thought power is too weak to trigger the appropriate mechanisms.

The practical question is whether meditation is strong enough to radically improve our thought power. Several studies conducted by scientists have shown that meditation may in fact induce profound change, far beyond the simple relaxation that most people use it for in the West, even beyond the medical applications of relieving stress, reducing blood pressure, and so on.

The first Western scientist to make any major breakthrough with the fourth state was an American physiologist, Robert Keith Wallace, who proved that it existed. In 1967, Wallace was a doctoral student at UCLA, where he began his Ph.D. research on the physiological changes that take place during Transcendental Meditation (a form of mantra meditation). Using the methods of modern biomedical research, he compiled data from meditators over a period of several years. Without causing any discomfort, he wired them up to measure their brain waves, blood pressure, heart rate, and other indices of physical change.

Wallace soon began to build a considerable body of unique results. First, he discovered that something real was indeed happening to the body in meditation. Within a few minutes of beginning their practice, his subjects entered a state of deep relaxation, marked by slower breathing and heartbeat, by the appearance of alpha waves in their EEGs (electroencephalograms), and decreased oxygen consumption detected in the breath. This last measure was particularly important because it showed that the body's metabolic rate, tied to the total consumption of fuel in the cells, had dropped—physiologists refer to this metabolic reduction as a "hypometabolic" state.

Meditators achieved their deepest relaxation quickly. It takes four to six hours after falling asleep to reach the period where oxygen consumption falls to its lowest levels, while meditators took only a few minutes. Moreover, in sleep the drop is usually less than 16 percent, whereas meditators achieved relative reductions that momentarily dipped almost twice as low. Wallace was impressed by these figures because such a deep state of relaxation had never been recorded before. What this showed was that the subjective feelings reported during meditation—inner silence, peacefulness, and relaxation—had a real physical basis. It was also very important that these subjects had not fallen asleep or gone into a trance. They were fully awake inside, even feeling a sense of heightened awareness. Wallace concluded therefore that meditation was a state of "hypometabolic wakefulness." Since his measurements were different from any seen in waking, dreaming, or sleeping, he concluded that he had verified an entirely new state of consciousness—the fourth state.

Certain of the meditators had exhibited physical changes that went far beyond the average. As with the yogis measured in India and the Himalayas, their breathing seemed to stop for long stretches. At the subjective level, these deeper states were experienced as absolute inner silence, a feeling of vast expansion, and a profound knowingness. The mind was emptied of all specific thoughts but left with the clear awareness of "I know everything." No one could explain these experiences, because scientific instruments are too crude to analyze or even detect them.

To anyone versed in the Vedic literature, however, it was obvious that these subjects were experiencing transcendental awareness of a deep sort. The Yoga Vasishtha, one of the greatest sources on direct experience of the transcendent, says of the fourth state, "When there is effortless suspension of breath, that is the supreme state. It is the Self. It is pure, infinite consciousness. He who reaches this does not grieve." It would be hard to find a better description of what the physiologists were seeing. Wallace looked at physical measurements made with Zen meditators in Japan and found comparable results; what was astonishing, however, was that his American subjects, most of them young, posthippie, and new to meditation, were achieving the same scores as Zen adepts who had practiced meditating for ten years.

Seen in a different light, what Wallace did was to legitimize the mind-body connection. It is now accepted fact that one's body spontaneously responds to one's state of awareness, just as the rishis said. The paradox is that we have to learn to dive inside at all. Meditation teaches us to control a process that is constantly influencing us every day, whether we realize it or not.

Recently I saw a Boston woman in her sixties who for several years had been suffering from a slow degeneration of the heart muscle called cardiomyopathy. There are various kinds of cardiomyopathy; hers was considered idiopathic, meaning that no cause could be found for it. Her main symptom at the time of diagnosis was shortness of breath whenever she exerted herself—she was experiencing heart failure from the enlargement of her heart. Medicine can do little or nothing for this disease, which greatly worried her, but when she had last seen her cardiologist two months earlier, he had suggested that she go into the hospital for an angiogram.

The purpose of an angiogram is to determine if the coronary arteries, the vessels sending oxygen to the heart, are blocked. The cardiologist was reasoning that if there was any blockage, some of her problem might be due to arterial disease, which is treatable. Apprehensively she underwent the test. The angiographer, who was also a physician, came to her room afterward.

"I have good news," he said. "Your vessels are clean—you don't have coronary artery disease. As far as I'm concerned, there is no need for surgery." As he was leaving, he turned to her and remarked, "If your condition gets any worse, the only thing that really can be done is to have a heart transplant."

The woman had never been told this before, and within a few days she began to have shortness of breath not just on exertion but whenever she lay down. Unable to sleep and getting more and more anxious, she returned to her cardiologist, who could find no reason for the worsening of her symptoms. Finally he confronted her one day, and she told him she was afraid of having a heart transplant. He assured her that her fears were groundless—her condition was by no means advanced enough for such a drastic procedure. From that day on, her new symptoms disappeared.

Once again we see that subjective reality and objective reality are tightly bound together. When the mind shifts, the body cannot help but follow. Objective reality looks obviously more fixed than our subjective moods, fleeting desires, and swings of emotion. Yet perhaps it is not; it is more like a violin string that can hold one pitch but also change pitch as your finger slides along it—that image occurred to me thinking about Chitra's case at the beginning of this book, but it holds true for all of us.

What the pitch on the string stands for is your level of consciousness. This is a very basic inner attribute, like a focal point on which all your thoughts, emotions, and desires converge, or a pair of green glasses that makes the whole world look green. Most people don't realize how consistent their pitch is, but others are quite aware of it—a depressed person radiates depression, even when he forces himself to act positive; a hostile person can set a whole room on edge, even if he says the most harmless things. One's level of consciousness fits into broad guidelines. Nobody is absolutely hostile or joyful, intelligent or dull, satisfied or discontent; dozens of subtle gradations exist in every personality.

The important point is that everything you think and do is determined by this point—you cannot think yourself to a higher or lower level of consciousness. This helps explain why meditation is not simply another kind of thinking or introspection, a mistake Westerners tend to make. It is actually a way to slide to a new pitch. The process of transcending, or "going beyond," detaches the mind from its fixed level and allows it to exist, if only for a moment, without any level at all. It simply experiences silence, devoid of thoughts, emotions, drives, wishes, fears, or anything at all. Afterward, when the mind returns to its usual pitch (level of consciousness), it has acquired a little freedom to move.

From a medical standpoint, a disease may represent a place on the violin string that is out of tune. Yet, for some reason, the mind-body system cannot find a way to let go, to slide to a healthier pitch. If that is so, then meditation may be a powerful therapeutic tool, allowing the body to get unstuck from the disease. Meditation researchers caught on to this potential in the late 1960s when they discovered that many college-age meditators who used alcohol, cigarettes, and recreational drugs spontaneously quit their habit within a few months of beginning to meditate. We can call this getting unstuck from an old level of consciousness that needed the drug; in terms of neuropeptides, it may be that the meditation freed up certain receptor sites by offering molecules that were more satisfying than alcohol, nicotine, or marijuana.

By 1978, Robert Keith Wallace had spent more than a decade validating separate mind-body effects on meditators. He decided to follow a new lead and investigate a more complex, holistic area, human aging. The aging process has traditionally been accepted without question as an inevitable aspect of normal life, and variations in it have been considered largely individual. Some people live longer than others owing to privileged genes, a strong immune system, or good luck, but there is no anti-aging factor that can be applied to everyone. If there were, then 70-year-olds would be more uniformly healthy in their bodily functions, just as most 20-year-olds are.

However, there is no scientific proof that aging is normal—it is just something we all happen to do. So many stresses are involved in "normal" living that the physiology might be considered under abnormal pressure all the time—from noise, pollution, negative emotions, improper diet, smoking, alcohol, and so on. Just "the disease of being in a hurry" hastens aging in almost everyone today. If meditation counters these factors, then it might reveal something entirely new about the aging process.

Wallace set out to measure a group of adult meditators for what is called biological age. Biological age shows how well a person's body is functioning compared to the norms of the whole population. It gives a truer measure of how the aging process is progressing than does chronological or calendar age, because any two people who are both 55 years old by the calendar will generally have very different bodies. Initially all that Wallace needed to test were three rather simple variables: blood pressure, acuteness of hearing, and near-point vision (the ability to see objects close-up). All three steadily deteriorate as the body biologically ages and therefore serve as convenient markers.

Wallace discovered that the meditators, as a group, were signifi-

cantly younger biologically than their chronological age. The difference between the two was not small, either—the female subject
who scored the best was fully twenty years younger than her chronological age. Strikingly, how much younger a person tested was
closely correlated to how long he had kept up his meditation practice. Wallace found a dividing line between those who had meditated fewer than five years and those who had meditated five years
or more. The first group averaged five years younger biologically,
while the second averaged twelve years younger. A backup study
conducted in England later calculated that each year of regular
meditation takes off roughly one year of aging. Another finding that
particularly impressed Wallace's team was that their older subjects
showed as good results as much younger people. A typical 60-year-
old meditating five years or more would have the physiology of a
48-year-old.

Another important point raised by this remarkable study is that
the subjects were not *trying* to age more slowly. They were simply
removing an invisible barrier, and then the desirable physical
changes took place of their own accord. This spontaneous flowering
seems to be quite nonspecific; a 1986 Blue Cross and Blue Shield
insurance study based on two thousand meditators in Iowa showed
that they were much healthier than the American population as a
whole in seventeen major areas of serious disease, both mental and
physical. This was a very significant improvement. For example, the
meditation group was hospitalized 87 percent less often than non-
meditators for heart disease and 50 percent less often for all kinds
of tumors. There were equally impressive reductions in disorders of
the respiratory system, the digestive tract, clinical depression, and
so forth. Although the study was limited to one group, this is very
encouraging news for anyone who wants to follow a holistic program
of prevention.

The fourth state may play an important role in our future. At the
source of human awareness lies a super-normal level of conscious-

ness—it can become normal, however, once we have accustomed ourselves to experiencing it. If turiya is the mind's birthplace, then why can't it be the mind's permanent home? This is the next area to explore, investigating whether nature is unified not just in Einstein's hypothetical model but in ourselves.

EXPANDING THE TOPIC

In hindsight, the practical side of this chapter, connecting meditation with positive changes in the brain, has only expanded.° Research into meditation continues apace, following the same lines I described thirty years ago. Vital signs are seen to improve, and various effects on brain function can be observed with ever-increasing accuracy. Skeptics have been thoroughly driven out of the debate on these issues, but not on the notion of unbounded awareness. Recognition of a fourth state of consciousness, beyond waking, dreaming, and sleeping, arouses fierce opposition because "unbounded" would mean that mind exists outside the brain.

The path to proving the reality of unbounded awareness isn't by introducing cosmic mind, not if you want to convince anyone who would suspect that God's in the wings. It's more convincing, especially to doctors, if you direct them to the intimate scale of the human body. When someone asks, "Where is the mind located?" they will automatically point to their heads. Why? Is it because we automatically expect to experience our thoughts in our heads? That seems to be the case. When dreaming at night, it gets a bit more ambiguous, since we feel that we are "inside" our dreams. But for

---

° As an example of today's sophisticated measurements, a November 2013 survey in *Scientific American* of the effects of meditation cited the following: Meditation not only changes brain neuronal interconnections, but it also increases brain tissue volume, decreases the volume of the amygdala, increases telomerase activity, and diminishes inflammation and other biological stresses that occur at the molecular level.

most of us, most of the time, "my head" is where "my mind" is located.

This response may feel true simply because so many sense organs are located there: eyes, ears, nose, tongue. But we can easily undermine the commonsense model of sight and sound taking place in the head. When a car backfires behind you, the sound can't be felt entering the ear canal, being processed in the inner ear and then in the brain's auditory center. There is no noise in the brain. Quite clearly the sound of the backfiring car comes from outside you. In some cultures, hearing is a faculty that goes from inside to outside, the opposite of what we assume. Think about driving down the highway and suddenly noticing the driver in front of you hitting the brakes. Your attention goes out in order to see his rear lights go on. The senses follow attention, which makes it plausible to say your mind went outside your body when you spotted the brake lights. We casually adopt this model for vision when we say that someone "shoots a glance" at someone else.

Babies, we are told, have a much more diffuse experience of the five senses, perhaps mixing them up in what are called synesthesias (for example, experiencing sounds as colors or tastes as shapes, an experience reported from hallucinogenic drugs and in deep meditative states). Some researchers contend that babies therefore have a poor sense of the boundary between themselves and the world. But infants turn into toddlers, and the separation between self and the world starts to harden. Society and family reinforce this habit as the toddler grows up, and eventually the mind takes its seat in our heads, or so it seems. In altered states, whether induced by drugs or in deep meditation, there are countless reports, echoed by Charles Lindbergh in his transatlantic flight, of the mind extending in all directions. There are even subjective reports of sitting in a chair and reaching out to touch some velvet drapes far across the room—the senses literally go where they are directed.

Neuroscientists would call such experiences anomalies, declaring resolutely that mind and brain have taken up residence together in a box called the skull. But it is undeniably possible to literally "think outside the box," beginning with the message system discussed in this book that connects every cell in the body with whatever is occurring in the brain. "Fine," a neuroscientist would argue, "but the brain is still the machine that makes mind. Take away the brain, and there is no mind." But this is the same as saying that if you turn off the radio, there is no music. You haven't destroyed the music, only the receiver.

One must be open to asking some culturally radical questions, including the most radical of all: Is a brain even necessary for "thinking"? There are different ways to explore this issue.

First, let's consider whether only human brains create minds. Few people who have pets or live on farms would say that the animals they encounter don't have minds. There is already abundant evidence that the genes, receptors, and neurotransmitters involved in human brain function are present in animals. Saying that different kinds of animal brains create minds is not so troublesome if you insist that the mind is rooted in these shared processes and chemicals. We aren't able to describe what animal minds are like (some may lack anything like human self-awareness), but we shouldn't have a problem conceiving that these creatures have one.

Second, there are nervous systems on the evolutionary ladder than don't require a central brain. Some creatures, like jellyfish, have neuronal nets distributed throughout the body. We, too, have such systems. Your gastrointestinal tract sends and receives signals from the peripheral nerves that branch out from the spinal cord. But digestion can function quite well when severed from the peripheral nervous system. As in the jellyfish, your gut constitutes a weblike intestinal nervous system. In the language of cell biology, specialized ganglion cells are located between muscle layers in the intestinal wall that act like a local brain. If one severs any peripheral nerves, these ganglion cells continue to instruct the intestine to move and absorb and secrete, working quite autonomously as a self-contained functional unit.

It turns out that the intestinal tract only takes advice from the rest of the body. It harbors its own reactions. When bad news gives you a sinking feeling in the pit of your stomach, you are experiencing an emotion as surely as you experience it in your head. In fact, your gut reaction precedes the thought. Does this mean that your intestinal nervous system creates such reactions on its own? That's unclear, but it's tempting to think so. Certainly many people trust their gut reactions over the confused and compromised responses that the brain is often saddled with.

The muscles of your face are directly linked to your brain. While we assume that the brain is telling the mouth and lips to smile when we're feeling happy, the reverse is also true. Seeing a smile on someone else's face can make you happy, and children are taught to smile as a way to break out of a sad mood. Whether this works or not varies from person to person, but it could be argued that the face is controlling the brain in those instances.

Findings about brainlike processes outside the skull have become common. The conduction system inside the heart, including pacemaker cells, which organizes your heartbeat, can be thought of as the heart's brain in the same way the ganglion cells in the gut are the brain of the intestines. The independence of the conduction system is shown when a transplanted heart keeps beating even though the nerves that connected it to the donor's central and peripheral nervous systems have been severed. The interaction between the heart's independent processing and the brain's is complex and not fully understood.

Still more mysterious are the trillions of bacteria that outnumber the body's cells by ten to one, living mostly inside the digestive tract but also on the skin and in the brain and other organs. We think of these bacteria as invaders, but over eons these microorganisms have actually been incorporated into vast stretches along the double helix of human DNA. The implications for what we call "being human" are enormous and largely uncharted. Taken as a whole, the bacterial component of the body is known as the microbiome. It doesn't sit passively on the skin or in the gut, nor does it invade the body. Instead, the microbiome is the border between "in here" and "out there," possessed of genes, receptors, and chemical messaging that make the same things possible for the brain. The function of the microbial DNA that is woven into our genes isn't known, but at the very least this is ancestral information we've assimilated as our own. More suggestively, this once-foreign DNA may be the switching agent for the genes in all higher life-forms.

These discoveries prove that our intelligence extends to the entire ecology. Mind has a physical basis everywhere. Any attempt to isolate it in the skull runs into serious objections. Instead of viewing unbounded awareness with skepticism, we need to see that every thought is unbounded. You cannot see, hear, or touch anything in the world without reaching beyond the illusory boundary of the isolated body. To watch a sunset is literally like watching yourself.

11

BIRTH OF A DISEASE

The rishis took a simple position in the mind-body debate. Everything, they said, comes from the mind. It projects the world exactly as a movie projector does. Our bodies are part of the movie, and so is everything that happens to the body. To a rishi, the wonder was not that we can make ourselves sick or well, but that we don't see ourselves doing it. If we could silently witness ourselves, we would see this and more. The very sky, ocean, mountains, and stars would be pouring out of our brains—they all belong in the movie, too. If the rishis' views are right, then we have been wrong to put so much faith in objective reality. And yet our objective frame of reference doesn't seem wrong. It serves us very well, on the whole; the sky and the stars seem to exist "out there," totally independent of us. Are we being fooled by our own movie?

To make the rishis' case, you have to adopt their perspective, which means stepping outside ordinary waking-state reality, at least slightly. If you can do that, then you begin to appreciate that the mind is indeed a powerful creator. I caught a small but revealing glimpse of this recently. I was in a crowded plane taking off from Bombay. Everything seemed completely normal except that the No Smoking/Fasten Your Seatbelt sign came back on at the same moment as the steward dashed furiously down the aisle toward the front of the cabin. The pilot announced over the intercom, "Ladies and gentlemen, please remain seated. We are going to return to Bombay for an emergency landing." His voice betrayed a tremor, and as we all sat tensely silent, a young Indian stewardess started sobbing loudly.

A few minutes later we bounced onto the runway, and three fire trucks sped to our side; we could hear their sirens wailing above the engine roar. Nothing else happened. No explanation was ever given for the incident. The passengers were quickly reboarded onto a different jet; about half elected to stay on the ground. I didn't feel too disturbed during the incident and got on the second plane. The next time I caught a flight, about ten days later, my mind was at ease. However, as soon as they flashed on the sign, No Smoking/Fasten Your Seatbelt, accompanied by that *ding* sound, my heart started to pound. At first I couldn't put two and two together; then I realized that I had created a small conditioned reflex in myself. Pavlov's dogs salivated at the sound of a bell, and I sped up my heart at almost the same thing. I then noticed that as soon as this explanation dawned on me, my heartbeat went back to normal.

For a few seconds I was present at the birth of one impulse that shaped my reality. It is plausible that I have unwittingly created myself by piling up millions of impulses just like it. These come too fast and furious for me to analyze them—as well ask a waterfall to analyze its drops—but the real sticking point is that they are so abstract. To the rishis, the whole world has been built up, layer by layer, out of sheer abstraction. Because you willingly give yourself over to it, a John Wayne western seems real, even though you know it is just beams of light bouncing off a flat white surface. A dream consists entirely of neurological impulses firing in your brain, but as long as you are in it, you are convinced by its reality. (Everyone is familiar with that faint, disappointing moment that comes when the dream stops being convincing. Instead of flying through the air, you begin to sense that "it is only a dream," and after a brief struggle, the waking world comes back.)

In the same way, the reality you accept in the waking state is known to you only from impulses firing in your brain. When you touch a flower, the act of touching brings together the force and matter fields in your hand with the force and matter fields in the flower. All of these fields are highly abstract, yet touch does not seem abstract to you. You are convinced by it. The rishis placed a huge emphasis on how much we all convince ourselves. A famous parable for this was given by Shankara, the greatest philosophical mind in the Vedic tradition:

A man is walking down the road in the evening and sees a large snake coiled in the dust. He runs away terrified and stirs up everyone with his cries of "Snake, snake!" The people of his village are also terrified; the women and children don't want to go outside because of the snake, and normal life begins to be overshadowed by everyone's apprehension. Then a brave person resolves to look at this snake. He asks the first man to take him to it, and when they get there, what they find is not a snake but a rope coiled in the middle of the road. All our fears, Shankara said, have been built up from just such a delusion. In fact, nothing real can be separated from what we tell ourselves is real.

This line of reasoning is not specifically Indian—it can be easily adapted to a modern frame of reference. Think of what happens when two bar magnets come together with their north poles facing each other. The magnetic field repels them apart. If these were thinking magnets, they would "feel" something solid in between themselves. They would create touch out of an abstraction, just as we all do.

The reason why, when you touch it, an object feels soft, hard, ragged, smooth, et cetera, is that such an interpretation is made in

your brain. Essentially, the five senses are just tools. Touch is really
the brain reaching out into the world, using specialized nerve cells
to register certain information—a very narrow band, we must remember, which is entirely different from what a snake "touches"
when its tongue flicks the air.

Similarly, the nerve endings coating the retina of your eye are
also extensions of the brain. Structurally, the retina is just a pool of
nerve endings fanning out like the frayed end of a rope, the rope
being the optic nerve, which gathers a million separate nerve fibers
into one bundled cord. Even though they are located deeper inside
you than the nerve endings under your skin, the eye's sensory cells
are also "touching" the outside world. There is no intrinsic difference between the field of light contacted by your eye and the energy
field you touch with your fingers—the real distinction between seeing and touching is made in the brain. And so it goes for every other
sense: hearing, smelling, and tasting involve specialized cells that
send impulses directly to the brain for interpretation, and without
that interpretation nothing could exist.

All things in existence are tied to our senses, and our senses are
tied to our brains. The commonsense notion that "this chair is hard
to the touch" is not true, until you restate it as "this chair is hard
because my brain made it that way." (The chair is not hard at all to a
cosmic ray, which zips through it like air. A neutrino zips through
the whole Earth with equal ease.) Using this insight, the rishis went
even further. They noticed that you do not have to touch an object
physically to know how it feels. Answer this question: Which is
softer, a starched linen napkin or a rose petal? You can easily compare the two in your mind, using an image of touch, without having
to go out and find a real napkin and a real rose.

The reason why you can do this is that you have gone to a subtler
level of the sense of touch. Similarly, there are subtle sounds, sights,
smells, and tastes. However, this level of the mind is not the end—in
meditation, one can reach even further back, beyond the five subtle
senses (called the *Tanmatras* in Ayurveda), until one arrives at con-

sciousness in its unified state—the Vedic texts compare this to following the hand's five fingers back to where they join at the palm. Subjectively, the visual image of a rose would grow fainter and fainter on the screen of the mind, until nothing was left but the screen itself. Then one would be at the true origin of the senses, the field of intelligence itself. In this way, the rishis reasoned, the whole world of physical reality comes into being.

We seem to be in deep philosophical waters here, but in fact every layer of touch, sight, hearing, smell, and taste influences our ordinary lives. If you like to eat oysters and I detest them, the difference is not in the oyster or in our taste buds. The contact between the molecules of the oyster and the taste receptors in our mouths is the same for both of us. Yet, in the process of tasting, your delight insinuates itself, and so does my disgust. All the raw data of experience must pass through the filter of intelligence, and no two people appraise it in exactly the same way.

When something seems to change in the world, the rishis said, it is really you that is changing. A friend of mine, also Indian, is a surgeon who has gained a reputation for being rather a gourmet. His specialty is omelets, the more exotic the better. The last time we had Sunday brunch together, however, he didn't order an omelet. Curious, I asked him about it, and he said, "I can't stand the taste of an omelet anymore." It turned out that his liking for them had changed instantly, earlier that week.

He was stirring up an omelet at home while his 6-year-old son, Arjun, looked on. As each egg was cracked, my friend tossed the shell aside. By chance a few of them fell into a small brown bag of birdseed that was going to be set out for the sparrows.

"Oh, don't do that," Arjun said seriously. "The birds will think their babies have died, and they won't want to eat." My friend is usually proud of his boy's precocious remarks, but all at once he couldn't abide the taste of the omelet he was making, or any other. Science would be at a loss to measure the change that occurred in him, because it is too ghostly and too individual. The idea that an omelet tastes good has no more weight than that it tastes bad. The same is true of every other sensation. Is a goose-down pillow soft? Not to someone with a migraine, who groans with pain when his head touches it. Does a jet move fast? Not if you view it from the moon. In short, there is no end to the way a sense impression can be interpreted, and no end to the ways that the body can respond to it.

The rishis said that life is built up by your participation in it. Nothing is good or bad, hard or soft, painful or pleasant, except as you live it. The same is true of disease. A disease is not the molecular contact of some outside organism with the molecules of your body. (As we saw, even if you put a drop of concentrated cold virus into a person's nose, his chances of getting a cold are no more than one in eight.) It is not even the flow of toxins in your blood or the action of runaway cells. In the rishis' view, a disease is a sequence of moments that you live through, during which you appraise every iota of the vast input that comes pouring in from all quarters of your world, including your body.

Your body is a world, too. When I first came to Ayurveda, I was deeply impressed by the following verse in the ancient texts:

> As is the human body, so is the cosmic body.
> As is the human mind, so is the cosmic mind.
> As is the microcosm, so is the macrocosm.

These words are subject to many interpretations. What they signify to me is that when I go about my everyday existence, I am in charge of two worlds, the little one in me and the big one around me. My appraisal of every minute detail "out there"—the sun, the sky, the chances of rain, the words other people say, the shadows cast by office buildings—is matched by an event "in here." Infinite choice is open at every second for me to alter the shape of the world, for it has no shape other than what I give it. The eminent neurologist Sir John Eccles stated this quite clearly when he wrote, "I want you to

realize that there is no color in the natural world and no sounds—
nothing of this kind; no textures, no patterns, no beauty, no scent . . ."
In short, nothing is so important about the universe as your participation in it.

The rishis' subjective approach found an enormously useful outlet in Ayurveda. Ayurveda is commonly classified as a system of
medicine, but with equal justice you could call it a system for curing
delusions, for stripping away the convincing quality of disease and
letting a healthier reality take its place. (The name itself suggests
that Ayurveda is meant to be medicine in the broadest sense. It
comes from two Sanskrit roots, *Ayus,* or "life," and *Veda,* which
means either "knowledge" or "science." The literal meaning, then,
is "science of life.")

Patients are curious to know what kinds of treatments are specifically Ayurvedic—are there new pills to try, exercises, diets, or
more arcane Eastern therapies? I say yes to all of these, but then
with some embarrassment I have to add that I spend much of my
time just talking, trying to get people not to be so convinced by their
disease. In Ayurveda, this is the first and most important step in
healing. As long as the patient is convinced by his symptoms, he is
caught up in a reality where "being sick" is the dominant input. The
reason why meditation is so important in Ayurveda is that it leads
the mind to a "free zone" that is not touched by disease. Until you
know that such a place exists, your disease will seem to be taking
over completely. This is the principal delusion that needs to be shattered.

It is undeniable that we all create scenarios and then become
convinced by them, down to our very cells. A young girl from Boston who went to college in Vermont was brought in to see me recently by her parents. They had become quite distraught when she
showed up in the middle of spring term with sharp chest pains.
These had set in while she was recovering from a cold and over a
period of a week became alarmingly severe. One night the girl had
a bad attack—she began to experience shortness of breath, palpita-

tions, and dizziness, eventually growing so frightened that her parents rushed her to the nearest emergency room.

By the time they got there, the whole family was in a state of near panic. The ER doctor listened to the girl's heart, detected that she had a slight heart murmur, and decided to run an EKG, or electrocardiogram. The EKG read-out showed occasional ectopic beats, meaning extra beats that were outside the heart rhythm. He then used ultrasound to perform a more sophisticated test, called an echo-cardiogram, from which he discerned an actual heart defect.

"She has mitral valve prolapse," he informed the family. This meant that when one of her heart valves closed, it ballooned inward, toward the chamber of the heart. "I want her to spend the night here in the intensive care unit," he continued, and within an hour the girl was taken upstairs, hooked to an intravenous drip of morphine for her pain, and supplied with extra oxygen through small tubes taped to her nose. Around her were heart-attack and stroke victims, some of them obviously dying. She found the whole experience highly distressing and began to hallucinate from the morphine as she drifted off to sleep.

The next morning, a careful examination of her tests led the doctors to diagnose that her pain was probably due not only to the mitral valve prolapse but to pericarditis, an inflammation of the pericardium, the covering around the heart. She was released on strong anti-inflammatory agents for this, as well as beta blockers to slow her heart rate. The pain in her chest subsided; however, she found it impossible to tolerate the beta blockers—besides affecting the heart, these drugs attach to receptors in the brain, causing drowsiness and mental disorientation.

Her medications were changed, only to bring on new side effects and expand her constellation of symptoms. The new prescriptions were meant to dilate her blood vessels, but this lowered her blood pressure too much, causing her to feel dizzy and nauseated; at times she would faint without warning. She managed to tolerate these side effects, largely because she wanted to stay in school at any cost. Every time she tried to cut back on her medication, even slightly, the original chest pain returned in full force, accompanied by her other symptoms. She came home for summer vacation and horrified her parents by clutching her chest one evening at dinner. She started to hyperventilate so severely that her mother went scurrying to find a paper bag for her to breathe into. Within a few minutes, she felt violent heart palpitations, began to vomit, and eventually passed out. Her parents sat up with her all that night and many nights to come.

Since there was nothing more that her doctors could do, the family cast about for other approaches. They hit upon a news story about Ayurveda, and one July day all three, mother, father, and daughter, came to the Lancaster clinic. I took a very detailed medical history from the girl, looked at her EKGs, and found myself quite surprised.

"Your pain isn't from your heart," I told her, and to prove it I pressed firmly on her sternum, the bone in the middle of the chest that covers the heart. She flinched. "You're still tender because what you originally had was an inflammation there, where the rib cartilage and the sternum meet. It is a condition called costo-chondritis, which can sometimes set in after a cold or other viral infection."

She and her parents looked startled, but I went on, taking apart the puzzle piece by piece. On the night they had rushed her to the ER, her high anxiety caused her to exhibit the occasional ectopic, or extra, heartbeats. Her main diagnosis, mitral valve prolapse, may occur in as many as 10 percent of young women with slender builds like hers. The reason for this is not known, nor is there conclusive evidence for why it should cause any pain, although in some patients it does. Similarly, the heart murmur that comes with it does not seem to be dangerous. Her pericarditis was a misreading of her EKG—the violence of her attack had probably made the ER doctor overanxious to find something wrong. The remaining symptoms—

nausea, vomiting, heart palpitations, dizziness, fainting, shortness of breath, and hyperventilation—were brought on either by the medications or directly by her.

"I have tried to go back to the moment when your condition was born," I said, "to show you how it built itself up, step by step. In its present form, your disease is a reflex. It is being kept alive by your own expectations."

At this point the girl's parents looked quite offended. I knew the anxiety they felt sitting up all night, worrying that she might be in real danger. To make the parents see that I wasn't blaming anybody, I told them about my experience on the airplane when the No Smoking sign set my heart going. Add a little more fear to the situation, and my pounding heart could have been the start of a "heart condition" just as convincing as their daughter's.

They were still uneasy. When their daughter suffered stabbing chest pains, they thought of her as a victim of illness; now I seemed to say that she was doing it to herself. The era of mind-body medicine has made this an extremely sore point. Life was simpler when a disease without a germ was considered "all in your head." The germs have largely been pushed back, but instead of leaving us free of disease, this has made disease far more enigmatic. Am I waiting for cancer to strike me, or is my personality giving it to me? This girl's case is a perfect example; A cardiologist might point to her heart defect as the cause of her pain; a psychiatrist could say that the defect didn't do anything—the girl simply panicked. The drugs she took induced vomiting, but she still vomits when they are removed. Her low blood pressure can cause fainting, but so can anxiety. Modern medicine has swung back and forth debating these points endlessly.

The result, according to patient surveys, is a huge increase in guilt. There is such a fine line between probing a patient's fears and fueling them. I have sat for hours counseling people with cancer. They listen attentively because "the doctor is talking." I tell them they can beat the cancer, and they quickly, anxiously agree. But when I am alone again, I am haunted by a terrible thought I see lurking in their eyes: "You say I'm sick, but really I did it to myself."

The girl had not spoken for quite a while. "So I'm creating this thing?" she finally said.

"No," I replied, "but you are certainly participating in it. Try taking away your participation—I bet things will change."

"How do I do that?" she asked.

"You have to break out of your own conditioning," I said. "The next time you have an attack, just stand back from it a little; let the pain be there, as innocently as you can." If she could do this, I told her, the whole thing would probably evaporate.

She listened and thanked me, then I heard nothing more for two weeks. Perhaps I had touched too many nerves. I had been making her disease more and more personal, when what the family desperately hoped for was that it was impersonal. Conventional medicine goes out of its way to put diseases into neat, classifiable boxes just so that the personal element is eliminated. I had noticed while interviewing her that this girl placed a huge importance on her diagnosis. She would preface each episode by saying, "When I get my mitral valve prolapse . . ." It was as if these words explained everything. They were like a net that drew together all her symptoms and held them tight. When I mentioned this, she looked very thoughtful. She had invested so much in the words *mitral valve prolapse* that they had acquired a kind of magic for her. It was essential to break the spell of this magic, which can be uncannily powerful.

I was wrong if I thought she hadn't taken our session to heart. Out of curiosity I phoned the family to see how she was doing. The news was very good: she was off all medications and her attacks were now limited to occasional bouts of chest pain. Her parents would sometimes see her sitting with her eyes closed. When they asked what she was doing, she said, "I just watch the pain until it goes away." The accompanying symptoms—dizziness, vomiting, fainting, et cetera—have disappeared.

In psychology there are certain extreme feelings—such as loathing, dread, horror, and awe—that many people cannot face. When these people grow horrified or struck with awe, they could swear that their emotion comes from outside themselves. In cases of paranoia, the person might even think that "they" are broadcasting such feelings into him through some kind of magic. ("They" can be Martians, communists, or next-door neighbors.) Freud called these our "uncanny" emotions and spent many years observing them in neurotic and psychotic patients.

But uncanniness is always present, I think. It is nature's way of putting a veil over our most secret fears; it hides inner pain from us until the moment when the pain breaks an invisible dam and comes pouring out. Then the twin thought arises, "Is this happening to me, or am I doing it to myself?" It doesn't really matter if the end result is a disease or just a sense of extreme discomfort. The important thing is to keep the patient from getting twisted up in his doubts—that way lies total paralysis.

Medicine has already paid a very high price for not dealing adequately with the personal nature of disease. For one thing, we have aroused guilt without being able to assuage it. People are horrified at the idea that they are to blame for their diseases. Doctors don't think they are stoking this guilt. Perhaps it was born out of being told over and over that no one is to blame. But if you say that living right will help prevent a heart attack or cancer, don't you have to accept that living wrong will help bring on the same diseases?

The whole issue of blame and responsibility is painful to untangle. When I had my private practice in endocrinology, I would see obese patients whose weight put them at high risk for becoming diabetic. I would warn them about the danger of continuing to eat too much; at the same time, I knew I was feeding their guilt, which would only lead to more eating. If a patient was a chain-smoker, I would be very firm and say, "My God, you know you have to quit smoking—think of the risks you are running." Many of these pa-

tients were ex-servicemen I saw at the V.A. hospital in Boston. After
listening to me, they could go to the PX upstairs, where government-
subsidized cigarettes were being sold at a steep discount. (I bought
mine there, too, having become a smoker during my night shifts as
an intern.)

In fact, no disease points up the paradoxes of blame and responsibility better than lung cancer. The public is well aware that this is
almost exclusively a smoker's illness. That puts the responsibility
squarely on the patient, but then a second thought enters. Aren't
these people addicted to nicotine? A 1988 report by the surgeon
general states that they are, and that their addiction may be harder
to break than addiction to heroin or alcohol. This means that one is
not dealing with a rational situation.

Sigmund Freud attempted for many years to stop smoking after
being informed by his doctor that twenty cigars a day—Freud's normal ration—was bad for his heart. He stopped once for seven weeks,
but his heart went into palpitations worse than before. He became
intolerably depressed and was forced back to his cigars. When he
didn't smoke, Freud told his biographer, "the torture was beyond
human power to bear." I have witnessed advanced lung cancer patients waiting for radiation who walk around a corner to smoke a
cigarette—this implies that prevention may be impossible, because
it would have to start before the first cigarette gets smoked.

In every disease, not just lung cancer, the patients are often too
hooked, too guilty, or simply too convinced to be helped. There is
no denying the deeply irrational streak in man. At the V.A. hospital
we took in every variety of alcoholic, including the dilapidated, mal-
nourished ones that were routinely swept in off the streets by the
police. One of the most frequent conditions in advanced alcoholism
is pancreatitis, or inflammation of the pancreas. Everyone brought
in with pancreatitis had to be treated with great care. They could
not eat or digest food, because calling on the pancreas only made it
more inflamed and extremely painful. Patients would vomit if they
tried to eat even one bite. We had to feed them by drip through an

IV tube, insert another tube into their stomachs to drain the digestive juices that continued to inflame the pancreas, and inject antibiotics to fight the infection that was often present.

It was all we could do to pull these men back from the brink of death, but when we had succeeded and they were discharged back onto the street, we often saw the same ritual. Looking out the second-floor window, we could see a tavern across the street from the hospital. Our patients walked out the door, barely tottered across the street, and went into the bar. Their first drink came ten minutes after their cure. Compassion for these people has its limits. Anyone could be forgiven for saying, "If you want to smoke and drink, if you don't exercise and insist on eating cholesterol, then too bad for you." Undeniably people do say such things, or at least think them. But the essence of compassion lies in recognizing how hard it is to be good. To forgive someone is to let him be free, even if he abuses that freedom beyond exasperation.

There is a story in India about the sadhu and the scorpion:

A man is walking down the road when he spots a sadhu kneeling beside a ditch. He approaches and sees that the sadhu is watching a scorpion. The scorpion wants to cross the ditch, but when he gets into the muddy water, he begins to drown. The sadhu carefully reaches down to pull him out of the water, but as soon as he touches it, the scorpion stings him. The scorpion goes into the water again, again it begins to drown, and when the sadhu lifts it out, he receives another sting.

The man sees this happen three times. Finally he blurts, "Why don't you stop allowing yourself to be stung?" The sadhu replies, "There is nothing I can do. It is the scorpion's nature to sting, but it is my nature to save."

The reason that society has set up the institution of medicine is to ensure that our instinct to save one another never dies. It is the same instinct that sees no blame in another person's weakness; it freely takes responsibility for troubles that are not its own. If I ever walked into a hospital and detected there that the spark of compassion had gone out, I could write the end of medicine—darkness will have won.

Modern medicine is still dominated by the notion that disease is caused by objective agents. A sophisticated analysis shows that this is only partly true. A disease cannot take hold without a host who accepts it, hence the current attempts to understand our immune system. Historically, both Greek medicine and Ayurveda were founded on the idea that the host is all-important. The Greeks believed that there was a fluid called *physis* that flowed in, out, and through all of life. The flow of physis tied the organs inside the body with the world outside, and as long as the two were in balance, the body would be healthy. (This premise is still reflected in our use of the word *physics* to explain the outer world and the related *physiology* to explain the inner.) In Ayurveda, it takes the balance of three elements, called *doshas,* to maintain health. The point is not whether physis or doshas exist, but that one's own state of balance determines whether one is sick or well.

Medicine is coming back to this notion, the oldest in all the healing arts, but I notice that an impersonal air still hangs over everything. We are setting up a concrete thing called the immune system and pinning our hopes onto it. The original idea, as voiced by the Greeks and by Ayurveda, was much more organic. A patient was not a collection of host cells but someone who ate, drank, thought, and acted. If a doctor wanted to change someone's doshas or his physis, he changed his habits. In this way, he got right to the root of the patient's participation in the world.

There are dozens of medical systems in the world, many of them deeply in conflict with one another. How can they cure people and yet disagree so completely? What is poison to me is cure to a homeopath. I think the answer is that all medicine works by helping a patient live through his disease, moment by moment, until the balance swings away from sickness toward cure. I cannot be more specific, because the process does not happen in books but in living persons. People have drunk grape juice and recovered from cancer. If you can successfully restore balance to the bodymind, then the patient's immune system will respond. The immune cells do not judge whether the doctor believes in conventional medicine, home- opathy, or Ayurveda. Insofar as it can change our participation in disease, every system is capable of working. I think Ayurveda will rise to prominence, however, because it recognizes the need to cure patients by curing their reality first.

More and more I feel the importance of the patient's personal reality. A middle-aged doctor, a radiologist, came to see me after he was diagnosed with leukemia. He was extremely sophisticated in his knowledge of the disease, an unpredictable form called chronic my- elogenous leukemia, meaning that it affected the white blood cells called myelocytes. As yet he felt nothing beyond some fatigue dur- ing the day, but the mortality statistics, which he also knew well, were grim. They said that the average survival was thirty-six to forty- four months. On the other hand, because the disease is unpredict- able, he could live much longer.

Before coming to me, he had consulted the leading cancer insti- tute in New York City. They had made extensive tests on his blood and offered him a choice of half a dozen experimental drug proto- cols. No single accepted treatment for his leukemia exists; none of the experimental ones came with any promises that his life expec- tancy would be lengthened.

Upon reflection, he had rejected treatment and began to read up voraciously on spontaneous remissions, including something I had written. He had sought me out for that reason. As we talked, I saw that one particular detail was a huge stumbling block for him.

"I want to believe I will recover from this," he told me, "but something really worries me. I read about a lot of remissions from cancer, but I didn't run across any spontaneous remissions from leu- kemia."

One could see how his medical mind was working. The variety

of leukemia he has is linked to a genetic component, called the Philadelphia chromosome. He had tested positive for this chromosome, and being a physician, that was the end of the story—he was genetically marked for doom. The only chance for Ayurveda would be if it promoted a miracle. But he couldn't find any reports of leukemia miracles in the journals.

"Look," I said, "you are obsessed with the statistics on this disease. Don't think about them—what you want to do is beat the statistics, don't you?"

"I know, I know," he said abstractedly, "but I can't find a single spontaneous remission in the whole literature. I could be the first, of course, but . . ." His voice trailed off.

I had a brainstorm. "Why don't you tell yourself you have some other cancer," I suggested. "Then at least you would have hope for a remission."

His face brightened, and he leaped at my suggestion. Then I had more good news for him. I had just stumbled across a review article that connected childhood leukemia and stress. This man had a totally different disease, but he also led an incredibly stressful life. His wife was divorcing him, his medical partners had filed a lawsuit against him, his children, now grown, did not speak to him anymore, and he had to support two houses and three Mercedeses. It was in the midst of his rancorous divorce that his diagnosis had been made, quite by accident, and now his wife insisted on staying with him. The reason she gave was her fear of being left alone after he died.

"I just read that stress is linked to childhood leukemia," I offered. He beamed when he heard this, because the scientist in him made a causal link between stress, the activation of "stress hormones" like cortisol, and finally a suppression of the immune system. Maybe that was happening to him. No one had actually shown a link between stress and his disease, but now he had one more straw to grasp.

He went away and continued to do well. The next time he came in, he asked me if he should go for a blood test. Leukemia causes a disastrous elevation in the number of white blood cells; a lower count would prove to him that he was really getting better.

"If the counts are bad," I reasoned, "then you will get depressed and put more stress on yourself. If they are good, then you will be getting better anyway. Why not postpone the blood test until you feel some symptoms?" He agreed to this and went away again.

The last time I saw him was last week. He told me that believing he has cancer instead of leukemia was working out well.

"You know," I said, "why bother to call it cancer? You could tell yourself that you have a chronic disease that has no name. If it doesn't have a name, then you won't have to worry about any statistics. People live a long time with mysterious diseases."

This final twist absolutely delighted him. With tremendous relief he shook my hand, and for the first time he agreed to come to the clinic to start Ayurveda. So far, I have done nothing for this man except change the label on his disease, but from that he changed his whole appraisal. Now we have a chance to witness the birth of a cure.

EXPANDING THE TOPIC

It was hard enough thirty years ago to float the proposition that every disease is personal. In medical school, doctors learn about the natural history of diseases, the course an illness normally takes in the average patient. (As the hoary medical student joke goes, "It takes seven days to get over a cold, but if you really take care of yourself, you'll get over it in a week." Imbedded in the punch line is the certainty that hard medical facts come first; personal differences come second and are largely a nuisance, because they skew the statistical sample.)

Now there's a new proposition to float that's even harder for doctors to swallow: All disease is personal. In fact, it has to be. This isn't blatant overconfidence on my part. The reason that all disease is personal is that reality is personal, and being sick or well is part of reality. The fact that a cold virus interacts with your immune system on a schedule that matches your neighbor when he has a cold is just a rough approximation. Some colds linger for a month. Viruses constantly mutate, and when they do, your immune system responds in kind—it learns what the virus has to teach.

Quantum Healing was written before the microbiome was explored, but I felt confident in saying that a bacterium or virus traveling around the world is the play of DNA talking to itself. DNA is sending messages constantly that pass in, out, around, and through the body. With present-day knowledge, we know that the microbiome isn't a camp of squatters who have parked themselves in our bodies. These microbes *are* the message, and it's constantly in flux. In 2014 a team headed by Dr. Patrick Schloss at the University of Michigan analyzed microbes gathered from three hundred people, in eighteen areas of their bodies. It was found that these microbes varied greatly. They changed, sometimes radically, for no known reason. There could be total population shifts in the course of a single day. In a sense the microbiome is the only bodily organ that can be replaced without surgery; in another sense it is a portable ecology, duplicating Earth's ecology microscopically. Every atom in your body came from soil, air, and water. Your microbiome retains the memory of this.

Even with the present imperfect understanding, everyone concedes that the trillions of microorganisms that interface with the outside world are major players in how life evolved and keeps evolving. No one has to catch a cold to participate in the self-interaction of life with life. In computer science (and rightly or wrongly), the brain itself is just an information processor. So when you catch a cold—or interact with any microorganism—you and the world are thinking as one.

What's your conversation like? You'll never hear a cold virus talking to you, but the exchange of messages isn't mysterious; it's just very, very complicated. I'm constantly astonished at how much meaning is contained in catching a cold. To let you in on this astonishment, I'd like to use a cold as the template for your entire life. So many file headings are needed just for this one experience.

Biology: The newly mutated cold virus is a new biological creation.

Environment: The new strain of cold was born at a certain place and time somewhere in the world.

Relationships: The virus's genes demand an interaction with your genome. In return, your genetic material has something to say about that.

Society: The cold hits a lot of people at nearly the same time, creating social implications, like a rise in sick days from work.

Core beliefs: When you catch a cold, your reaction to it depends on how tough or fragile you think you are, how dangerous or innocuous it is to get sick, and other personal beliefs.

Desires: Catching a cold affects what you wanted to do that week if you hadn't gotten sick. You may have to put some desires on hold, such as going on a vacation.

Memories: In your immune system, the virus awakens the memory of colds you've had in the past. Antibodies are released coded by these past illnesses.

Psychological conditioning: You have personal memories of catching a cold over the years, and your reaction this time is likely to be almost identical to your reaction last winter.

Microbiome: The new arrival in the virus family interacts with the massive colony of microorganisms that are already present in and on our body.

Gene expression: Depending on everything listed above, genes in your brain, immune system, and various organs respond to all the changes occurring or threatening to occur.

It's a little exhausting to contemplate this list, but that doesn't mean that the possible implications of catching a cold have been exhausted. For that, you'd have to interview trillions of cells, each of which has its own story. Yet if we back away to a larger perspective, the point is simple: All disease is personal because reality is personal. No one, not even identical twins who begin life with the same genetic scorecard, inhabits a reality that's the same as another person's. How could they? The messages delivered by the common cold are like one grain of sand on the beach, and the tide never stops coming in, depositing new grains of information.

Colds take care of themselves, but what about cancer, heart disease, diabetes, and other severe disorders? They are influenced by everything on the list, too, and it seems utterly blind to ignore them. A materialist can't duck out of the argument by reverting to medical school textbooks. A liver enzyme may be a fact, but so are the receptors on the outer membrane of a liver cell, and these are responsive to every single influence I've listed. There's no such thing as being halfway in the game; your total being is committed to participating.

How you see yourself is perhaps the most important influence on your state of wellbeing, or its absence. Life on this planet goes back about 3.5 billion years, and your body retains all the evolutionary knowledge accumulated over the eons. So you can justifiably see yourself as all life, which means that every interaction with the world is actually an interaction with yourself. What then? "Who am I?" becomes a very different question.

In *Quantum Healing* I offered a better way to manage personal reality. As much as I delighted in discovering countless new facts, simplicity held the key. (I recall a guru saying there are a thousand reasons to pick a pin up off the floor and a thousand reasons not to—no one can live like that.) At some point you simply have to accept the reality of cosmic intelligence and surrender to it.

Surrender connotes defeat to some people, who therefore hate the idea. It connotes drifting through life carelessly to other people, who therefore love the idea. But when it comes to managing your personal reality, surrender involves specific choices, and each must be tested to find out if it's viable.

1. You relax and relinquish the desire to control.
2. You trust that you are cherished in creation, and you act on this trust.
3. You accept your own being as a source of infinite intelligence.
4. You approach every problem as having a level of solution that can be found.
5. You focus on personal growth, which is eternal, and minimize personal setbacks, which are temporary.
6. You ask for and receive support from Nature.
7. You resist the endless demands and unceasing insecurity of the ego.

That's the agenda, not just for the spiritually inclined or the mystically gifted, but for anyone who grasps how personal reality really is. A supreme intelligence is responsible for creating order out of chaos, shaping every waking moment into "my" life. The paradox is that if you really want reality to be entirely yours, a unique creation, you must offer it up as a gift from the cosmos.

12

"WHAT YOU SEE,
YOU BECOME"

When pressed for the ultimate truth, the Vedic seers uttered two words that overturn all our accepted notions of reality: *Aham Brahmasmi*. A free translation would be, "I am everything, created and uncreated," or more succinctly, "I am the universe."° To be everything, or even something beyond the confines of one's physical body, sounds very strange to the Western ear. A story is told about an English lady traveling through northern India who was taken to the caves along the Ganges where yogis sat in deep meditation. She was pleasantly received by one yogi outside his cave. At the end of the visit, she said, "Perhaps you don't leave here very often, but I would be happy to show you around London."

"Madam," the yogi calmly replied, "I *am* London."

In their teaching stories, the rishis also showed a talent for beguiling the intellect. One of the most famous concerns a youth

---

° The Sanskrit literally says, "I am Brahman." Brahman is an all-inclusive term and therefore untranslatable; it signifies all things in creation—physical, mental, and spiritual—as well as their uncreated source.

named Svetaketu, who was sent away from home to study the Veda. In ancient India, this entailed staying with the priests and memorizing long stretches of sacred text. Svetaketu stays away for twelve years. When he at last comes home, he is very puffed up with his own learning, and his father, half-dismayed and half-amused, decides to deflate him. Here is an excerpt from the dialogue that ensues:

"Go and pick a fruit from that banyan tree," Svetaketu's father said.

"Here it is, sir."

"Split it open and tell me what you see inside."

"Many tiny seeds, sir."

"Take one of them and split it open and tell me what you see inside."

"Nothing at all, sir."

Then his father said, "The subtlest essence of this fruit appears as nothing to you, my son, but believe me, from that nothing, this mighty banyan tree has sprung.

"That Being, which is the subtlest essence of everything, the supreme reality, the Self of all that exists, That art thou, Svetaketu."

This is quite a quantum story, actually. The universe, like the huge banyan, springs from a seed that contains nothing. Without a metaphor like the seed and the tree, our minds cannot even grasp what such a nothingness is, since it is smaller than small and earlier than the Big Bang. The deeper mystery of the tale is that Svetaketu himself is composed of this same all-pervading, unimaginable essence. To find out what Svetaketu's father means, one has to explore the expanded sense of awareness that is central to the rishis' knowledge.

"I am everything" implies an ability to transcend the normal flow of time and the normal confines of space. Despite his intuitive brilliance, Einstein did not step outside the river of time, except mentally. He said that he had experiences of self-expansion in which there was "neither evolution nor destiny, only Being," but such episodes did not enter his scientific work directly. Like all physicists, he adhered to the objective method and scrupulously excluded his own consciousness from his theories. His search for a unified field that would embrace all of time and space was a strictly mathematical enterprise.

To the rishis, this is the very attitude that makes physics incomplete. We are not onlookers peering into the unified field, they said—we *are* the unified field. Every person is an infinite being, unlimited by time and space. To reach beyond the physical body, we extend the influence of intelligence. As you sit in your chair, every thought you are thinking creates a wave in the unified field. It ripples through all the layers of ego, intellect, mind, senses, and matter, spreading out in wider and wider circles. You are like a light radiating not photons but consciousness.

As they radiate, your thoughts have an effect on everything in nature. Physics already recognizes this fact for sources of physical energy: any light, whether a star or a candle, sends its waves throughout the quantum field of electromagnetism, going as far as infinity in all directions. The rishis took this principle and made it human. Their nervous systems actually registered the distant effect that a thought produces; this was as real for them as seeing light is for us. But we are bounded in our awareness; being confined to the waking state keeps us from perceiving the subtle changes we are producing everywhere.

Yet these changes are always present. For thousands of years, the rishis declared that man lives, breathes, and moves in the cosmic body. If this is so, then nature is as alive as we are; the whole distinction between "in here" and "out there" is a false one, as if the heart cells disregarded the skin cells because they were not on the inside.

Knowing this, the rishis became extremely powerful individuals, but not in the ordinary sense. Where most men are interested in material power, the rishis were interested in the power of awareness. To them, the material level of the world was quite crude. The real power in nature lies closer to the source, and the ultimate power must lie right at the source.

Favoring mind over matter is not a mystical notion. If you want to build a skyscraper today, you don't start by piling up concrete and steel; you go to an architect, whose intellect prepares the plan that must exist before construction begins. His plan contains more of the power to build a building than is contained in the labor. Certain fields, such as music, mathematics, and quantum physics, can make almost no progress without geniuses who work deep in silence— Einstein's preferred method of investigation was not to work in a lab but to perform thought experiments in his head. He was in the habit of doing this long before he achieved any degree of fame and position. He was placing clocks around the universe, he once recalled, before he could afford to buy a real one for his house.

To the rishis, it would seem peculiar that we portion out our intelligence into so many small, isolated fields of knowledge. Our social conditioning forbids the cosmic perspective, not by condemning it but by providing so much distracting busy-work. If you are caught up in bricks and mortar, it is difficult to learn architecture. A field like medicine is now so incredibly complicated that if you say, "This patient can be treated through the flow of intelligence," sheer momentum would be against you as much as disbelief.

The unbounded state is not frequently seen in our society, while its opposite is absolutely epidemic. Psychiatrists see patients every day who are crippled by boundaries, people who have programmed guilt, anxiety, and unnameable insecurities into themselves. Those who have acquired phobias are extreme examples of this, since their deadly fear is out of all proportion to any actual danger. If you take an agoraphobe—someone who fears open spaces—out for a drive, he will show intense anxiety. If you stop in an open field and ask him to step out of the car, he will be as paralyzed as a normal person who is asked to jump off a cliff. Try to force him and he will struggle for his life, literally.

The keenest anguish of a phobic is knowing that he has created his own condition, but his will is not enough to break the pattern he has programmed into his physiology. (One agoraphobe in England grew so miserable and ashamed of his phobia that he decided to end his life. The method he chose was to drive two miles in his car, an action he was sure would be lethal! When this failed, he felt terrified at first, but then he discovered that his phobia had lessened. He had accidentally hit upon the therapy called "flooding," which psychiatrists sometimes use to wrench far-gone phobics out of unreality.)

Boundaries created in silence are the most confining. People who have never heard of Veda generally know the word *Maya,* or illusion—in Sanskrit, it literally means "that which is not." Maya is greatly misunderstood—the rishis did not call the world Maya to say that it does not exist, like some mirage. Maya is the illusion of boundaries, the creation of a mind that has lost the cosmic perspective. It comes from seeing a million things "out there" and missing one thing, the invisible field that is the origin of the universe. Reading the great rishis, it is no wonder that they considered Maya a poor substitute for the cosmic perspective. The Yoga Vasishtha said, "In the infinite consciousness, in every atom of it, universes come and go, like particles of dust in a beam of sunlight shining through a hole in the roof."

Quantum reality leaps from Vasishtha's pages, because he found the perspective which showed him, "In every atom, there are worlds within worlds." Demolishing one's own boundaries does not make the relative world vanish; it adds another dimension of reality to it— reality becomes unbounded. When the walls are down, the world can expand. And that, according to the rishis, makes all the difference between a world that could be a heaven and one that becomes a hell.

The mechanism behind phobias can be used in exactly the opposite way, to take down a wall rather than build one. We could just as easily, and far more happily, talk about people who overcome fears that are supposed to be normal. The construction workers on skyscrapers used to include a large proportion of Mohawk Indians, who were raised without a fear of heights. The same courage can be gradually built into oneself by practice—for example, by walking a tightrope.

Such flexibility is not limited to psychological states. Nutritionists have abundant scientific evidence to show that the body must be given certain vitamins and minerals every day in order not to fall prey to deficiency diseases—the classic instance is scurvy, which afflicted the British navy when sailors were fed solely on hardtack biscuits and grog and deprived of the vitamin C in fruits and vegetables.

Nonetheless, native cultures around the world have existed for centuries without rigorous daily vitamin requirements and have adapted perfectly well. The Tarahumara Indians of northern Sonora in Mexico have become famous in physiological circles because they can run twenty-five to fifty miles a day in high altitudes without discomfort. Whole tribes run these marathons every week; when the winner of one race was tested two minutes after crossing the finish line, an American physiologist discovered that his heart rate was slower than when he began.

What amplifies this inexplicable feat is that the Tarahumara typically live on two hundred pounds of corn a year for the average family, half of which is made into corn beer. Other sources of nutrition, such as root vegetables, become available in small quantities during the limited growing season. By being able to thrive on an absurdly substandard diet, these people show the nearly infinite flexibility of the mind-body system. Ironically, their adaptation is so perfect that when placed on a "balanced" diet fortified with vitamins and minerals, many native people develop heart disease, hypertension, skin disorders, and rotten teeth, none of which they had before, in epidemic proportions.

Obviously, these examples throw down a challenge to our whole conception of what is normal. We have ample evidence in our own culture that what is most normal about us is our ability to create our own reality. As Sir John Eccles told the parapsychologists, it is incomprehensible that our thoughts can move molecules, and yet we live quite comfortably with this impossibility all the time. The rishis simply extend our comfort zone all the way, into the normality of the infinite.

We already know that if an impulse of intelligence wants to do something, then it does it, using intellect, mind, senses, and matter to find its outlet. Intelligence can create a physiology where healing thoughts take place, but it can also create the reverse. If we were "hard-wired" like a computer, then every physiology would be predictable; in reality, no physiology is. Intelligence creates new circuitry at will, and this makes each person unique. Every experience in life changes the brain's anatomy. The new dendrites created in the brain cells of active old people are just one instance.

Even more extraordinary is the following experiment: Dr. Herbert Spector of the National Institutes of Health took a group of mice and gave them poly-I:C, a chemical known to stimulate the activity of natural killer T-cells in the immune system and thus strengthen the animal's defense against disease. Every time a mouse received his dose of poly-I:C, the smell of camphor was released in the vicinity at the same time.

For a few weeks the pattern continued, injecting the chemical and releasing the camphor smell. When the chemical was taken away, Spector exposed the mice to only the camphor, and he found that their immune-cell count again increased, even without the chemical. In other words, the smell alone made them stronger against disease. Could he have done the reverse and lowered their immunity with a smell?

A team at the University of Rochester later showed that this is possible. They took a group of rats and fed them cyclophosphamide, a chemical known to diminish the efficiency of the immune response. At the same time, the rats were given saccharine-sweetened water, which substituted for camphor as the neutral agent. When the drug was withdrawn, the animals still dropped their immune-cell count just by tasting the water. What excited the researchers at the time was the realization that the immune system has learning ability. It directly responds to outside stimuli, not just to the internal environment of the bloodstream.

In a larger sense, however, these experiments tell us that the body is not tied to predictable responses. The intelligence of a cell is creative. The predictable mechanism that responds positively to poly-I:C and negatively to cyclophosphamide can transform itself and respond to anything. Moreover, it can turn around and respond with opposite results—the smell of camphor could have been associated with either drug.

There is no fixed connection, then, between what kind of experience you put into the body and the result that comes out—your nervous system is set up for unboundedness. The more we dwell on this, the more remarkable the implications are. The smell of camphor did not do anything to cause the change in immune cells: the mice could have smelled roses or listened to a Mozart quartet. What actually happened inside them was the creation of an impulse of intelligence, a totally fluid entity that coordinates a piece of the non-material world with a piece of the material world. The ancient rishis understood this very well. A verse from the Veda says, "What you see, you become." In other words, just the experience of perceiving the world makes you what you are. This is a quite literal statement. Children growing up in homes where there is inadequate love can show a variety of symptoms—they may be unhappy, neurotic, schizophrenic, sickly, angry, or any number of other responses. But one of the strangest is a condition called psychosocial dwarfism. Such children do not grow up; they induce in themselves a deficiency of growth hormone from the pituitary, and as a result, they remain small and undeveloped in their physiques.

Ignoring the biological clock, the onset of puberty can be delayed; so can the acquisition of mental skills associated with older children, which is not directly controlled by the pituitary. It is not a dysfunction of the pituitary that is at fault, for when these children

are placed in loving surroundings, their condition can spontaneously reverse, and they quickly catch up with their peers in size.

Growing up is a built-in, genetically programmed outcome of
being born—yet these children defy it simply because they feel unloved. Even if a doctor injects them with growth hormone, many
refuse to grow. A study with adult male victims of heart attacks
showed that the most significant factor in their recovery—meaning
whether they lived or died—was not anything to do with diet, exercise, smoking, or a will to live. The men who lived felt that their
wives loved them, while those who felt unloved tended not to survive; no other correlation the researchers could find was as strong.

For years I have been haunted by the memory of one of my first
patients, an Indian villager named Laxman Govindass. I was still a
medical student in New Delhi, confined to the drudgery of working
up physicals on the patients whom the hospital staff doctors were
too busy to see. The hospital in question was a teaching hospital attached to my school, the All-India Medical Institute, and the aca-
demic doctors there had scant interest in a broken-down alcoholic
like Laxman Govindass.

He was a peasant farmer whose drinking had gotten out of hand
to the point where his family deserted him. One son had bundled
him off to the door of our hospital and left him there with the words,
"Here's where you will probably die." Like all villagers consigned to
us, Mr. Govindass was very apprehensive and totally out of his element. The interns took good enough care of his cirrhosis of the liver,
but without spending any time to become acquainted with him personally. I got to know him only because as a student I had most of
the day free; I made a habit of following the orderly who brought
around the evening curry so that I could chat with the patients.

I struck up a rapport with Mr. Govindass, sitting by his bed and
exchanging an occasional word; mostly we just looked out the window together. Day by day he wasted away a little more, and nobody
gave him longer than a week or two at most, including me. In a short

while it was time for me to rotate from the city to a village dispensary sixty miles away, so I came in to wish him good-bye. To keep up a good front, I told him that I would be back to see him in thirty days.

In reply, he looked at me very seriously and said, "Now that you are leaving, I have nothing more to live for—I will die." Without thinking, I blurted, "Don't be silly. You can't die until I come back to see you again." Since Mr. Govindass was extremely emaciated—he weighed less than eighty pounds—his doctors were surprised that he was even alive.

I left for my posting in the country and in a little while had no more thoughts about him. A month later, on my return to New Delhi, I was walking down the hospital corridor and saw the name Laxman Govindass on one of the doors. I rushed in, feeling strangely apprehensive, and there he was, curled on his bed outside the sheets in a fetal position. There was nothing left of him but skin and bones, but when I gently touched him, he turned his huge eyes toward me. "You have come back," he muttered. "You said I could not die without seeing you again—now I see you." Then he closed his eyes and died.

I recounted this incident, one of the most important in my life, once before; at that time, I felt two emotions—a lingering guilt that I had sentenced this man to so much protracted suffering and a deep respect for the mind-body connection that had kept him alive. Now I realize that I was seeing the truth of unboundedness, the ability of our impulses of intelligence to do what they want, despite all the rules that might have to be broken. The impulse that I shared with Laxman Govindass was love. Though it arose in a wasted body, his love had the power that love always has—it gave new life. It pierced through the Maya of his body and defied death to claim him. On the delicacy of that impulse, a gossamer thread as strong as steel, a new medicine could be founded.

The possibility that each person is an infinite being is becoming more real now. Gifted with total flexibility in our nervous systems, we all have the choice to build boundaries or tear them down. Every person is continually manufacturing an infinite array of thoughts, memories, desires, objects, and so on. These impulses, rippling through the ocean of consciousness, become your reality. If you knew how to control the creation of impulses of intelligence, you would be able not only to grow new dendrites but anything else.

"What you see, you become" is a truth that shapes the whole physiology, including the brain. This was brought home by an ingenious experiment devised by psychologists Joseph Hubel and David Weisel, again involving newborn kittens. Three batches of kittens were placed in carefully controlled environments as they were opening their eyes. The first was a white box painted with horizontal black stripes; the second was a white box painted with vertical black stripes; the third box was simply left white.

After being exposed to these conditions during the critical few days when sight develops, the kittens' brains conformed to them for life. The animals raised in a world with horizontal stripes could not correctly see anything vertical—they would run into chair legs, whose verticality had little or no reality for them. The batch from the vertical-stripe box had exactly the opposite problem, being unable to perceive horizontal lines. The kittens from all-white surroundings had a larger disorientation and could not relate to any objects correctly.

These animals became what they saw, because the neurons responsible for sight were now rigidly programmed. In the case of humans, too, the brain sacrifices some of its unbounded awareness every time it perceives the world through boundaries. Without the ability to transcend, this partial blindness is inescapable. For each of the senses, not just sight, impressions are constantly being laid down on our neurons. Although we customarily call the heavier impressions "stress," in fact all impressions create some limitation.

To illustrate: researchers at M.I.T. in the early 1980s were probing into how human hearing works. Hearing appears to be passive, but actually every person listens to the world quite selectively and puts his own interpretation on the raw data that come into his ears. (A trained musician hears pitch and harmony, for instance, where someone who is tone-deaf hears noise.) One experiment involved having people listen to short, simple rhythms (1-2-3 and 1-2-3 and 1-2-3), then training them to hear the rhythm in a different way (1, 2, 3-and-1, 2, 3-and-1, 2). After they started to hear the rhythms differently, the subjects reported that the sounds seemed livelier and fresher. Clearly, the experiment had taught people to slightly alter their invisible boundaries. However, the really interesting result was that when they went home, these people found that colors looked brighter, music sounded happier, the taste of food was suddenly more delicious, and everyone around them appeared lovable.

Just the slightest opening of awareness caused a reality shift. Meditation, because it opens more channels of awareness and opens them to a deeper level, causes a bigger shift. The change does not depart far from the normal way we use our awareness. Building boundaries will still be a fact of life. The twist the rishis gave was to infuse this activity with freedom, raising it to a level that transcends the petty thoughts and desires of the isolated ego. Ordinarily, the ego has no choice but to spend life desperately erecting one boundary after another. It does this for the same reason as medieval cities erected walls—for protection.

The ego finds the world a dangerous, hostile place, because everything that exists is separate from "I." This is the condition known as duality, and it is a great source of fear—the Veda calls it the only source of fear. As we look "out there," we see every kind of potential threat, all the trauma and pain that life can inflict. The ego's logical defense is to wall itself in with the friendlier things—family, pleasures, happy memories, familiar places and activities. The rishis did not propose tearing down these defensive boundaries, although many people believe that was their intention. In both East and West, the idea that Indian sages condemned the "illusion of life" has taken root, and yet, Vedic reality was not based on such an absurdity.

Duality does exist, and because of its existence the recognition of a higher unity is made meaningful. Two polar opposites fuse into a whole—this principle puts the silent and active fields of life into proper perspective. When the rishis found unity, the silent field of intelligence, they found the other pole that makes life complete. The ancient texts explain this as *Purnam adah, purnam idam*—"This is full, that is full."

The highest goal of existence, then, is to achieve "two hundred percent of life." The human nervous system can accomplish this because it is flexible enough to appreciate both the diversity of life, which is infinite but full of boundaries, and the unified state, which is equally infinite, but completely unbounded. Just from a logical standpoint, no other possibility could exist. No one was given a cosmic computer and told, "Remember, you can use only half of it." No one gave us any limitations on the patterns of intelligence we can make, change, blend, expand, and inhabit. Life is a field of unlimited possibilities. Such is the glory of total flexibility in the human nervous system.

This is a tremendously important point. It says that we can bypass the limited, bounded choices that we are used to making and go directly to the solution of any problem. The basis for this assertion is that nature has already structured the solution in our consciousness. The problems are in the field of diversity, while the solutions are in the field of unity. Going straight to the field of unity automatically hits upon the solution, which the mind-body system then carries out—that was the rishis' shortcut.

Robert Keith Wallace's studies on aging are an excellent example of how the shortcut works. The current scientific wisdom holds that aging is a complicated, poorly understood area. Gerontology, the study of old age, has become a specialization only since the 1950s, when the mapping of DNA made it possible to consider that there might be special genes for aging (none have appeared so far, although certain aging mechanisms are known to be genetically coded in lower animals). Now that gerontology is in high gear, it is swamped with conflicting theories and huge data banks amassed from research projects that will take decades to finish.

This intensive research effort has not made people age more slowly. The major advance in the field has been to document that healthy people do not have to deteriorate automatically as they grow older, a point that has been made for centuries without data banks. Gerontology has had some valuable medical applications, such as the recognition that many senile symptoms once thought permanent are reversible. They are not signs of brain decay but the by-product of poor nutrition, isolation, dehydration, and other factors in the person's environment. Otherwise, gerontology proceeds bit by bit, forging tiny links in theories that are conjectural to begin with. As for getting the American people to eat better, exercise sensibly, and practice disease prevention, the whole field is in agreement with the rest of medicine.

Wallace's research, however, proceeded on the assumption that people do not age by bits and pieces but as whole human beings. Therefore, aging contains a large element of choice. If old people can retain their mental faculties by continually using them, then the practice of meditation, which opens the awareness completely, should do even more. Wallace's basic finding, as mentioned earlier, was that long-term meditators did decrease their biological age by five to twelve years. (High levels of a little-understood hormone called DHEA [dehydroepiandrosterone] were also found; it has been speculated that DHEA somehow helps to retard aging and perhaps inhibit the onset and growth of cancer.)

This research suggests that aging is controlled by consciousness. Operating at the usual level of superficial, confused thinking, we speed up the aging process in our cells, but as we move to the silent region of the transcendent, mental activity stops, and apparently cell activity follows accordingly. If this is true, then aging can be programmed from different levels of awareness. If we program ourselves to deteriorate, which was the rule in earlier generations, then that becomes the reality. Programming of this kind is not a matter of simply thinking or believing. Positive attitudes, mental alertness, the will to survive, and other psychological traits can ease old age; they certainly help crack the rigid social conditioning that old people are often trapped by. But actually changing the aging process itself is another, far deeper matter.

Officially, gerontology recognizes no means to reverse or retard the aging process—a rather stringent position, when you consider that aging has not even been adequately defined. The rishis would counter by saying that science has failed to reach the level of awareness where aging can be defeated. In 1980, a young Harvard psychologist, Charles Alexander, went into three old-age homes outside Boston and taught about sixty residents, all at least 80 years old, some mind-body techniques. Three were used: a mainstream relaxation technique (the kind used in typical stress-management programs), Transcendental Meditation, and a set of creative word games performed every day to keep the mind sharp.

Each person learned only one technique, and the groups were allowed to use them without supervision. When the three groups were tested on follow-up, the meditators scored highest on measures of improved learning ability, low blood pressure, and mental health—all of which should decline with age. The people also reported that they felt happier and not as old as before. But the really striking result did not come to light until three years later. When Alexander returned to the old-age homes, about one-third of the residents had died since he left, including 24 percent of the participants who had not learned meditation. Among the meditative group, however, the death rate was zero.

These people had now lived to an average age of 84, one of the rarest and loveliest instances where science has performed an experiment that immediately conferred the gift of life. Although limited in scope, this is one of the most hopeful results in the whole aging field and a victory for the rishis' shortcut. It says that expanding your awareness is enough to extend your life. What will be the life span of meditators who began in their twenties instead of their eighties? Time will tell.

The assumption that smothers life is to feel that you are a prisoner in your body. The human body seems to work in a mechanical fashion. One of the best studied of its mechanisms is the homeostatic feedback loop, a self-regulating device like that used in thermostats. A thermostat is given a set point, such as 70 degrees F., which is like the set point of body temperature. The apparatus is sensitive to a temperature range extending a few degrees too high or too low. By turning the heat or air conditioning on or off, it maintains a nearly even temperature. The know-how in a thermostat is quite limited; you could call it an intelligent switch, but it has only one idea on its mind, whereas the body's feedback loops manage to balance not just body temperature but blood pressure, water levels in the cells, glucose metabolism, oxygen and carbon dioxide concentrations, and on and on, not leaving out the thousands of separate chemicals produced with exquisite precision everywhere in the physiology.

Since the thermostat always returns to its norm and so does the body, isn't this a kind of hard-wiring that cannot be denied, that in fact is necessary to our existence? The greatest of nineteenth-century physiologists, Claude Bernard, made the famous statement, "Free life is the fixity of our interior milieu"—in other words, the ability of our thermostats to hold their position makes us free. Brilliant as this insight was, a drastic mistake has crept in with it. When a thermostat senses that the room is 65 degrees or 75 instead of 70, those variations are mistakes; only 70 degrees is right. In us, on the other hand, many settings can be right; normal is just the point we return to most of the time. If you ran a marathon without your blood pressure, heart rate, glucose metabolism, and sweat production rising drastically above "normal," you would collapse.

"Normal" is just the zone we like to live in. It is not a rule but a preference. The Tarahumara Indians, perhaps because they descend from ancient runners who carried messages across the Andes to the Incan empire, have adjusted to a "normal" that is different from ours, more suited to their way of life. In defiance of a meager diet, what they wanted to do—to run fifty miles a day—was more important than mere bodily norms. Their bodies adapted to intelligence, no questions asked, and not the other way around. Thanks to the habit of following one style of living, it may be difficult to adapt instantly when the mind desires a change—obese people should not jump from their armchairs to join marathons—but the power of adaptation can never be totally sacrificed. For all our internal "hardwiring" and thousands of homeostatic mechanisms, we can change our skills, forget them, acquire new ones, and so on. That is the ultimate glory of being a human being, and it cannot be attained without total freedom.

The West clearly has mixed feelings about the whole idea of higher consciousness, compounded of longing, bafflement, and distaste. I travel at least two days a week, year round, talking about Ayurveda to many kinds of audiences, both medical and nonmedical, and very quickly I learned how sensitive a chord I was striking. A CBC interviewer in Canada introduced himself to me by demanding, "Can you give me five reasons why you are not a fraud?" A more congenial interviewer in Los Angeles leaned toward me with mystical anticipation and said, "Tell me, Doctor, have you been here—before?" I was so startled I blurted, "We're all here all the time."

Since the 1960s, the proliferation of casual knowledge about the East has been a blessing and a curse, for although many people have picked up a few catch phrases like *nirvana, Atman,* and *dharma,* and almost everyone can let the word *karma* pass by in conversation without blinking an eye, the actual sense of these words has been garbled. I have tried to show that Vedic knowledge is systematic and sound; that it is as far-reaching as our most advanced science; and that many of the things we most desire for ourselves, such as freedom from disease and an unimpaired old age, can be approached through this great body of understanding about human existence.

But I would betray the rishis' knowledge if I did not present its final expansion, which has no clearly defined precedent in the West—or at best is confined to religious doctrine. The rishis were after a state of total awareness. For them, this was not philosophy or religion but a natural form of human awareness. The fourth state, it turns out, is not an end point but a doorway. And what is on the other side? The only complete answer would have to come from the thousands and thousands of pages of Vedic texts, which function as the encyclopedia of experiences the rishis recorded. The simplest answer is to say that what each rishi encountered was the Self. An extremely accurate depiction of meeting the Self was given by a meditator from Connecticut:

> One of the most regular experiences in my meditation is of expanded awareness, of no longer being confined to the inside of my head, but being as infinite or more infinite than the universe. Sometimes I feel the boundaries of the mind being pushed out, like the ever-widening circumference of a circle, until the circle disappears and only infinity remains.
>
> It is a feeling of great freedom, but also one of naturalness, far more real and natural than being confined to such a small space. Sometimes the sense of infinity is so strong that I lose the sensation of body or matter—just infinite, unbounded awareness, an eternal, never-changing continuum of consciousness.

Everyone will have to respond to this in his own terms. I hope that we have laid enough solid groundwork so that the account can appear in its true light, not as a self-delusion but as an actual encounter with the silent field of intelligence. Earlier, we noted that the body in its real nature is non-change mixed with change. The reason why that is so is that all of nature exhibits these two paradoxical yet complementary states. As awareness expands, the huge scope of change and the equally huge scope of non-change dawn on the mind. An ancient Chinese poem by Hsu Hsu says:

> The first wave is receding
> The second wave promptly arrives
> So many layers of time
> So many lives.

Can we grant this beautiful openness of perception, at once serene and all-encompassing, to an ordinary person from Connecticut? I think we have to, for the same biochemistry that sustains such an experience is available to anyone, regardless of time. Our DNA has remembered all the things that have ever happened to human beings. It would be ridiculous to suppose that only Chinese or Indian DNA can trigger higher states of consciousness; it would be impoverished to claim that they are not real. The meditator's statement ends with this wonderfully exact appreciation of quantum reality: "Sometimes there is an interesting paradox of activity and rest all in one, and I feel within my awareness that I am moving infinitely fast and remaining perfectly still at the same time. This is the experience of the ever-changing along with the never-changing."

Anyone who wants to take the full benefit of the Vedic knowledge must come to grips with the fact that such normally inconceivable states as infinity, eternity, and transcendence are real. These words do not belong to the vocabulary of the ordinary waking state, but they are not so distant from it, either. We all have the power to make reality. Why make it inside boundaries when the boundless is so near?

EXPANDING THE TOPIC

I often refer to skeptics in these expanded topics because *Quantum Healing* caused the skeptical beehive to buzz rather violently. Skeptics view themselves as guardians of scientific truth. They can just as easily be seen as the society for the suppression of curiosity. Yet I sympathize with anyone who can't buy into *Aham Brahmasmi,* the

Vedic assertion that "I am the universe." From the viewpoint of everyday life, this simply seems impossible. At best, *Aham Brahmasmi* might be the otherworldly state reached by enlightened sages long ago and far away.

Yes and no. A person's consciousness has to shift in order to realize, in a higher state of awareness, that "I am the universe." But the statement can't apply simply to these few people. Only someone with medical school training can look through a microscope and identify T cells from the immune system, yet everyone has T cells. So it's not the truth of *Aham Brahmasmi* that we should doubt; either it's true or it isn't. The real issue is how to arrive at the state of consciousness that reveals this truth.

A Buddhist maxim holds that it takes a thorn to remove a thorn. In other words, the mind encloses us in boundaries, but only the mind can get us beyond boundaries to experience the unbounded. In modern terms, we can refer this paradox to the brain. The brain is the receiver of mind, the instrument whose physical processes parallel every thought, feeling, sensation, and image that passes through our minds. The Buddhist maxim applies to it, too. The brain is a thorn in that it reduces reality to fixed boundaries, but it is capable at the same time of registering the unbounded.

In this regard, I became fascinated by the work done by the Polish-American mathematician Alfred Korzybski (1879–1950), because he worked out what the brain does when it processes reality. Billions of bits of data bombard our sense organs every day, of which only a fraction gets past the brain's filtering mechanism. When people say, "You're not hearing me" or, "You only see what you want to see," they are expressing a truth that Korzybski tried to quantify mathematically.

Sometimes the things a person can't see are simply outside the range of human experience, like our inability to see ultraviolet light. But a great deal more depends on expectations, memories, biases, fears, and simple closed-mindedness. If you go to a party and someone tells you that you are about to meet a Nobel Prize winner, you will see a different person than if you had been told he is a reformed mafia hit man. When all the filtering and processing is complete, there is no doubt that the brain doesn't actually experience reality but only a confirmation of its model of reality.

The model of reality you are following right this minute is wired into the synapses and neural pathways of your brain. Some of this is so-called hard wiring, which means it belongs to the brain's intrinsic structure, such as the wiring that leads from your eyes to the visual cortex. Other wiring is formed through personal experience and is much more fluid; this is known as soft wiring. Between them hard and soft wiring deliver a model of reality to you, and whatever is outside the model doesn't exist. Korzybski was one of the first analysts who pointed out that if the brain is capturing only a fraction of the raw data being fed to it, one cannot claim that the brain is an accurate vehicle for experiencing reality.

Two interesting points follow:

1. All models are equal as viewed from the level of the brain.
2. Reality transcends any model we can possibly make of it.

These two points allow God, the soul, and all other spiritual experiences back into the picture. The first point demolishes the notion that science is superior to religion because it gathers facts while religion deals in beliefs. In truth, science filters out and discards a huge portion of human experience—almost everything one would classify as subjective—so its model is just as selective, if not more so, than religion's. As far as the brain is concerned, neural filtering is taking place in all models, whether they are scientific, spiritual, artistic, or even disturbed and psychotic. Seeing little green men is a brain phenomenon just like seeing green trees. The brain is not a mirror of reality.

There is no way anyone can claim to know what is "really" real. You can't step outside your brain to fathom what lies beyond it. This limitation is much more severe than people suppose. The brain operates in time and space. Your thoughts, for example, come one after another, like boxcars in a train. So whatever is outside time and space is inconceivable, and unfiltered reality would probably blow the brain's circuits, or simply be blanked out.

Yet here is where the Buddhist notion of using a thorn to remove a thorn comes in, because the mind can look beyond the brain's filtering process. Consider this short poem by William Blake.

> To see a world in a grain of sand
> And a heaven in a wild flower,
> Hold infinity in the palm of your hand,
> And eternity in an hour.

This is a perspective that goes beyond everyday perception. How did Blake arrive at it? His lines resonate with me—I find them quite thrilling—because Blake had inner vision, which looks beyond the limited model that the brain creates. People who are completely adapted to constricted awareness still find themselves confronted with glimpses of unbounded awareness. This came home to me when Michael Shermer, founder of *Skeptic* magazine, had his worldview overturned by a mysterious event.

Shermer, with whom I've had many debates, fell in love with a German woman, who moved to the United States after they agreed to marry. On her wedding day she was very happy, but with one deep regret. Her grandfather, with whom she was very close, had died and therefore would never witness her wedding day. The ceremony took place. Shermer and his bride returned home. That night over dinner, there was the sound of music coming from the next room. The newlyweds followed the sound. A broken transistor radio that belonged to the bride's grandfather had suddenly come to life on its own—it was previously dead—and it not only played music but classical music, her grandfather's favorite. Mystified and deeply moved, the couple went to sleep hearing the radio play. The next day the room was silent, and the radio returned to its previous unusable state.

Shermer published this anecdote on the back page of *Scientific American*, where he writes a regular column, always from the skeptical point of view. It took some courage for him to admit that an inexplicable event had shaken his skepticism, but what had happened to him was a classic example of synchronicity, a meaningful "coincidence" that is far too unlikely to be random. Predictably, Shermer's skeptical followers weren't buying the story. They told him to take the transistor radio to a good electronics shop, where he'd find a rational explanation. Just as predictably, these commenters ignored the timing of the incident, the congruence with what his bride wanted, and the fact that a radio suddenly turned on and was tuned to a station playing music her grandfather loved. As the philosopher Leibniz pointed out, theories are correct about what they include but wrong about what they exclude. In this case, the radio is the least of it. The really important parts are excluded if you stubbornly view the event through skeptical spectacles.

Perhaps not as dramatically, we all get glimpses of reality that defy the limited model residing in our brains. Experiences that go beyond everyday reality are wide-ranging. Ask yourself if any of the following have occurred to you.

You felt that your awareness extended beyond your body.
You felt safe in your own being.
You had a sudden insight that came out of nowhere.
Your body felt physically light and buoyant.
You felt at home in the world.
You knew with certainty that you are loved.
You felt energy bubbling through your body.
You had a random thought, and it materialized.
Events came together perfectly to reach a goal you set for yourself.

You felt intuitively that everything happens for a reason.

You felt a connection with a higher intelligence.

You experienced the presence of God or the soul.

These are moments when reality peeks through the iron grille. No filter is ever perfect; no censor can catch every infraction. When Buddhism speaks of using a thorn to remove a thorn, nothing is more important than paying attention to glimpses like these, where expanded awareness takes over, if only briefly, from constricted awareness. As esoteric as spirituality can be, to escape from the brain's limitations all you need to do is say "yes" to moments of expanded awareness instead of "no." You are the one who ultimately decides how much reality you want to experience, and every time you say "yes," you are giving instructions to your brain. In time, it will adapt to any level of awareness you want.

This point was validated by studies of the brain function of a group of Tibetan Buddhist monks. They had meditated for years on the value of compassion (one name for the Buddha is "the compassionate one"), and if this value had grown in their lives, some change should appear in their brains. In fact it did. The monks showed increased delta waves, representing so-called slow-wave sleep. Considered to be unconscious activity in most people, slow-wave sleep is associated with remaining self-aware even when you are in deep sleep. This is a noted attainment in yoga. In addition, the monks showed unprecedented activity in the prefrontal lobes, especially in regions associated with higher emotions like compassion.

As startling as these findings were, they could have been predicted once you accept that the brain must follow where the mind goes. Meditation creates beneficial changes in brain functions you would never be aware of, because such things as heart rate and blood pressure don't register in our minds as conscious choices. Saying "yes" to experiences of expanded awareness is different. You make a conscious choice to favor a range of experiences that your brain either ignores, shuts down, or censors.

I wish in hindsight that I had emphasized how faulty every model of reality, including the quantum model, must be. Korzybski held that even mathematics was a model, subject to the limitations of all models that the brain constructs. Not everyone would agree— holding on to mathematics as a universal truth gives advanced physics its toehold on the quantum world. But I am not using any of these ideas as bludgeons to bash science with. Korzybski simply pointed out, using the language of science, that whatever reality is, it transcends the brain.

13

BODY OF BLISS

There is no more beautiful experience than when the world expands beyond its accustomed limits. These are the moments when reality takes on splendor. The Veda calls such an experience *Ananda,* or bliss; it is said to be another quality inherent in the human mind but covered over by layers of dulled awareness. *Bliss* is an uncomfortable word in the West; like transcendence, it needs to be demystified. Let's start with a personal reaction to what bliss feels like. A beautiful first-person account is given by physiologist Robert Keith Wallace. The scene is Nepal, where Wallace went in 1974, taking a break from a conference being held in India:

Along with a physicist friend, I made my way up from Katmandu, the capital, to be nearer the Himalayas. We found a beautiful alpine lake, which Nepalese princes once favored as a summer retreat. For less than a dollar, we rented a boat and pushed out onto the water. It was a windy day with clearing skies, a perfect day to fly kites. I had bought one at the bazaar, painted a fierce red and built for acrobatics. I stood up, and it jumped out of my hand as I let it loose on the wind.

The tiny kite floated up into the high, thin air. I stood looking up toward the great mountains around us. Though they hid their heads in the clouds, they gave off an aura of grandeur and peace. As I watched, the clouds lifted all at once. I was absolutely in awe. What I had taken for mountains were only foothills! Beyond them, like ancient gods, rose the true Himalayas, unbelievably mighty and majestic.

We could hardly speak, so much power and beauty was concentrated in that breathtaking scene. The sense of having a small, isolated self disappeared, and in its place was the delicious sensation of flowing out into everything I beheld. I felt a sense of complete fullness contained in my own silence. Fittingly, the tallest peak before us was Annapurna, whose name means "fullness of life."

Standing there on the lake, I saw directly into the reality where time really is timeless. The same power that reared these mountains was flowing through me. If I wanted to find the source of time and space, I only needed to place my fingers over my heart. The single adequate word to describe my sensations at that moment is bliss.°

What stands out unmistakably in this experience is *its* sense of revelation. People who have been directly touched by bliss feel that they are suddenly being exposed to life as it really is. By comparison, their ordinary view was flat and distorted; they had been accepting a dingy image for the real thing. To experience bliss every hour of the day would be a sign of complete enlightenment, but even a brief encounter is significant—it permits you to actually feel waves of consciousness as they well up from the field of silence, cross the

° Adapted from Robert Keith Wallace's *The Physiology of Consciousness* (M.I.U. Press, 1993).

gap, and are infused into every cell. This is the body's own awakening.

In Ayurveda, bliss is the basis for three extremely powerful healing techniques. The first is meditation, which we have already discussed. Its importance is that it takes the mind out of its boundaries and exposes it to an unbounded state of consciousness. The other two techniques are more specific. The first is the Ayurvedic psycho-physiological technique—the term *psycho-physiological* simply means "mind-body" (we often use an informal name, the bliss technique). The second healing technique is called primordial sound.

To explain how such healing works, let me take an example from hypnosis. One of the most surprising findings of hypnosis research is that subjects can make their hands warm or cold, raise rashes on their skin, and even form blisters in a matter of a few minutes after the hypnotic suggestion is introduced. This is not, strictly speaking, a peculiarity of the hypnotic trance—subjects hooked up to biofeedback machines can do similar things in their normal state of awareness. What is being demonstrated here is the power of attention to alter the body. Ayurveda has made use of this principle for thousands of years. Indeed, since the basic premise of Vedic knowledge is that consciousness creates the body, it is only natural that techniques for focusing attention should have been discovered.

The bliss technique and primordial sound fall into this category. Consciousness is nothing but awareness. You can be aware that your hand is hot, which is passive awareness, but as the hypnosis research shows, you can also make your hand hot, which is active awareness, or attention. When you "pay attention" to something, you shift from passive to active awareness. Attention exerts far more control than people ordinarily realize. That is because we are victims of passive awareness. A person in pain is aware of the pain but not that he can make it increase, diminish, appear, or disappear. Yet all this is true. (People can walk on fire, for example, because they can control their level of pain; more remarkably, they can control whether their feet actually get burned—that too is under the control of attention.)

In Ayurveda, each and every symptom of disease, from a minor neck pain to a full-blown cancer, is under the control of attention. However, between us and the symptom lie barriers—the veils called Maya—that prevent us from exercising our attention in a therapeutic way. All mind-body medicine attempts to remove these obstacles so that healing can take place. Outside Ayurveda, the word Maya is not used, but any term that amounts to the same thing is applicable. I have used other phrases, such as "barriers in silence," "the ghost of memory," and "the mask of matter." In the current environment, where mind-body medicine is just proving itself and has to beware of stepping on the toes of science, techniques for breaking through Maya are still rather rudimentary. Fortunately, nature has set up things so that mind-body approaches of all kinds will work. Laughter can defeat a fatal disease; so can drinking a glass of grape juice every day, if you believe strongly enough in it.

It would be much better, however, to have a science of awareness. Ayurveda supplies just that. It would also be helpful to have a theory that supplies this science with a firm grounding in philosophy; the Vedic knowledge supplies that. When I teach people Ayurvedic healing techniques, I am not inducting them into a Vedic world, or into some mystery. I am trying to let them realize that their own awareness creates, controls, and turns into their bodies. This is a fact, not just a Vedic view of things.

When the body is in pain, a distorted area of awareness is crying out to the rest of awareness for help. Our natural instinct is to bring the help. The way we mobilize the platelets and clotting factors in the blood to heal a cut is nothing more than awareness bringing in help. A bruise heals because intelligence goes to work on it. I think that much has become abundantly clear by now.

Some people are fortunate in being such natural creatures that when they get cancer, they do not block the innate urge to get well.

No doubt there are thousands of such people in the world who have not come under scrutiny. Rather than being branded miraculous by religion or science, they stand as the mute, inglorious Miltons of the healing process.

Ayurveda extends their ability to everyone. The Ayurvedic approach is to take a process already going on in the body and assist it naturally and without strain. Any pain or disease you have is like an island of discomfort surrounded by an ocean of comfort, for in comparison to any one disease, your healthy awareness is as big as an ocean. Assuming that you are normally constituted, there is no innate reason why you cannot heal any disease with awareness. (In old age, or in cases of chronic illness, our inner abilities get depleted; therefore, Ayurveda cannot guarantee a cure because sometimes it is not there in nature's scheme.)

The bliss technique gives the patient the experience of himself as pure awareness, the ocean of well-being that is our basic prop and sustenance. With this technique alone it is possible to "drown" a disease in awareness and cure it. However, like the hypnotic subjects who can focus their attention to make a blister appear, it is also useful to focus attention more precisely to heal. For that, the primordial sound technique exists. With it, a specific tumor or arthritic joint can be attended to; a weak heart or clogged arteries can be zeroed in on. You are not attacking the disorder with the primordial sound but paying closer attention to it—so close that the distortion of awareness lurking at the bottom of the disorder falls back into line. In earlier chapters I called this process banishing the ghost of memory.

Together, meditation, the bliss technique, and primordial sound are the practical application of all that I have been building up to, the tools of quantum healing. Let me illustrate them with a case study, and afterward I will explain their connection to bliss.

Laura is a young woman from Boston who contracted breast cancer in her mid-thirties. Confronted with her diagnosis, she elected for personal reasons not to undergo any conventional treatment, despite her doctor's anxious insistence that without treatment she would be dead in less than two years. Today, three years later, she is still alive and on the surface appears perfectly normal. Her X rays reveal that the tumor has not shrunk, but its growth, if any, has been slight. This implies that Laura is still in considerable danger, but in her own mind, her present state is a great victory.

Although her cancer is still present, it has not followed what doctors call the "expected natural history" of the disease. Dr. Yujiro Ikemi, one of Japan's leading experts in psychosomatic medicine, has surveyed sixty-nine patients whom he considers to have had spontaneous regressions of cancer. It is not necessary for the cancer cells to disappear entirely, Dr. Ikemi notes—he looks for other signs, such as that the tumor is growing abnormally slowly, the patient has not wasted away, and the malignancy has not spread to other parts of the body. These signs are enough to indicate a spontaneous regression in Ikemi's view, and Laura fits them all.

Laura was already meditating when I first saw her. In 1987 she went through two weeks of inpatient Ayurvedic treatment and was taught primordial sound and the bliss technique, both of which can be used during meditation. Let us say that the mind has settled down in meditation and is experiencing itself as silence. Bliss is in that silence, just as intelligence is. You cannot "feel" that you are intelligent, but you can feel bliss. The bliss technique brings it out for the mind to register in various ways—as warmth in some part of the body, tingling, a flowing sensation, or several other physical manifestations. Bliss remains abstract, but a sort of "afterglow" is being picked up during the technique. Primordial sound, on the other hand, is quite focused—it brings the awareness of bliss directly to the diseased area of the body. (One does not have to think of all this as happening separately. The bliss level of awareness is always present; the techniques simply draw the conscious mind to it. Once bliss is experienced, the mind-body connection has been made.)

As soon as she learned the techniques, Laura felt immediate

positive effects. The primordial sounds went right to the breast area, she told me. At times they induced a throbbing feeling, heat, or even pain; most of the time, however, she would sit down with pain in that area and the technique would cause it to go away. The most dramatic results, subjectively, came from the introduction of bliss. I asked Laura to write out her experiences for me, whether joyful or painful or just indifferent, and she agreed to. The latest report says this:

> The experiences during the bliss technique are not as profound as when I started one and a half years ago, but then there was such deep-rooted fear and sorrow, a feeling of helplessness and intense anxiety, so the contrast was quite great when I began to experience such joy and bliss.
>
> At that time there were large black holes experienced in my awareness. I do not see the black holes anymore, and the feeling of constant happiness is more stable. Yet days still come when the joy and bliss are so powerful that I can hardly contain them. I rarely experience fear anymore, just some general anxiety that I can usually control with a little attention.

While other women in her position are devastated by their treatments and left with the deepest scars, physically and mentally, it is amazing that Laura, though still suspended between life and death, can end her letter this way:

> A year and a half ago, I was only 99 percent sure that the cancer would be eliminated. It has only been in the last month that I have grown 100 percent sure. I have no doubts now. I feel confident in the support of nature. I still don't know the exact form nature's help will take, or the timing for it, but I am less concerned about the final manifestation than I am about the breakthrough in consciousness. I can see clearly in my awareness the perfect breast.

Laura is a sensitive observer of her own awareness, and she sees its flow very exactly. To her, there is a huge difference, from the inside, between being sick and becoming well. The techniques she is using do not call for visualization, but she says that she can see the tumor grow whenever she feels anxious or sorrowful. This image represents, I believe, a direct link between her awareness and the progress of the cancer.

What will the final outcome be? She and I agree that the process itself is the outcome; every day is a whole—not a step toward some dreamed-of recovery, but an end in itself, to be lived in its fullness as if no disease existed. Because I am much more indoctrinated by my past medical experiences with cancer than Laura is, I often think that she is far ahead of me in her joyful confidence.

Bliss is both objective and subjective. You can feel it as a sensation, but it also effects measurable change—it can alter the heart rate, blood pressure, hormone secretions, or anything else for that matter. This is what allows bliss to be useful medically. The patient is using the Ayurvedic techniques "in his head," but the bliss being experienced is re-creating his body at the same time. What is happening is that the body is receiving a signal from its own blueprint, not a material blueprint but the one that exists in consciousness.

Because the blueprint is invisible, it has to find a way to cross over into material existence. To do that, nature employs bliss—it is a vibration that bridges mind and matter, allowing each bit of the body to be paired with a bit of intelligence:

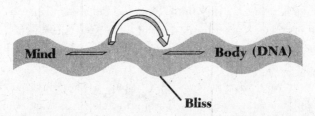

This diagram shows the mind-body connection as being like a radio broadcast: mind is sending out impulses of intelligence, DNA receives them, and bliss is the carrier signal. On paper, these three elements have to be separated, but in reality they are completely fused. The message, the messenger, and the receiver are one. Of course, we have looked at the mind-body connection dozens of times before, but we didn't have the "glue" that keeps mind and body from flying in separate directions—bliss.

DNA now takes on special importance. A single neuropeptide, or any other messenger molecule, carries only a tiny bit of the signal that mind is sending. Adrenaline, for example, is correlated to fear. This seems to imply that each thought activates one molecule, but that would be like saying that 101.5 on an FM radio receives only one song. In fact, the body can receive an infinite variety of signals, thanks to DNA.

We are used to thinking of DNA as an unchanging blueprint, albeit "the blueprint of life." DNA is nowhere near so static. I was sitting quietly two days ago when I had a glimpse of DNA in my mind's eye. I saw DNA speeded up so that one human lifetime, from the moment of inception to the moment of death, fit into the space of a few minutes.

What I saw wasn't a chemical but a process of incredible richness and dynamism. Everything in life pours out of DNA—flesh, bones, blood, heart, and nervous system; a baby's first word and a toddler's first step; the maturing of reason in the brain's cortex; the play of emotions, thoughts, and desires that flicker like summer lightning through every cell. All of this is DNA. To call it a blueprint is to take the husk and miss the fruit. Imagine yourself going to a Mercedes dealer, paying thirty thousand dollars, and having him hand over a car's blueprint instead of a car. Now imagine the blueprint actually turning into the car—not only that, but starting itself, driving down the road, and replacing its own spare parts. Then the blueprint would be equal to DNA. (It would also need another quite amazing talent: any part—the carburetor, the tires, even a chip of paint on the door—would have to know how to turn into a whole car.)

Whatever it is that makes DNA so dynamic is not visible in its material makeup; molecules themselves are passive participants in time. They can change, as oxygen and hydrogen change when they combine to form water, but DNA actively shapes the course of time. This is such an important feature that I need to explain it at length; otherwise, the real miracle of DNA will be lost on us.

In the past few years, researchers have been intrigued by one particular gene, called the per gene, in the DNA of a fruit fly. As part of their inherited behavior, fruit flies sing in the evening to call their mates. Normally, they repeat their call quite rhythmically, once every 60 seconds.

Ronald Konopka, a research professor at Clarkson University, first linked the rhythm of the fruit fly's song to the per (for "periodic") gene. He also found that the rhythm could change. When the per gene mutates, it produces faster or slower intervals between calls: one fly sings every 40 seconds, another every 80 seconds.

What is so fascinating about this discovery is that each kind of fly times its existence to a different length of day. The normal, 60-second fly follows a 24-hour day; the faster, 40-second fly a shorter day of 18 to 20 hours; and the slower, 80-second fly a long day of 28 to 30 hours. The conventional interpretation is that the per gene establishes the insect's daily rhythm. A similar effect is seen in us; if confined to a cave where he cannot see the sun and is not allowed to look at a clock, a man will sleep and wake up on a regular cycle, not of 24 hours but generally of 25 hours—this seems to be the daily, or circadian, rhythm that our DNA has built into us. Similarly, the fruit fly does not care when the sun rises or sets; when its song changes, the day changes. That means that its sense of time comes from within, activated by the per gene.

This is a far more stunning conclusion than the conventional one. The conventional one says that DNA is controlling a rhythm inside the cell, but I am saying that it controls time itself. The per gene is the link between time "out there" and DNA "in here"; it literally creates time as the fruit fly knows it. In physics, Einstein demonstrated that there is no fixed yardstick for time in the relative world; a space traveler would think that the clock on his spaceship is ticking normally, just as it does on Earth. But if he attained a velocity near the speed of light, the clock would in fact be going slower than Earth-bound clocks. This would not be an illusion; every biological process, including how fast the space traveler ages, would also slow down. Aren't these fruit flies the insect equivalent of Einstein's space travelers? They are experiencing time as either slow or fast, not from traveling near the speed of light but simply from their own internal signals.

A fast-singing fruit fly would have no way of knowing that it is living in "fast time" (assuming that it is isolated from the other kinds of flies). It emits the same number of calls per "day" as either the normal or the slow singers, without realizing that its day (18 to 20 hours) is entirely determined inside itself. But what is the per gene actually doing?

Another investigator, Michael Young of Rockefeller University, joined Konopka and discovered that the per gene works by coding certain proteins in the cell that regulate rhythm. It is these proteins, coming and going in cycles, that make the day seem long or short to the fly. Similar genes and coded proteins have also been found in mice, chickens, and human beings. This brings us remarkably close to seeing how the DNA is creating all of reality. It is manipulating the molecules into rhythms, or vibrations, that we decode into time. Other vibrations are decoded into light, sound, texture, smells, et cetera. Sir Arthur Eddington calls all of these "fancies of the mind," for essentially none of our sensory input is anything but a signal transmitted to us via DNA—pure, abstract vibrations that we turn into "real" events in time and space. If a gene can regulate time, then it is only a step away from regulating space, too. There is nothing to time and space, from a subjective point of view, except one's own participation in it. Like the fruit fly, we measure an hour by the clock, and the clock is in us.

Here we come to a fork in the road. Biologists realize that if the proteins in a cell regulate the cell's rhythms, then something must regulate them. What is it? One road leads to a materialistic explanation. Naturally, this is the one science prefers. Some biologists believe that the cell wall lets chemicals through only at a certain rate, and this rate is our yardstick for time, our molecular clock. Others say that the clock is actually a chemical code imprinted on the DNA, which is read in sequence from the moment of conception until death. Neither explanation has been worked out in satisfactory detail. If the rishis are right, they never will be—no answer exists on the level of molecules alone.

As is obvious by now, the rishis would take a different road and say that the clock inside us is intelligence. The per gene is just a mechanical part, a wire or tube in DNA's radio. Through it, time expresses itself, just as an emotion expresses itself through a neuropeptide. Time is riding on a molecule, and once again we mustn't mistake the rider for the horse. The signals for time, space, motion, texture, smells, sights, and all the rest of the world come from the level of silent intelligence. That is where we really live, and the miracle of DNA is that it can turn so many totally abstract messages into life itself.

If you go walking through the woods on a warm autumn day, feeling the fallen oak leaves under your feet, smelling the ripe, dank earth, and watching the October light as it plays in the branches overhead, you are experiencing the world through your DNA. It imposes a definite selection on things. You are not smelling the argon and xenon gases in the air or seeing the sun's ultraviolet emissions. You can walk through leaves but not through the wood of the trees. The incredible complexity of green moss registers on your mind as a patch of fuzz; and of the pollen, spores, bacteria, viruses, and other microbes that fill the air by the hundreds in every cubic centimeter, you register nothing. The reason for this special focus resides in you. Those are humanized leaves, trees, smells, and light.

If your senses were refined enough, you would go even further and realize that you *are* the woods. It is not just sending signals to you from "out there"; rather, you are blending your own signals with its. None of your sense organs is separated from nature's continuum. Your eye is a specialized light receptor that merges into the light it perceives. If the light failed, your eye would atrophy as surely as the blind cave-fish's eye; if your eye's structure changed—for example, if each eye swiveled independently, like a chameleon's— every object would acquire completely different relations in space. That would be your experience, and nothing in the relative world exists outside experience.

A bee approaching a flower sees the nectar and blocks out the petals—as far as the bee's eye is concerned, this is what exists. For us, to see a bar magnet means seeing the sharp outline of the iron but not the radiating magnetic field around it. Therefore, the iron is what exists, as far as vision goes. Add in all the other senses, and you have the world that you are creating. It was built up over 600 million years by your DNA; ultimately, however, this world expresses your inner intelligence, with DNA the adroit servant. It serves you in your way, as it serves other creatures in theirs.

DNA turns the vibrations of light into eyes and sound into ears. It turns time into a mating song for fruit flies and into the march of history for man. It gives bats their sonar and snakes their sensitivity to infrared light. In each and every case, however, the DNA is merely the radio. One will never discover the secret of space-time looking at DNA, or any other material thing. The attempt is just as doomed as tearing apart a radio's wiring to find where the music is. The rishis found the level of music—it is bliss.

Bliss is the vibration that intelligence sends into the world. In fact, we can map our existence in terms of a single diagram that compresses mind, body, DNA, and bliss into one undivided whole:

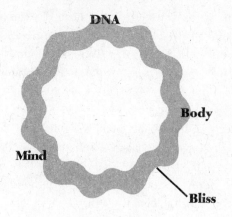

With good reason one could call this picture the circle of life. In it we see bliss as a continuous signal, a loop that connects mind, body, and DNA in a lifelong conversation. All three participants share equally in what gets said—what the mind knows is also known by the body and DNA. Your experiences resonate on all three levels. You cannot be happy or sad, sick or well, awake or asleep, without sending a message everywhere in inner space.

You may not think that you can "talk" to your DNA (another prejudice that comes from seeing DNA as only a material blueprint), but in fact you do continually. The fleeting chemicals that race through you at the touch of thought, the receptors hanging out on the cell wall waiting for their messages, and every other speck of life are manufactured by DNA. (I realize that I am truncating a long process. DNA directly manufactures only genetic material, but using its active twin, RNA, it gives rise to all the proteins, cells, and tissues we have.) Thinking happens at the level of DNA, because without the brain cell sending out a neuropeptide or other messenger, there can be no thought.

The Ayurvedic technique called primordial sound takes direct advantage of this. I drew bliss as a circle to represent a constant, unbroken signal. However, there can be breaks in the circle. These occur when the DNA, the mind, and the body are not perfectly synchronized. Ayurveda would say that many diseases begin where there is such a break—bliss slips out of its groove, so to speak, throwing off the cell's intelligence. To repair the break, a specific signal needs to be inserted back into the circle—a primordial sound. In this way, a vibration is used to cure a vibration.

Treating disease with a mental sound is highly unusual, I know. To understand it, we need to make a closer connection between bliss and the quantum field. By the 1970s, the world's atom smashers had been busy for forty years, and now there were hundreds of "hadrons," a class of subatomic particles that were proliferating far too abundantly to be considered elementary by any standard. Didn't the universe have simpler building blocks than this? The way out of the dilemma was found by theorizing that all of these particles were variations not on a smaller particle but on an underlying wave form.

This wave form was dubbed a "superstring," because it behaves very much like a violin string. The superstring theory holds that billions upon billions of unseen strings pervade the universe, and their different frequencies give rise to all the matter and energy in creation. Certain vibrations also turn into time and space—the prefix *super* indicates that these strings actually reside far beyond our limited four-dimensional reality. No one will ever see them, no matter how powerful our instruments become.

To clarify what a superstring is, physicist Michio Kaku gives an analogy to music: imagine that a violin is enclosed out of sight in a box. As its strings vibrate, different pitches, chords, sequences of notes, and timbres are produced. If you were an alien who did not know what music is, you would find each of these things completely different from one another—the note C might be like a hydrogen atom, while E-flat was a photon. Only by opening the box and seeing that indeed every sound came from one violin would you be convinced that they had a unified source.

In the same way, nature's fundamental field is constantly vibrating and producing variations upon the same "notes," but our senses are set up so that they turn this sameness into differences. We perceive iron as a solid note, hydrogen as a gaseous note, gravity as a heavy note, and so on. Only by exposing the superstrings would the underlying unity be evident. They are exposed not by opening the box but by mathematical formulas that show that all forms of matter and energy fit the super-string model—as so far they all do. Therefore, quantum physics now has its first good candidate for a unified field theory, justifying Einstein's faith in the order of the cosmos.

Amazingly enough, the Vedic rishis also perceived that the cosmos was pervaded by strings. These strings were called *sutras*, from which surgeons get the word *suture*. In Sanskrit, sutra can mean a stitch (or suture), but also a thread or a verbal phrase. If you think of a sutra as a thread, then the whole universe is woven like gossamer from threads of intelligence, billions and billions of them. Like notes played on the unseen violin, the fundamental level of the whole world, according to the Vedic rishis, is made of sounds. Because they arise before anything else, they are primordial—hence the term *primordial sound*.

It takes more than one sound to make the universe. However, the rishis did have just one sound to begin with, a vibration called Om, which appeared at the time we would call the Big Bang. Om is a meaningless syllable—it simply stands for the first wave that breaks the cosmic silence. As it breaks up into many tinier waves, Om subdivides into different subfrequencies that compose the matter and energy in our universe.

Once you open your mind to the possibility, it is no more surprising that stars, galaxies, and human beings can be created from Om than from a superstring. Both are abstract. Going back to the hidden violin, Kaku wrote, "The tones created by the vibrating string, such as C or B-flat, are not in themselves any more fundamental than any other notes. What is fundamental, however, is the fact that a single concept, vibrating strings, can explain the laws of harmony"—or in the case of the universe, the laws of nature.

Om can be pictured as a straight line whose pitch rises into infinity, like the most super of superstrings. It is no accident that the syllable Om sounds like the English "hum"; when the rishis tuned in to the sound of the universe, they actually heard it as a cosmic hum. If you were enlightened, you would be able to hear the vibration that is your own signature; for instance, you could "hear" your DNA as a specific frequency vibrating in your awareness. Likewise, each neuropeptide would grow out of a sound, as would every other chemical.

Starting with DNA, the whole body unfolds into many levels, and at each one the sutra, or sequence of sound, comes first. Therefore, putting a primordial sound back into the body is like reminding it of what station it should be tuned in to. On that basis, Ayurveda does not treat the body as a lump of matter but as a web of sutras.

Needless to say, it has taken me some time to explain all of this to myself. When I first began to administer the Ayurvedic programs at the inpatient facility in Lancaster, I kept one foot firmly planted in my private endocrinology practice—although I felt in tune with Ayurvedic theory, I was still nervous about its results. Every week I shuttled back and forth from my office to the clinic. One October day I walked into the dining hall and noticed one of the cancer patients, a middle-aged man who was sitting quietly in the corner, eating lunch with his wife. He had cancer of the pancreas, a fatal condition that is also extremely painful. When he had come in the door five days earlier, his face was gray and creased after months of suffering. I walked over now to say a few words. As I approached, he casually looked up at me. It was one of those moments that stops the heart. His face looked peaceful and relaxed; his eyes were unmistakably touched with bliss. I asked him how he felt. He said that he had no pain at all; after four days of Ayurvedic treatment, he had taken himself off all his pain medication. A few days later he left, and until the time he died, he remained largely free of drugs.

This is not yet a cure, but it is a huge step toward one. Consciousness would be curing people today, I am convinced, except that we diagnose disease too late, after years of stress have hardened the physiology and made it difficult for bliss to penetrate. But the gate is always open, even if only by a crack. All the Ayurvedic healing techniques operate on the premise that one treats the patient first, the disease second.

The prospect of becoming a well person again, as opposed to fighting against a disorder known to be incurable, gives hope to people who otherwise have nothing to hold on to but grim statistics. One AIDS patient in Germany has been treated with Ayurveda for two years as part of a pilot program conducted in Europe. Diagnosed in 1984, he is still alive at the time of this writing in August 1988 (80 percent of AIDS patients die within two years of diagnosis); he leads a normal life and is without overt symptoms.

A similar program is under way in California, treating AIDS patients under clinical observation to see if both the latent and active phases of the disease can be affected. Both groups are small, and the subjects know that Ayurveda is not promising a cure, but the supervising physicians feel that they are seeing improvements, particularly in the patients' ability to withstand the debilitating fatigue that saps the strength and will of AIDS patients.

Just to extend the latency period, giving a patient more years before the disease produces symptoms, would be a major breakthrough. However, I met one patient, not connected with the clinic, who seems to have done better than that. A musician from Los Angeles in his early forties came to be taught the bliss technique two years ago; I did not see him again until this year, when he came to learn primordial sound. I asked how he was doing, and he answered that he had something important to tell me—he had AIDS.

The diagnosis had been made four years earlier after he came down with pneumonia. Rather than the typical pneumonia caused by the pneumococcus bacteria, his came from a protozoa known as *Pneumocystis carinii;* this disease is one of the most common that strike AIDS patients when their immune systems collapse. He recovered from the attack and decided to change his life. He learned to meditate, and for the first time in his adult life he gave up the habitual routine of long nights, heavy drinking, pills, smoking, and promiscuity that had been attached to his career. (Interestingly, a survey of long-term AIDS survivors shows that all of them have made this kind of "take charge" decision over their disease. Standard medicine cannot explain why this should be such a lifesaver, but it is.)

By the time he learned the bliss technique, two years later, his health had improved to the point where he looked totally normal. The bliss technique became a major focus of his determination to overcome AIDS.

"I don't think of myself as fighting my sickness," he remarked. "I'm just learning that all the unhappiness and anguish I used to live with was wrong." Inside, he began to experience a much more positive range of emotions—he told me that he had never suspected that he could get hooked on happiness. Today, four years after the original diagnosis, he looks completely healthy, and except for a certain amount of fatigue, he lives as if the AIDS were not there.

Each year's international symposium on AIDS discloses deeper gloom about defeating it. AIDS is caused by the HIV virus, plus its related mutations, which are a researcher's nightmare, because they belong to a particularly baffling, elusive class of organisms called retroviruses. Even a normal virus, such as the one responsible for colds, has remarkable powers to elude the body's immune system.

Contrary to the way it responds to bacteria, our DNA mysteriously forgets how to fight against an invading virus—in fact, it actually appears to cooperate with it. When a virus comes near the cell wall, it melts through, penetrating as if without resistance; it is next ushered directly to the cell's nucleus, where the DNA obligingly shuts down normal operations and begins to manufacture the proteins for making new viruses.

A cold or flu virus is content to let DNA build proteins for it, but a retrovirus like HIV goes one better by blending into the DNA's own chemical strands, masking itself as the host's genetic material.

There it sleeps until the day, which may come years later, when the DNA is triggered to fight another disease. Then the retrovirus awakens and begins to replicate itself by the millions, using the host cell as an incubator and eventually resulting in the host cell's death. The cell bursts open, loosing a horde of lethal viruses into the bloodstream. Every step of the cycle is so mysterious and complicated that the AIDS virus has quickly earned a reputation for being the most complex disease organism ever discovered. No drug is capable of treating it; AZT, which helps postpone the active phase, is riddled with major side effects, making it impossible for some patients to take the drug.

This is not to deny Western medicine its own approach. When a life-threatening disease arises, it is necessary to take drastic measures—on this point there is no disagreement. But I believe that viewing disease as a distortion of intelligence might represent a move toward a deeper level of understanding, and therefore of treatment.

Both cancer and AIDS seem to be cases where the proper sequence of sutras must be unraveling at the deepest level. In other words, they are failures of intelligence, like "black holes" where bliss gets distorted out of its normal pattern. What makes both diseases so intractable is that the distortion runs so deep—it is locked inside the DNA's own structure. This causes the cell's self-repair mechanism either to break down or turn against itself. In the case of cancer, DNA actually seems to want to commit suicide by ignoring its knowledge of proper cell division.

In both diseases the distortion apparently penetrates as far as the very force fields that hold DNA together. (Cell physics is a complex field, but it is believed that a cell senses and interacts with viruses in the first place by detecting their chemical and electromagnetic resonances; such signals are interpreted by the DNA and presumably can also fool it.)

From the perspective of the sutras, or Vedic sounds, there must be a distortion in the proper sequence of intelligence as it unfolds into the relative world. "Hearing" the virus in its vicinity, the DNA mistakes it for a friendly or compatible sound, like the ancient Greek sailors who heard the siren's song and were lured to their destruction. This is a believable explanation once one realizes that DNA, which the virus is exploiting, is itself a bundle of vibrations.

If this explanation is valid, then the remedy is to reshape the improper sequence of sounds, using Ayurveda's primordial sound (known as *Shruti* in the Sanskrit texts, from the verb that means "to hear"). These sounds are basically like pottery molds—by placing the mold back over the distorted sequence, one guides the disrupted DNA back into line. This treatment is subtle and gentle in its effects, but some preliminary results have been quite dramatic. Once the sequence of sound is restored, the tremendous structural rigidity of the DNA should again protect it from future disruptions.

In the near future Ayurveda will blossom, I believe, and help us to create a new medicine, one of knowledge and compassion. At its best, current medicine already contains these ingredients—the medical system is in trouble, but its woes are transcended by caring individuals. They will be the first to see that Ayurveda is not in conflict with their work as doctors; it can only help the process of recovery and bring healing under our control.

EXPANDING THE TOPIC

Looking back, I realize that the concept of a universe based on vibrations, leading to the concept of the human body as a bundle of vibrations, was a bridge too far for many. There have been "vibrational healers" in every culture, if by vibration we include light, sound, music, mantras, chants, and shamanistic rituals. Probably the most comprehensive "science of vibrations" is found in the area of Vedic knowledge known as *shabda*, the Sanskrit word for "speech." The intriguing feature of *shabda* is that it fits the demand of Western science for a reductionist model—every phenomenon is reducible to a unique vibrational state—while at the same time fitting the "top-down" Eastern approach, which sees all phenomena emerging from the field of consciousness.

Yet anyone in a gotcha state of mind would find it easy to accuse vibrational healing of being a sham—the underlying concept is too alien to materialistic thinking. Once again quantum theory may bolster speculation, since there are physicists now toying with the idea that if the universe exists in Hilbert space (a strictly mathematical concept) and if Schrödinger's equation holds true (the classic equation that accounts for quantum probabilities throughout the universe), there may be an elegant way to reduce creation to a single wave function. (The legendary physicist Richard Feynman long ago speculated that all electrons may be reducible to one electron.) Once again this would be pure mathematics, yet by reducing the physical universe to a single wave function that gets entangled with itself to break down into the infinite waves that underlie infinite particles, something unique happens. There is no longer a split between reductionism and a top-down approach. One wave would give us a singular source from which everything else can be derived. The entanglement of the wave into countless subdivided waves would satisfy the demand for specific data that can be built up into complex explanations for higher-order forms like atoms, molecules, stars, galaxies, and so forth.

Anyone who isn't fully conversant in advanced mathematics can only watch from the sidelines before such a theory is accepted or rejected. *Shabda* gives everyone a chance to get back in the game, however, because of its practical extension into healing and the power of consciousness in general. A thought "in here" is vibrationally connected to a result "out there," and so two worlds, mind and matter, are bridged. A gotcha mentality is rarely fair, but skepticism has no rebuttal to the unshakable fact, stated by Sir John Eccles in an earlier chapter, that every thought performs telekinesis by influencing the chemical state of the brain: We cross the mind-body barrier every time we think.

Shabda also says that higher states of consciousness are vibrational. This greatly simplifies the whole issue of enlightenment, making it a natural phenomenon like weather, the stars, and hydrogen atoms. Vibration is the great leveler. Therefore it fascinated me when Dr. Jeffery A. Martin started publishing results from his Ph.D. work in psychology showing that higher consciousness is so natural that it exists all around us.

Martin posted an online message asking for responses from people who thought they were enlightened. He got more than 2,500 replies, and from this pool he intensively interviewed around fifty subjects. At first it was hard to find a common language. Feeling that you are enlightened is personal, and it also sets you apart from normal society. Martin found that his subjects often were sensitized by being outsiders, and revealing their unusual mental state had led to such things as being sent to a psychiatrist, put on medication, or even being committed to a mental hospital.

However, very early on he realized that as different as each person was, their experiences fell onto a continuum. There wasn't a single enlightened state but rather a sliding scale. To find neutral ground, and to fit the accepted model of what doctoral research must look like, he adopted the cumbersome tag Persistent Non-Symbolic Experience. "There is a shift in what it feels like to be you," Martin notes. "You move away from an individual sense of sense, which is considered normal, to something else."

Defining what "something else" is wasn't easy, because these people came from different backgrounds and were influenced by cultural factors. However, Martin was able to identify four areas of change.

If you found yourself shifting into Location 1, it would be typical to report that you have fewer thoughts than before. "You might say something to me like 'All of my thoughts are gone,' and the kinds of thoughts that go away are ones that refer to the individual self," says Martin. Which isn't surprising if you are experiencing a loss of "I" as a separate isolated being.

Putting ourselves in their shoes, these people don't keep a running story in their heads about what's happening to "me." When they think about themselves, it fades away as soon as they notice it. The same is true for their emotions, which are fewer and more spontaneous. When anger arises, it fades almost immediately. Emotions were still positive and negative but rarely if ever extreme. The person could be irritated when stuck in traffic, yet they didn't carry the residue of stress around with them afterward, and it would never build into road rage. They felt a sense of inner peace that could be interrupted, but quite soon it would return.

Such a person is operating in a bigger "self space," rather than being cramped inside the narrow confines of the ego. They feel freer and more expanded. This applies to their bodies as well; they often report that the body has no fixed boundaries but extends in all directions. Once they arrived in Location 1, people usually kept progressing—the highest state Martin calls Location 4—and they rarely slipped back or jumped ahead. Everything happened internally, and for many the shift wasn't spiritual. It was just the way they experienced themselves.

"If you sat in a roomful of people and a small percentage belong to this altered sense of self," says Martin, "you wouldn't be able to spot them. To all outer appearances they are just like you and me."

At the outset, before Martin's research began to expand to many other universities and countries, his typical subject was a white male from the United States or Europe, because women, for unknown reasons, were not eager to volunteer as enlightened or to discuss what their experiences were. Religious backgrounds were diverse, spanning Eastern and Western faiths, yet most of the subjects had done some kind of spiritual practice—they wanted to be in a higher state of consciousness. Curiously, around 14 percent had done nothing of this kind. They had spontaneously popped into higher consciousness or, more typically, drifted into it. They reported being in their new state anywhere from forty years to as little as two or three.

Martin's research base has expanded to more than a thousand subjects, which means we must ask ourselves if "normal" isn't a fixed state but a spectrum, with consciousness evolving much further than anyone has previously predicted. At the very least, higher consciousness has become much less exotic. It's no longer the province of sadhus and yogis in the Himalayas. Martin's study focused on body, emotions, sense of self, and thoughts, which are value neutral, making his work acceptable in the academy. But he found that the spiritual dimension had also opened up. Some subjects reported the kind of open, clear, silent awareness associated with Buddhism; others experienced the bliss I discuss in this chapter. Still others had no idea what to make of their state of awareness. But they were amazed at the amount of wellbeing they were experiencing, and this grew as they moved further along the spectrum. (Paradoxically, in Location 4, all emotion fell away, even love, and the richness of bliss was replaced by what Martin calls complete freedom. Yet his subjects report that they don't miss the experience of emotions and bliss, because in freedom they have found the very highest state of wellbeing.)

If it is startling to realize that enlightenment is all around us, and that it's a natural progression, even more intriguing is the prospect that enlightenment is personal. The way that you create your own reality doesn't suddenly come to an end; enlightenment isn't like jumping off a diving board. There are as many kinds of enlightenment as there are people, one might suppose. In a word, evolution itself is evolving, like everything else.

"Normal" won't be valid until it broadens to include everyone on the spectrum of consciousness. We will also need to revise the old definitions of enlightenment, in fact, to conform to the present age. The West has almost no formal institutions, outside monasteries and convents, geared for people who want to pursue higher states of consciousness or who have already arrived there. Here's what "normal" should encompass.

Feeling unbounded

Being at peace

Having a loose attachment to your personal history

Living in the present

Becoming free of negative thought forms and emotions

Breaking away from traumas and wounds from the past

Accepting that higher consciousness is natural, part of the
    human continuum

Experiencing more and more self-awareness as you evolve

Living in a state of wellbeing that continues to grow and deepen

A venerated spiritual teacher was once asked, "What does it take to be enlightened?" His reply: "You no longer have a personal stake in the world." If you identify with the boundaries erected by "I, me, and mine," this sounds like a death sentence. Having a personal stake in the world is what life is all about, isn't it? But with a longer view, across the entire spectrum of consciousness, the opposite is true. When you no longer identify with "I, me, and mine," you are ushered into a new world of experience that transcends the individual. This is the second birth that the Vedas extol as the true beginning of life.

Finally, I find it very touching that Martin's enlightened subjects, as amazed as they were by their new state, thought that nothing could be better. "This is as real as it gets" was a common reaction. But they were wrong. Reality is infinite, and what makes it infinite isn't the edge of the universe racing away faster than the speed of light. The universe matches human aspirations, and its infinity reflects the infinity inside us once we wake up and realize that it exists.

14

THE END OF THE WAR

f asked for an exact definition of quantum healing, I would say this: quantum healing is the ability of one mode of consciousness (the mind) to spontaneously correct the mistakes in another mode of consciousness (the body). It is a completely self-enclosed process. If pressed for a shorter definition, I would say simply that quantum healing makes peace. When consciousness is fragmented, it starts a war in the mind-body system. This war lies behind many diseases, giving rise to what modern medicine calls their psychosomatic component. The rishis might call it "the fear born of duality," and they would consider it not a component but the chief cause of all illness.

The body will send many signals to indicate that a war is going on. Recently a young French-Canadian woman came to see me suffering from Crohn's disease, a severe intestinal disorder characterized by chronic and uncontrollable diarrhea, accompanied by painful inflammation. Although the cause of Crohn's disease is unknown, it strikes mostly among young adults and may be connected to a deficiency in the immune system. What is well known is that the intestinal tract is highly sensitive to emotional states; in this patient's case, it was not surprising to hear that she worked long hours under the high pressure of a downtown Boston advertising firm.

After talking to her for a while, I discovered that she had learned to meditate several years before. I asked her if she still kept it up. No, she answered, there wasn't much time for it; when she did sit down to meditate, it didn't do much good, because she usually fell asleep in a few minutes.

I then asked if she had adjusted her diet to help her condition, slowed down the pace of her life, or considered moving on to a job with less stress. Looking somewhat impatient, she said no again— she wasn't going to allow her disease, which caused her many difficulties, to rule her life.

"Look," I said, "you have a very serious condition. If this inflammation persists, you may have to have parts of your intestine surgically removed. What are you going to do about that?" She was quite knowledgeable about her disease, and I didn't have to tell her that some grim choices lay ahead. The surgery in question involves considerable disfiguration, since with part of the intestine removed, a tube has to be extended out of the abdomen to handle elimination. Even then, the disease is not cured and tends to recur in other parts of the intestine.

"That's why I'm here," she answered. "I want a mental technique to help me continue to lead a normal life."

I was seeing the result of what the rishis called *Pragya aparadh,* the mistake of the intellect. This woman's body was crying out for healing, and it was telling her so every time she had an attack. She couldn't even close her eyes to meditate without her body desperately grabbing some relief in the form of sleep. Yet, her mind interpreted these attempts at healing as either irrelevant or troublesome. She insisted on leading a "normal life" of high stress that her system wasn't equipped to cope with.

"This is not the kind of disease you can fight," I said, "because there's no one on the other side but you." I explained that the same neuropeptides that registered stress in her brain were produced in her intestines. When she felt fear, frustration, and worry, the identical emotions were being experienced in her abdomen.

I told her that in my opinion she didn't need any new mental technique—she needed to let her body do what it wanted to do, which was to get well. The best way to cooperate with that was to give her body the rest it was demanding, continue to meditate, change her diet, and realize that no rewards from her job could possibly outweigh the danger she had put herself in. Nature was trying to tell her something very important, and once she paid attention, her problems would correct themselves.

"In a case like yours," I said, "you already have the best medicine you could possibly hope for—it's your own attention. Right now, the quality of that attention is fearful and tense, which is why you aren't getting better. But as soon as your awareness becomes settled and loses its fear, your body will recover—it's up to you."

She listened to me with interest, but I sensed that she resented hearing these things. The mistake of the intellect is insidious. The intellect refuses to believe that everything is happening inside one mind-body reality; it creates the fiction that the sick body is somewhere else, anywhere else but in the same situation as itself.

Illness is obviously a sign that there is a war going on. According to Ayurveda, the conflict is being waged "in here," contrary to the germ theory of disease, which tries to tell us that the war was started "out there" by invaders of every kind—bacteria, viruses, carcinogens, et cetera—which are lying in wait to attack us. Yet, healthy people live amid these dangers quite safely. Only when the immune system collapses, as in the case of AIDS, do we realize that our skin, lungs, mucous linings, intestines, and many other organs have learned to coexist with outside organisms in a delicate balance. The pneumonia that an AIDS patient typically catches is caused by a variety of *Pneumocystis* that is present in everybody's lungs all the time. The AIDS virus activates such diseases from the inside by demolishing one part of the immune system (the helper T-cells), thus breaking apart the network of information that holds us together.

In fact, we *are* this network, which projects itself into the world as our bodies, thoughts, emotions, and actions. Nor does the network stop with us. The simplistic idea that germs are our deadly enemy is a half-truth, because germs are part of the network, too. The whole living world is bound up in DNA, which has evolved along one channel as bacteria, along another as plants and animals, and along still another as man. The environment "out there" cooperates with the one "in here" like two polarities, in one sense totally opposed but in another totally complementary. If you look at reality from the viewpoint of all DNA, not just ours, then there is an entire global information network that has to be kept alive and healthy.

Viruses, for example, are capable of mutating very quickly—that is why a shot that immunizes you from this year's flu will usually not be effective next year. The flu virus will have mutated somewhere around the world into a completely different strain. (One of the AIDS virus's many unprecedented talents is its ability to mutate a hundred times faster than a typical flu virus.) Researchers have recently speculated that the reason why viruses mutate so rapidly is to keep pace with new variants of bacteria, thus carrying to all parts of the globe the news that life is changing.

Getting the flu, therefore, is like getting a news update. Your own DNA learns about alterations in the world's DNA that are challenging it, and your DNA then meets the challenge, not passively but actively. It must prove its viability by surviving the virus. The immune system rushes to meet the invader, and they engage in battle, molecule against molecule. The whole operation is timed to the split second and leaves no room for error. The macrophages rush to discover the identity of this new life form, probe it for vital weaknesses, and then mobilize the genetic material in their own DNA that will collapse the molecules of the virus, rendering them harmless.

At the same time, the immune cells also destroy any of your own cells that have played host to the invader. These infected host cells have not yet died from the flu. They are engorged with living viruses that pose a threat after the immune cells have wiped out all the flu that is gushing through the bloodstream. To kill an infected host cell, certain immune cells (killer T-cells) latch onto it from the outside and puncture holes in the cell wall. Like a deflating tire, the host cell spills out its liquid content, collapses into an empty bag, and dies.

But the host cell is not just eliminated; its DNA is actually dismantled by other signals from the attacking immune cells. This is an absolutely fascinating aspect of the whole process. What is really happening is that one bit of your DNA (the immune cell) is dismantling another bit of your DNA (the host cell), which in fact is just a copy of itself! The only difference between the two is that the second bit of DNA, in the host cell, has made the mistake of cooperating with the flu virus. No one knows why this occurs. As we saw in the last chapter, our cells mysteriously allow themselves to be killed from within when viruses attack them. Physically, the virus is no match for the cell, being thousands of times smaller and less complex—as one medical writer put it, it is as if a basketball came through the window of a skyscraper and the whole building fell down.

You would think that such mistakes show the imperfection of the body's intelligence, but that is too superficial. What is actually happening here is an exquisite example of quantum healing at work; in fact, the idea that a war is going on is just another half-truth, for when one bit of DNA dismantles another, we are witnessing a totally self-enclosed process. Every part of a disease reaction, from the scavenger cells that first meet the invader, to the host cells that take it in, to the macrophages, killer T-cells, helper T-cells, B-cells, and so on, are all the same DNA expressing its various abilities. In other words, the DNA has decided to stage for its own benefit a drama in which every part is played by itself.

Why should DNA put on one mask to succumb to the flu virus and another to rush in and destroy it? No one has answered this profound question, but it must have its logic in the whole scheme of life, the larger drama enacted by all the DNA in the world. I can make a speculation that we are watching DNA enrich life by adding as many variations as can possibly exist on one planet.

Nothing that happens to DNA is lost; it all stays within the self-enclosed system. Once the flu virus is defeated, the DNA records the encounter by producing new antibodies and specialized "memory cells" that float around in the lymph system and bloodstream for years afterward, adding to the immense storehouse of information that DNA has been accumulating since life began. This is how DNA makes you a player on the world scene.

If I look out my window, I can see a multilane highway with cars rushing by. Occasionally a jet flies over, sending a flock of birds twittering into the sky. Gulls circle overhead, thirty miles inland from the sea, and in the air is the distinct smell of the ocean, rich with marine life. All of this spectacle, including me, is the play of DNA. It has been projected from a molecule whose responsibility is to unfold new life without ever compromising life as a whole. Someone once estimated that all the separate DNA of every person who has ever lived would fit comfortably in a teaspoon, and yet if the tightly wound DNA in even a single cell nucleus of your body were uncoiled and the pieces laid end to end, they would stretch out to five feet. This means that the genetic thread contained in the body's 50 trillion cells is 50 billion miles long—enough to reach the moon and back 100,000 times. The Veda says that the universe's intelligence extends "from smaller than the smallest to larger than the largest," and DNA is the physical proof of it.

Therefore, it must be wrong to think that conflict is the norm. In general, a state of peace exists between your DNA and the other DNA "out there." For every time that you actually have to fight off a disease by getting sick, there are dozens, if not hundreds, of times when your body has warded off sickness without any overt symptom. It is only when there is a distortion "in here" that the immune system loses its ability to silently defend, heal, and remember.

We tend to forget that peace is the norm. Psychiatrists and sociologists take it as a given that modern man is deeply divided in his psyche. The rise of stress-related disorders, depression, anxiety, chronic fatigue, and "the disease of being in a hurry" is a sign of the times. The hectic pace of work, and life in general, has accustomed us to turmoil. By now, people are thoroughly indoctrinated by the idea that a certain degree of internal conflict is normal. The war, it seems, was started by us, and it is taking its toll in a frighteningly ordinary way.

All of this is what I wish I could have expressed to Chitra, the young woman with breast cancer whose story opened this book. She was fortunate enough to receive a cure that seemed miraculous, but as I was writing these chapters, her case became very different. The cancer cells had been defeated but not their memory. Because Chitra remained extremely anxious about having her cancer recur, she and I agreed that conventional therapy should continue. At the same time, she promised to keep up her meditation and the bliss technique I had taught her. I heard nothing for a month, then she called with bad news: her doctors had detected a dozen small shadows in her CAT scan that they interpreted as brain cancer. In a state of extreme fear, she began an intensive course of radiation, this time accompanied by experimental chemotherapy.

Weakened by the earlier bout with breast cancer, Chitra endured severe side effects, including depression. She stopped meditating and no longer returned for Ayurvedic treatment. Her platelet count dropped severely—platelets are blood cells critical in the clotting process—which meant that it was too dangerous to continue the chemotherapy. Chitra's doctors determined that her bone marrow was producing antibodies that attacked her own platelets (probably in reaction to the many transfusions she had received).

They considered a bone marrow transplant, but tried first to exchange the blood plasma. During the procedure, she had a seizure and soon developed severe anemia and various infections.

At this point Chitra's case was turning into a mounting disaster. She refused a blood transfusion, being horrified at the thought of getting AIDS. Because of her agitation, she had to be placed on an intravenous drip of morphine and Valium. Her awareness became duller and duller, and she slipped into a coma, probably induced by shock, followed by the onset of pneumonia. The doctors informed her husband that she would probably not recover, and a day later, without regaining consciousness, Chitra died. She was the victim not of her cancer but of her treatment, and I cannot help but think death from cancer would perhaps have been more humane.

The passing of this beautifully innocent and devoted young woman came as a great blow. Although I had no consolation to offer, I immediately called Raman, her husband, who was completely shattered. For months we had both watched Chitra pass into the light of life and back into the shadow of death, sharing extremes of joy and despair. Sincere efforts had been made to save her, yet I cannot expel the bitter taste that comes from knowing, as all doctors know, the barbarity of our current approach to cancer.

Every day, a physician in practice sees patients who have undergone some devastating cancer treatment that has been declared a success because the cancer cells are now gone, disregarding the weakening of the entire body, the looming danger of recurrent cancer caused by the treatment itself, and the state of lasting fear and depression that so often comes with the cure. To live in constant fear, even without cancer in your body, is not a good state of health. The war is not over; it has merely moved from open skirmishes to underground terrorism.

The underlying philosophy in cancer treatment is that the mind will just have to stand by while the body endures devastation. In other words, an open clash is actually encouraged in the mind-body system. How can this be called healing? In a clash between mind and body, the patient is fighting on both sides—there is only his body and his mind. Isn't it obvious that when a loser emerges, it will be he?

The vital issue is not how to win the war but how to keep peace in the first place. The West has not arrived at this insight, or comprehended that the physical manifestation of a disease is a phantom. The cancer cells that patients dread and physicians battle against are just such phantoms—they will come and go, raising hopes and despair, while the real culprit, the persistent memory that creates the cancer cell, goes undetected. Ayurveda gives us the means to go directly to the level of consciousness that exorcises this memory. Thinking of Chitra, I wonder how long it will be before we broaden our outlook. We ask for heroism from patients at a time when they have little of it to give, or else we treat them as statistics, turning survival into a game of numbers. Ayurveda tells us to place the responsibility for disease at a deeper level of consciousness, where a potential cure could also be found.

To say that a patient's awareness is responsible for his cancer is very troublesome to many people—and so it should be. Ayurveda as I view it does not agree that there is a so-called cancer personality, nor does it accept that superficial emotions, styles of behavior, and attitudes cause cancer. Some researchers are convinced that patients who react with helplessness and depression to their cancer are more likely to die from the disease than those patients who have a strong component in their personalities called "the will to live." This seems unarguable, but is it any help?

A person afflicted with cancer naturally goes through cycles of emotion; his will to live is susceptible to wild swings from one extreme to the other; and there is no reason to expect that any "typical cancer personality" profile should emerge. (Some of the original research that supposedly verified the "typical cancer personality" was based on insignificantly small patient groups, as few as twenty-five subjects, all of whom had only one type of cancer—typically breast cancer.) Why should the psychologically healthy, who already have such a great advantage, be the only hopeful cases?

This is not an empty question. Recently I was on a plane and happened to sit beside a very lively woman in her sixties. She struck me immediately as a Yankee of the classic type—very vigorous, no-nonsense, and full of strong opinions. Her family had lived in Maine for generations and had become quite prosperous. Since my head was full of all the issues involved in cancer treatment, we began to talk about them.

The old lady lifted her chin. "I don't believe any of these doctors know what they're talking about," she declared. "My mother was diagnosed with breast cancer in 1947. She went and had the lump removed and then came home to look after her four children. My father begged her to return to Boston for a mastectomy, but she said she was too busy for it, and she was too busy to be sick, too. She went on perfectly normally like that. After a while my father won out, and she did go back for the mastectomy, but there wasn't any radiation or chemotherapy back then."

"What happened to her?" I asked.

"Nothing happened," the woman answered. "She lived twelve more years, until she was over seventy, when she contracted pneumonia. The whole family gathered around her bed, she told us goodbye, and three days later she died."

Listening to this story, I suddenly saw, with a combination of wonder and sadness, what it was about—the paradox of being normal. It is absolutely normal to be too busy to be sick, for that is exactly the kind of awareness that the immune system thrives on. When you are just yourself and not a "cancer patient," then the complicated chain of the immune response, with its hundreds of precisely timed operations, goes to work with a vengeance.

But once you give in to helplessness and fear, this chain breaks apart. You start sending out the neuropeptides associated with neg-ative emotions, these latch onto the immune cells, and the immune response loses its efficiency. (Exactly how this happens is not known, but the decreased immune status of depressed patients is well documented.) Here is where the paradox comes in: if you reacted to cancer as no great threat, the way you react to the flu, you would have the best chance of recovering, yet a diagnosis of cancer makes every patient feel totally abnormal. The diagnosis itself sets up the vicious circle, like a snake biting its tail until there is no more snake.

The reason I felt sadness and wonder at the same time is that it suddenly dawned on me how infinitely beautiful the immune system is and how terribly vulnerable at the same time. It forges our link with life and yet can break it at any moment. The immune system knows all our secrets, all our sorrows. It knows why a mother who has lost a child can die of grief, because the immune system has died of grief first. It knows every moment a cancer patient spends in the light of life or the shadow of death, because it turns those moments into the body's physical reality.

Cancer, or any other disease, is nothing more than the sequence of these fleeting moments, each with its own emotions, its own mind-body chemistry. In other words, the diseased cells are but one ingredient out of countless others; the others are just more intangible. Ayurveda maintains that many different conditions interact to create disease—the disease organism plays one part, aided by the patient's immune resistance, age, diet, habits, the time of year, and many other factors that contribute to the eventual clinical result. Western medical studies have also abundantly proved that a person's lifestyle and emotional makeup are implicated in his state of health, but we lack the omniscience to evaluate all these factors. A cancer patient has a whole life behind him, populated by thoughts, actions, and emotions that no other person shares exactly.

The fact that emotions lie so deep does not mean that cancer patients cannot alter them. People can be rescued from their feelings of helplessness and despair by going to a still deeper level. It does not matter if one is caught in the throes of either despair or huge self-confidence. Either one could be a phantom. Ayurveda therefore pays much less attention to surface emotions than does current mind-body medicine. The whole rationale for treating cancer (or AIDS) with primordial sound and bliss techniques is that they reach the deep levels of consciousness common to everyone, the weak as much as the strong.

The following case study is the most complete success to date of treating cancer with these techniques. The patient is a woman in her late thirties named Eleanor. In 1983, while living in Colorado and working for a computer company there, Eleanor was diagnosed with advanced breast cancer that had metastasized to the lymph nodes under her arm. She underwent one radical mastectomy, followed by a second; her reaction to chemotherapy afterward was extremely poor. Finding the side effects intolerable, she abandoned conventional treatment altogether, even though her doctors made her well aware that the cancer had now spread to her bones. Patients in this category of metastasis have about a 1 percent chance of survival.

As it happens, Eleanor was advised by her family doctor to start meditating in 1986, in the middle of her disease. Through her meditation practice, she heard about Ayurveda. She came to Lancaster for inpatient treatment, where I met her and instructed her in the primordial sound for treating cancer. The results were remarkable. Her severe bone pain disappeared (this incident was mentioned earlier, in chapter 9), and whenever she returned home to be X-rayed, her radiologist found fewer and fewer pockets of bone cancer.

It was far too late for these regressions to have been caused by her earlier treatment. Generally, if a tumor is being bombarded with radiation or chemotherapy, it shrinks very quickly. If Eleanor survives for two more years, she will enter the privileged ranks of patients who beat all the odds. But what I want to portray here is the overall change she has undergone. I asked her to write down the history of her disease as seen from the inside. What she sent me is a very remarkable document. It begins at the most harrowing mo-

ment of her life, when she is about to enter the operating room to
have breast surgery:

> Undrugged, I am lying in the pre-op holding area by the doors
> of the O.R. at City of Hope Hospital. A nurse walks by carrying
> a huge breast in a clear plastic bag. My breasts seem so small,
> helpless, and innocent. I had nursed my baby sons and felt so
> good about my breasts; they were feminine, soft, and pretty—I
> trusted them. Now I am just lying here, waiting for someone to
> cut away at least one of them.
>
> I am scared and shaking. Every nerve in my body seems to
> be screaming for action, wanting to run away before it is too late
> and I am pushed through the doors to the O.R. I feel like I am
> betraying my body to a rape of degradation. I am 35 years old,
> and this whole thing is going against my sense of what is right.
>
> When it's over, the emotional impact starts to set in. My
> image of my body is bad—I don't want the doctors to see me, let
> alone my husband. I am past naked. I am stripping off my fem-
> inine shape, infected for weeks afterward, hooked to drains
> whose tubes are sewn to my body. The red-topped glass tubes
> rattle whenever I try to walk.

Eventually Eleanor healed enough to begin six months of chemotherapy. She was told that her chances of recovery were high, but
when a mammogram was taken of the remaining breast, it was
found to be cancerous as well. A second mastectomy was scheduled:

> Now I really want to escape. For months I have heard that I had
> cancer, then didn't have cancer, then had cancer again. I am so
> weary of surgeries and uncertainty. I am sick from fever, horri-
> ble night sweats, pain, humiliation, doubt about my body, my
> spirit, my gender—everything. All that I have trusted has let me
> down.

Bilateral breast cancer, bilateral mastectomies, and eventually bilateral breast reconstruction. I hope this is the end, and I can get on to recovering from my other symptoms. Then on to wellness again, despite my odds.

Soon afterward, Eleanor began to practice meditation. At first she approached her meditation with reservations and even outright skepticism, but these gave way to "a sense of inner acceptance." Four months later, in June 1986, she found that she was accidentally pregnant. Eleanor's doctors had told her that her chemotherapy had made her sterile, which happens to about 25 percent of younger women, rising to 85 percent for women over 40. For those who are not rendered sterile, giving birth is extremely risky, but to Eleanor, the idea of having another child held a special importance:

This pregnancy was symbolic to me of wholeness and blending with nature. It was a miracle, and I was happy. Then when my doctors said that I should abort this child to save my own life, it seemed like a nightmare. As the pregnancy continued, I got even sicker. I was told that my tests now indicated estrogen positive cancer, and my chances for survival were slim. I protested these facts and carried the baby, a decision that I lived with in peace.

After the successful delivery of a baby boy, Eleanor discovered that her cancer had returned, this time to her bones:

Back to cancer, and the roller-coaster ride began all over again. The City of Hope doctors predicted that I would live "perhaps six more months, but probably not more than two years." (This was fourteen months ago, in March 1987.) The cancer had advanced well into my bones (the X rays revealed a dozen cancerous sites, principally in the ribs and vertebrae), and I felt very sick, literally to the bone. The treatment plan was full doses of chemo "for the rest of your life." That didn't sound like I'd be around too long.

Eleanor responded poorly to chemotherapy, and on the recommendation of her family doctor, who had suggested meditation before, she visited Lancaster for Ayurvedic treatment in June. When I reviewed her case, I recognized that she was gravely ill; I couldn't promise her a cure, but I told Eleanor that there were more possibilities than she realized—the inner core of herself had not been violated by cancer, and we would try to bring her in touch with that core. After two weeks, she began to feel much better, both physically and mentally, and she left with no bone pain. Apparently this was the turning point:

After returning back to work, to chemotherapy and doubts, a special thing happened. A wild dove had flown inside the company warehouse one morning and would not leave. Two or three hours later, when I came in, the bird followed my path upstairs, through the halls leading toward my office, and landed quietly on my desk in front of me. I gently picked him up and all at once felt overwhelmed as we shared each other's comfort.

A few months passed after we turned him loose in the country. In September, I found that my bone scans were not good, but not worse either. Chemotherapy was causing multiple side effects. I didn't really mean to quit chemo, but I had consistently bad blood counts, and that meant that the chemo temporarily had to stop. I immediately started feeling better and realized that I wanted no more chemo, even at the risk of dying.

In December I visited Lancaster again. My time there was wonderful; some special herbs had come in for me, and I was given a primordial sound technique to use at home. At the end of December, another bone scan showed no change. This confirmed my belief that chemo was superficial. I continued my techniques, and when I returned in March, three months later, the bone scan showed that all but one tiny pocket was gone.

The radiologist smiled and said he didn't know how this could have happened without chemo. He hugged me, and when I left, he said, "This will make history." My family doctor called the radiologist for a full interpretation of the scans; he got off the phone and told me that I was almost completely recovered.

As I got the news, I couldn't stop the tears from welling up. I wondered how I could have ever doubted this result. Touched by love and nature's perfection, I had one quiet, soft desire, to go sit again against the earth, surrounded by peace in a celebration of spring flowers, and to enjoy all that has happened and all that I am.

In closing, I have to add that I am realistic; I understand the typical Western approach to this event. I also know that there are great possibilities here. All the truths of my experience somehow add up to one truth, but when I think I've grasped it, it slips away. It leaves me feeling humble and rather silly for trying to take apart the wholeness. But I am very, very peaceful and comfortable, having been assured again and again that the wholeness is perfection.

Eleanor has come a very long way. Last year she was in the worst category for surviving her disease; now many authorities like Dr. Ikemi would consider her case a spontaneous regression. Her general health is good; there is no sign of the body wasting away. Eight months after undergoing the last chemotherapy, her bone cancer has dwindled until there is only one small shadow on her X rays, and this has not definitely proven to be cancerous. Her blood chemistry, which became abnormal as the result of active disease, has now returned to the normal range—this is much stronger proof than the X rays that Eleanor is getting well.

I have no fear for her now, even if she had to begin her battle again. Eleanor is beyond battles—she radiates the peacefulness she writes about, and spending time with her makes me feel happy and secure, all the more because I understand how rare her peace is. From the despair of disease she has discovered joy. At the moment when the memory of health returned, it brought her enough power to last a lifetime.

EXPANDING THE TOPIC

The simple definition of quantum healing given in this chapter is that quantum healing brings peace. I believe this is still true, perhaps more than ever. At the time I was writing, inflammation hadn't been connected to cancer, heart disease, and a host of lifestyle disorders. Inflammation is a mystifying phenomenon, because it's needed as a crucial part of the healing system (bringing extra blood to the diseased or injured area, triggering a cascade of complex chemical interactions at the site) while in its most acute state, such as the inflammation that occurs during severe burns, it can be fatal.

The most troubling kind of inflammation is chronic and low level, which is one reason it took medical science so long to identify it as a culprit. But the internal war I wrote about is chronic, too, whether we are speaking of inflammation, stress, or imbalances that lie below the level of producing symptoms. (In my view, inflamed emotions are likely to be just as damaging to cells.) Western medicine is catching up with Ayurveda in this regard. Thousands of years ago Ayurvedic physicians focused on subtle imbalances that pushed the body out of its natural balance and ease.

Saying that your body needs to be aligned with Nature sounds very nonmedical. It's more like homespun philosophy. In the fifteen years I practiced endocrinology before looking into meditation and alternative therapies, I would have shrugged off this piece of advice. Thirty years later, it resonates very deeply. I see the human body as having cosmic implications. It is the interface between a single individual and Nature as a whole. In the early part of the twentieth century a poor boy from India named Jiddu Krishnamurti was scooped up by spiritually minded Westerners and for a time declared to be the next "world teacher" after Buddha and Jesus.

Krishnamurti's life story is fascinating, because although he renounced the grandiose title being foisted upon him, he seems to have been someone Jeffery Wright would place in Location 4, where consciousness becomes free of boundaries. At the very end of his long life—he died in 1986, at age ninety—Krishnamurti became a public figure for a second time. Now he was a white-haired figure of wisdom, an image that fit a little awkwardly. He was too tart and impatient, too rational and inquisitive, to be anyone's idea of a comforting, otherworldly guru.

You can see a YouTube video[*] from Madras, India, in 1980 where a very frail but alert Krishnamurti is asked a written question. "You often switch over from mind to brain. Is there any difference between them?" Krishnamurti's reply begins with an apology. If he used the words *mind* and *brain* interchangeably, it was a slip of the tongue. He muses for a second before answering the question with a question. "Is the mind something untouched by the brain? Is the mind not the result of time, while the brain is?"

In a nutshell he has described the mystery of time and the timeless. As creatures of the brain, human beings live in the realm of time, and yet our minds keep returning to the timeless. Quantum physics offers one lens for examining how spacetime came about, but ultimately, the investigations of science run into a contradiction. The brain, in trying to examine the quantum field, is itself a quantum phenomenon. Every atom in the brain is reducible to a quivering vibration in the quantum field, and each wave vanishes into multidimensional Hilbert space, whose existence is purely mathematical.

In other words, relying on a quantum object to explain quantum reality is like asking a robot to build itself from scattered parts

[*] https://www.youtube.com/watch?v=FqGXEFhsjtA&list=UU88A5W9XyWx7WSwthd5ykhw

lying around the floor. You have to have a plan—instructions, a blueprint, a conception—for the robot to follow before it can do anything. If someone produced a robot that could build itself from scratch, the machine would be a hoax or a delusion. Somewhere behind the physical apparatus, a mind must set the agenda. The same is true of the brain. It is just a thing in a world of things, with no privileged position. The atoms in your cerebral cortex aren't smarter than the atoms in a lump of sugar or in the dust picked up by a vacuum cleaner, because atoms aren't smart to begin with. Only mind is.

It's not hard to grasp that a robot can't build itself from scratch without instructions, but the human brain doesn't come with a manual, and we witness it doing all kinds of things on its own, like a player piano that produces the infinite variety of music without anyone touching the keys. For this reason, neuroscience will continue to be materialistic for quite a while longer; it's much easier to take apart a player piano than to explain the invisible pianist.

Krishnamurti, like the ancient Vedic sages, found a way beyond the duality of mind and brain. It begins with self-awareness. If you look at how your brain is operating, he says, you'll see what a narrow groove your thinking follows and how mechanical it is. Our education and careers, the perspective of science and engineering, our memories—all contribute to conditioning our thoughts. (In a wry aside, Krishnamurti remarks that neuroscience is beginning to view all of life as conditioned by the brain, "which we have been talking about endlessly." He spent decades trying to get his listeners to break away from the conditioning of the brain, but few understood what he meant.)

"A thought is a material process. There is nothing sacred about thought," Krishnamurti points out. When you go to a temple, when you project a happy future, when you entertain idealistic hopes, all of this is a material process. Saying such things is quite ruthless. Krishnamurti's audiences frequently found themselves squirming under his barbed challenges. Perhaps it was futile for someone who had arrived at the freedom and clarity of Location 4 to explain what he saw to people who hadn't even experienced Location 1. Yet in the simplest everyday words, he wanted them to see what was really happening: "thought has created the architecture and everything inside the building."

If we are aware of this, he says, we must move in a totally different direction. The past is constantly being repeated in the present. Tradition, however noble, offers no help. "If we accept tradition, it makes the mind extraordinarily dull." Imagine the shock to audiences who thought that Krishnamurti himself belongs to the tradition of Hinduism and gurus and enlightened sages—he swept all of that away. With so much pain, disorder, and chaos in the world, he says, how can we simply turn to tradition? He even torches the sacred Bhagavad-Gita: Reading it is repetitive and convenient, but meanwhile the brain becomes dull, routine, and stupid.

So what was his totally different direction? Taking the mind to its source in the timeless. This begins by observing your own actions and behavior. In a word, Krishnamurti asks his listeners to stop looking at the content of their consciousness and instead at consciousness itself. In the Gita, Lord Krishna declares, "Curving back on myself, I create again and again." To understand this passage, you must substitute "pure consciousness" for "Lord Krishna," and then a seemingly religious statement makes universal sense. The whole of creation is consciousness working within itself. It never stands apart from its creation. How could it? There is nowhere else to go.

This realization, the very foundation of Eastern wisdom traditions, has recently become a hot idea in cosmology, under the name of panpsychism, which holds that the universe is conscious. If you accept panpsychism, you no longer have to explain how matter learned to think. You aren't limited by the notion that consciousness is a late arrival in the cosmos, coming on the scene only when the human brain evolved. A host of dilemmas is solved when mind is everywhere. But a nifty theory that has caught everyone's fancy doesn't meet the challenge posed by Krishnamurti: How do we deal with a world in chaos and disorder?

There must be peace at every level—body, mind, and world— for healing to be complete. When you're sick, getting well isn't theoretical. The same holds true in a Middle East battle zone or in a conflicted soul. "Is love, is compassion, the product of thought?" Krishnamurti asks at the end. By implication, it isn't, but he wants every listener to look inside and discover this truth on their own. Accepting it blindly amounts to no more than another nod to tradition, which dulls the mind. Every spiritual tradition extols love and compassion, but we don't live in a world where they've taken root to defeat hatred and discord.

For the truth to set us free, it must happen one person at a time, through a journey of self-awareness. The gurus, sages, and seers cry, "Wake up!" with one voice. But they can't walk the path for us. Since the appearance of *Quantum Healing* I believe I've witnessed a wave of interest in waking up, and it continues to swell. Krishnamurti wasn't optimistic, however. "I'm afraid that love doesn't exist in this country," he mourns, referring to India. When asked if there was a spiritual revival in the New Age, he conceded only that perhaps there were more good beginners.

The problem with love, he pointed out, is that "the word is not the thing. . . . That which is the product of time, of thought, which is not the material process is the mind." If this one idea seizes hold of people, one at a time, there is a way out of our distress and the chaotic world produced by the worst in human nature. The brain can be trained in any direction, for better or worse. Healing results when it is trained for better. But only by finding our source in the timeless will we reach the level where all solutions emerge. If you need to be inspired by the prospect of waking up, look as I do, to the poets. I'll let Rumi, then, have the last word.

Oh God,
I have discovered love!
How marvelous, how good, how beautiful it is!
I offer my salutation
To the spirit of passion that aroused
and excited this whole universe,
And all it contains.

ACKNOWLEDGMENTS

To Gautama, Mallika, and Rita for their unconditional love and acceptance of all I do.

To Carla Linton for her dedication to create a better world.

To Muriel Nellis, who inspired my confidence as a writer from the very beginning.

To Toni Burbank, whose editing brought clarity to my thinking and improved every chapter of this book.

And especially to Huntley Dent—our deep friendship, the insights we shared together, and his literary guidance were all evolutionary experiences for me.

READING LIST

I felt that readers would appreciate a short list of highly readable books on the major subjects I refer to in this book: physics, mind-body medicine, and Veda. I enthusiastically recommend the following nine books, all of which entered into my own education on these fascinating subjects.

Davies, Paul. *God and the New Physics*. New York: Simon & Schuster, 1984.

Dossey, Larry, M.D. *Space, Time, and Medicine*. Boston: Shambhala, 1982.

Franklin, Jon. *Molecules of the Mind*. New York: Atheneum, 1987.

Hawking, Stephen M. *A Brief History of Time*. New York: Bantam, 1988.

Kaku, Michio, Ph.D., and Jennifer Trainer. *Beyond Einstein*. New York: Bantam, 1987.

Locke, Stephen, M.D., and Douglas Colligan. *The Healer Within*. New York: Dutton, 1986.

Murchie, Guy. *The Seven Mysteries of Life*. Boston: Houghton Mifflin, 1978.

Smith, Anthony. *The Body*. New York: Viking, 1986.

Wilber, Ken, ed. *Quantum Questions*. Boston: Shambhala, 1984.

BIBLIOGRAPHY

The literature devoted to every topic in this book, once scarce and scattered, has ballooned into something vast. As the era of the Internet dawned, numerous websites and blogs arose to address mind, body, and spirit.

I began to write books that focused on topics first addressed in *Quantum Healing*. Here are some selected titles.

Perfect Health (1990) offers a practical guide to Ayurveda, adapted to the daily needs of modern life in the West.

Ageless Body, Timeless Mind (1993) explores the mind-body connection as the best way to prevent premature aging and reverse the effects of the aging process.

The Seven Spiritual Laws of Success (1994) is a pocket guide to the principles of yoga, adapted for everyday use.

The Book of Secrets (2004) goes deeply into the teachings of Vedanta and the wisdom tradition of consciousness.

Reinventing the Body, Resurrecting the Soul (2009) describes the process of self-transformation from the deepest level of consciousness, the soul.

In the intervening years since *Quantum Healing* appeared, I eagerly embraced these new opportunities. You will find extensive, updated discussions at www.deepakchopra.com and wide-reaching sites like www.huffingtonpost.com, where I've contributed weekly for several years. These posts are completely indexed, although not divided into topics yet.

The most comprehensive cataloging of spontaneous remissions is also available online. It was compiled by Caryle Hirschberg and Brendan O'Regan for the Institute of Noetic Sciences, with literally thousands of references. Available in hard copy, the text is online at the institute's website, http://noetic.org/library/publication-books/spontaneous-remission -annotated-bibliography/.

Finally, as my exploration into quantum healing deepened, I felt that I should coauthor papers with credentialed scientists who understood the implications of the mind-body connection as applied to medicine, biology, genetics, and physics. Following is a list of collaborations with one of my most admired and widely published colleagues, physicist Menas Kafatos, in the form of peer-reviewed articles. I'm enduringly grateful that he and the other scientists have coauthored posts and blogs with me in recent years—see the index at *Huffington Post*.

Deepak Chopra, Menas C. Kafatos, and Co-workers' Papers

1. Kafatos, Menas, Rudolph E. Tanzi, and Deepak Chopra. "How Consciousness Becomes the Physical Universe." *Cosmology* 14 (2011): 1318–28, http://journalofcosmology.com/Consciousness140 .html.

2. Attila Grandpierre, Deepak Chopra, P. Murali Doraiswamy, Rudolph E. Tanzi, and Menas C. Kafatos. "A Multidisciplinary Approach to Mind and Consciousness." *NeuroQuantology* 11, no. 4 (2013): 607–17, http://dx.doi.org/10.14704/nq.2013.11.4.703.

3. Chopra, Deepak, and Menas C. Kafatos. "From Quanta to Qualia: How a Paradigm Shift Turns into Science." *Philosophy Study* 4, no. 4 (2014): 287–301, http://www.davidpublishing.com/ show.html?16636.

4. Kafatos, Menas C. "The Conscious Universe." In Deepak Chopra, ed., *Brain, Mind, Cosmos: The Nature of Our Existence and the Universe,* ebook. New York: Deepak Chopra, c/o Trident Media Group, 2014.

5. Chopra, Deepak, Menas C. Kafatos, and Rudolph E. Tanzi. "A Consciousness-Based Science: From Quanta to Qualia." In Deepak Chopra, ed., *Brain, Mind, Cosmos: The Nature of Our Existence and the Universe*. ebook. New York: Deepak Chopra, c/o Trident Media Group, 2014.

6. Chopra, Deepak, Murali P. Doraiswamy, Rudolph E. Tanzi, and Menas C. Kafatos. "Your Brain Is the Universe." In Deepak Chopra, ed., *Brain, Mind, Cosmos: The Nature of Our Existence and the Universe*. ebook. New York: Deepak Chopra, c/o Trident Media Group, 2014.

7. Kafatos, Menas C., and Deepak Chopra. "The Time Machine of Consciousness, Cosmology of Time, Quantum Physics of Time Travel." *Cosmology* 18 (2014), http://cosmology.com/Contents18 .html.

8. Kak, Subhash, Deepak Chopra, and Menas C. Kafatos. "Perceived Reality, Quantum Mechanics, and Consciousness." *Cosmology* 18 (2013): 231–45, http://cosmology.com/ConsciousTime107.html.

9. Kafatos, Menas C., and Deepak Chopra. "The Nature of Reality, the Self, Time, Space and Experience." *Cosmology* 18 (2014): 456–60, http://cosmology.com/ConsciousTime115.html.

10. Grandpierre, Attila, Deepak Chopra, and Menas C. Kafatos. "The Universal Principle of Biology." *NeuroQuantology* 12, no. 3 (2014): 364–73, http://www.neuroquantology.com/index.php/journal/article/view/747/667.

11. Kafatos, Menas C., Gaetan Chevalier, Deepak Chopra, John J. Hubacher, Subhash Kak, and Neil D. Theise. "Current Physics Perspectives." *Global Advances in Health and Medicine,* forthcoming.

INDEX

G

Gash, Don M., 52

Gastrointestinal tract, 224–26

Genes, xiii, xiv, xvii, 14, 69, 94
  depression and, 102, 104, 106
  lifestyle and genetic
    changes, 56

Germ theory of disease, 105, 302

Gerontology. *See* Aging

Goleman, Daniel, 138–39

Goswami, Amit, 150

Govindass, Laxman, 257–58

Gravity, law of, 121

Green, Elmer and Alyce, 185

Guilt, patient's feeling of, 236–37, 238

H

Hallucinations
  after open-heart surgery, 76–77
  from digitalis, 75–76
  See also Schizophrenia

Hahnemann, Samuel, 136

Hawking, Stephen, 9

Healing, xvii
  in Ayurveda, 232–33, 278
  consciousness and, 9, 10–11, 12, 14
  holistic, 181
  intention and, 195–99
  love and caring to heal, 181
  mechanisms, 39–40
  Nature and, 40, 125–27
  negativity impeding, 180
  normal vs. "miraculous," 12, 14, 16, 35, 41, 183–85, 278, 306
  prayer and, 195

positive attitudes promoting, 185–86

quantum events in, 115, 116, 117

Hearing, 223, 260, 286

Heart
  brain of, 225
  cells, 194, 225

Heart attacks
  case history, 114–15, 233–37
  mind-body relationship in, 114–15
  personality types and, 25–26
  recovery from, 257
  statin drugs and, 129
  See also Coronary disease

Heraclitus, 47

Hinduism. *See* Rishis; Sadhus; Veda/Vedic tradition

Hippocrates, 24, 40

Hoffman, Donald D., 79

Holistic medicine, definition of, 5

Homeopathy, 136–37, 149, 242

Homeostatic feedback loop, 264

Homunculus, 30

Hormones
  mechanisms for producing, 42–43
  and mental illness, 29–30
  transmission of, 68
  See also Adrenaline

Hoyle, Fred, 131

Hsu Hsu poem, 266–67

Hubel, Joseph, 259

Human Genome Project, 128

Hydrocephaly, 166

Hypertension, 57
  diuretics and, 43–44

Hypnosis, 276, 278

INDEX

ABOUT THE AUTHOR

As a global leader and pioneer in the field of mind-body medicine, DEEPAK CHOPRA has been transforming the way the world views physical, mental, emotional, spiritual, and social wellness. Known as a prolific author of more than eighty books with twenty-two *New York Times* bestsellers in both fiction and nonfiction, his works have been published in more than forty-three languages.

With medical training in internal medicine and endocrinology, he is a Fellow of the American College of Physicians and a member of the American Association of Clinical Endocrinologists. He serves as the Founder of the Chopra Foundation; co-founder and chairman of the Board of The Chopra Center for Wellbeing; founder of The Chopra Well on YouTube; adjunct professor of Kellogg School of Management at Northwestern University; adjunct professor at Columbia Business School, Columbia University; assistant clinical professor in the Family and Preventive Medicine Department at UC San Diego Health Sciences; faculty at Walt Disney Imagineering; and senior scientist with The Gallup Organization. GlobeIn acknowledges Chopra as "one of the top ten most influential spiritual leaders around the world." *Time* magazine has described Dr. Chopra as "one of the top 100 heroes and icons of the century and credits him as "the poet-prophet of alternative medicine." The World Post and The Huffington Post global Internet survey ranked Dr. Chopra #40 influential thinker in the world and #1 in medicine.

deepakchopra.com

AS SEEN ON PUBLIC TELEVISION!

The authors of the *New York Times* bestseller *Super Brain* present a bold new understanding of our genes and how simple changes in lifestyle can boost genetic activity. The leap into "radical well-being" is a promise waiting to be fulfilled.

"You are not simply the sum total of the genes you were born with," write Deepak Chopra and Rudy Tanzi. "You are the user and controller of your genes, the author of your biological story. No prospect in self-care is more exciting."

Learning how to shape your gene activity is at the heart of this exciting and eagerly anticipated book. Begin your journey to optimum health and well-being today.